The Mufti and the Fuehrer

By the same author

Under the Sign of Palestine

The Jews and the Ukrainians

The Pogroms of the Volunteer Army

The Pogroms in the Ukraine Under the Ukrainian Governments

Transjordan Within the Frame of the Palestine Mandate

European Population Transfers

The Arab Refugee Problem

Rebel and Statesman: The Vladimir Jabotinsky Story— The Early Years

Fighter and Prophet: The Vladimir Jabotinsky Story—The Last Years

On Wings of Eagles: The Plight, Exodus, and Homecoming of Oriental Jewry

Star in Eclipse: Russian Jewry Revisited

Postwar Population Transfers in Europe, 1945-1955

The Refugee in the World

Haj Amin el-Husseini, the Grand Mufti of Jerusalem.
(Zionist Archives and Library)

The Mufti
and
the Fuehrer

The Rise and Fall
of Haj Amin el-Husseini

Joseph B. Schechtman

New York · Thomas Yoseloff · London

Preface

TWO IMPORTANT QUESTIONS MUST BE ANSWERED BEFORE beginning this study of the political career of Haj Amin el-Husseini, former Mufti of Jerusalem. The first is: Does his life and public record warrant a full-length political biography?

The answer is unhesitatingly in the affirmative.

Between 1920 and 1948, Palestine was governed by Great Britain under an international mandate stipulating that that country was to become a Jewish national home. Yet, says John Marlowe in his challenging study, *The Seat of Pilate: An Account of the Palestine Mandate* (1959), "the dominant figure in Palestine during the inter-war years was neither an Englishman, nor a Jew, but an Arab—Haj Amin Mohammed Effendi al-Husseini, Mufti of Jerusalem and President of the Supreme Moslem Council." The term "dominant" is used in this connotation not in the sense of actually controlling, let alone officially ruling, the country, but of being the central single person constantly exercising dynamic, powerful influence, occupying the fore of the troubled and often tragic Palestine scene. This pivotal position was enhanced rather than weakened when the Mufti fled Palestine in October 1937, to seek refuge in

Lebanon as a political émigré. Later, in Baghdad, which became his residence from October 1939 until May 1941, he was the gray eminence behind the abortive pro-Axis coup of Rashid Ali el-Gailani, had established an efficient pan-Arab shadow "government" of his own, and conducted high-level negotiations with Axis leaders. When the Iraqi rebellion failed, he managed to escape to Teheran and from there to Rome and Berlin, openly and definitely joining the Axis camp. During the three and one-half years (October 1941–May 1945) of serving the Axis, he built up a truly world-wide network of anti-Allied activities, including broadcasting, espionage, formation of Arab and Moslem military units. After the collapse of the Third Reich he flew to Switzerland and then spent some twelve months of relative inactivity in a villa near Paris, under the benevolent French surveillance, only to "escape" once more to Cairo, where he was greeted by the entire Arab leadership as the greatest Arab patriot and hero.

Since then, Haj Amin has been, in one way or another, in the forefront of all major events in the Arab and Moslem world. Altogether, for more than four decades, he influenced the turbulent Middle East political scene as few leaders before him had done. His name was prominently linked with every major stage of the dramatic Arab-Jewish and inter-Arab conflicts in the area. No other Arab leader before him has been so passionately revered and enthusiastically followed by partisans and so fiercely hated and vehemently denounced by antagonists—Jews, Britons, and Arabs alike.

Irrespective of one's evaluation of the merits of the policy Haj Amin was pursuing and of the methods he was applying in the incessant struggle for his goals, hardly anyone can fail to be fascinated by the truly dramatic vicissitudes of his checkered career. His was an eventful, stormy life of high adventure, with a recurrent pattern of spectacular ups and downs which is not easily matched in recent history.

The second question is: Is the author, Joseph B. Schechtman, a Jew and a confirmed Zionist, the proper person to write an objective and fair biography of so strongly and violently anti-Zionist an Arab leader? The answer to this query is more difficult.

I would not claim that I am the *most proper* biographer of the Mufti. Yet I do believe that there is nothing impossible or improper in my undertaking such a task. My reasons are as follows:

(1) There is to my knowledge no up-to-date full-length biography of the Mufti by either an Arab or pro-Arab, nor for that matter by a "neutral" author. In 1942 there appeared in London a thirty-six-page brochure by M. P. Waters, *Mufti Over the Middle East;* and in 1947, Maurice Pearlman published, again in London, a ninety-one-page booklet, *Mufti of Jerusalem, The Story of Haj Amin el-Husseini.* Both publications contain valuable factual material which is partly used in this study, but they are vastly outdated, polemical in style, and consistently hostile, even derogatory, toward their subject.

Nothing of importance was added in the last fifteen years to these two booklets. Without trying to explain this odd gap in the abundant literature on the tempestuous Middle East scene, I feel that my attempt to fill it is both timely and legitimate.

(2) I cannot promise an "objective" biography, but I have done my best to make it "fair."

There hardly exists in the world of letters such a phenomenon as an "objective" life story of a controversial figure, political or otherwise. As a rule, biographies are written either by admirers or by detractors of their subjects. But even authors who do not belong to either of these two categories, who have no axe to grind, and who approach their subjects without prejudice, can claim objectivity only to the extent that they do so without deliberate prejudice; that they are honestly endeavoring to collect and assess *all* available material likely to enable them to tell the story *in full;* that they studiously avoid adjusting a date or an event, retouching any detail to fit a preconceived purpose or to produce what they might deem to be a convenient version.

At that point, their "objectivity" inevitably ends. Ultimately, a biographer cannot help but present an image which emerges in his mind after close and intense study of the gathered material as a whole. He can only portray his subject in the light of the knowledge and understanding he gained from this study. He then recreates the life story of his subject to the best of his ability, with all its inherent conflicts and its recurrent themes of accomplishment and failure, creating an over-all perceivable pattern into which single parts can be woven to make an organic entity.

This is the purpose and the method I have conscientiously tried to apply to the preparation of this biography. It is not a eulogy of the former Mufti of Jerusalem, nor has it been conceived as an indictment. I let the facts, presented in a pragmatic narrative, speak for themselves; and I am in a position to vouch for the factual accuracy of every single item in this narrative. There is no attempt at twisting or perverting actual events to suit a preconceived scheme. I felt both entitled and duty bound to judge the events but not to sit in judgment, thus presenting the reader with a pre-cooked verdict. The stormy life of the man whose political trajectory I undertook to trace is too complex and fascinating to be portrayed in black and white colors only;

to assess him either as "knight in shining armor" or un-
mitigated arch-villain would be an oversimplification.

It is not for me to judge whether or to what extent I
succeeded in implementing the purpose of this study. It
does not claim the distinction of being a "definitive biography" of Haj Amin el-Husseini. Yet I believe that it makes
a contribution to a significant and badly neglected chapter
of recent Middle East history.

I am indebted to the Zionist Archives and Library in
New York for providing abundant documentary material
from both Jewish and Arab sources. To the head of this
institution, Mrs. Sylvia Landress, and to the entire staff
goes my wholehearted gratitude.

Mrs. Renee Cohen, my wife Rachel, and my daughter
Miriam Gottlieb, have been eminently helpful in the preparation of the manuscript.

JOSEPH B. SCHECHTMAN

Jamaica, New York
June 1964

Contents

ILLUSTRATIONS

The Mufti and the Fuehrer

1

Ascendance in Palestine
1920–1937

Origin

ONE OF THE ACE CARDS AMIN EL-HUSSEINI HAD BEEN CON-
sistently playing was his alleged descent from the Prophet.
He had, however, no valid claim to this distinction.* He
is simply a member of one of the Arab patrician families
of Palestine who, until the 1920's, had exercised little influence outside the city of Jerusalem. The main branch of
the family was not of Palestinian stock. They were the *al-
Aswads* (i.e., "The Blacks"), who had come to Palestine
from Yemen via Egypt some three hundred years ago and
rose on the local Moslem social scale after one of them

* When, speaking to the Sheikh-President of the famous Al-Azhar
University in Cairo, Pierre Van Paassen referred to Haj Amin's claim to
have descended from the Prophet, the reaction was both negative and
indignant: "Son of the Prophet, is he? A son of Satan, that is what I
call him for making such a claim. There are ten thousand descendants
of Fatima in Arabia, and their names are known, but they do not bear
titles to distinguish them from ordinary Moslems. That would mean a
sort of spiritual aristocracy. There is no room in Islam for such things."
(M.P. Waters, *Mufti Over the Middle East* [London, 1942], p. 9.)

had married into the family of Sheikh Abugosh, who owned much land around Jerusalem. Later, one of the male members of the Aswad clan married the daughter of a Moslem notable named el-Husseini, who claimed descent from Hussein, son of the Caliph Ali, and Fatima, only daughter of the Prophet Mohammed. Contrary to Moslem custom, this Aswad assumed his wife's name which conferred prestige and influence. Apparently in order not to effect a complete break with his own name, he went under the double name Aswad-Husseini. But Amin's grandfather, Mustapha, apparently concluded that the hyphen was distracting from the value of the addition and dropped the Aswad altogether. Henceforth the family was known as el-Husseini.

For some two centuries the Husseinis played a minor role as provincial aristocrats until the aforementioned grandfather Mustapha, who was on good terms with the Turkish authorities of the country, became, in the late 1890's, Mufti of Jerusalem. His appropriation of the distinguished name, Husseini, angered many leading Arab families. The story goes that they had persuaded the Turkish governor of Jerusalem to forbid the new mufti the use of that name. But the family saved themselves from disgrace by getting one of their relatives, Shukry Bey el-Husseini, who was then in the Turkish capital, to "fix" the matter with the government. And Husseini they remained.[1]

Education and Haj

It was an event of importance solely to the Husseini household in Jerusalem when blue-eyed Amin entered this world in 1893. By all accounts he was an average youth

who showed little inclination for study. His education was limited. He went first to a local Moslem school and then to the government school in Jerusalem. For about a year he attended the school of the Alliance Israélite Universelle, where he acquired his first knowledge of French.*
At the age of nineteen, his family thought it was time for some serious coaching. Amin was sent to Cairo and was admitted to the Azhar University, the main curriculum of which was Islamic philosophy. But he never completed his studies. After just a year in Cairo, he managed to acquire enough money to finance a pilgrimage to Mecca and Medina, the Holy Places of Islam. The pilgrimage gave him the right to use the surname "Haj" (Arabic for "pilgrim"), a title which carried in Moslem society more weight than years of study.

Humble Early Career

From Mecca he returned to Jerusalem as Haj Amin. Yet, whatever plans for advancement he had in view, they were interrupted in 1914 when Turkey entered the First World War as a belligerent on the side of the Central Powers. Amin obtained a commission in the Turkish Army, with a safe billet at an office in Smyrna. After the war, he returned to British-ruled Palestine and for a time served as a clerk in the office of Gabriel Pasha Haddad, Arab advisor to the military governor of Jerusalem.

In 1918, Haj Amin and a Palestinian-born Jew, I. A. Abbady, were designated by the Arab and Jewish communities to translate for public circulation Reuters' press messages into the country's two languages. For five months they had been working together in a tiny room at

---

* The author owes this information to the New York office of the American Friends of the Alliance.

the Jerusalem Governorate, so that Abbady became one of the few non-Moslems who had know Haj Amin personally. The young Amin at that time "cut a dashing figure," was "consciously and always the man-about-town, dapper, perfumed, bejeweled and over-dressed." But already at that early stage he was a fanatical nationalist. "Remember, Abbady," he used to say, "this was and will remain an Arab land. We do not mind you [Jewish] natives of the country, but those alien invaders, the Zionists, will be massacred to the last man. We want no progress, no prosperity [deriving from Jewish immigration]. Nothing but the sword will decide the future of this country." While some Arab intellectuals—among them such future collaborators of Haj Amin as Auni Bey Abdul Hadi, Aref Effendi el-Arel, and Riad Bey Solh (the latter two received their education in Paris, largely subsidized by Baron Edmond de Rothschild) used to meet with Abbady and a young brilliant Hebrew writer, Itamar Ben Avi, and discuss plans for Arab-Jewish cooperation, Haj Amin was violently opposed to any such course. An evening school for the teaching of Hebrew to the Arabs, Arabic to the Jews, and English to both, which was established as a result of these talks, with an enrollment of over one hundred students from both communities, lasted a year-"until Amin succeeded in killing it," relates Abbady.[2] Later, Haj Amin was transferred first to the Department of Public Security, then to the Customs Excise Office at the small town of Qalqilieh. For a time he held a minor civil service position in Damascus, but was soon discharged and again returned, jobless, to Jerusalem.

Here he obtained a tutor's position in the Rashidieh School, a Moslem teachers' seminary, and began to seek the limelight of public life, writing for the local Arab paper *Suriyah al-Janubiyah* (Southern Syria) and addressing gatherings of Arab nationalists. In both capacities he displayed a passionate hatred of both Britain and the Jews, scoring spectacular success in rousing his audiences and readers to ardent anti-British and anti-Jewish animosity. He also showed considerable organizing ability.

The Pogrom of 1920

The Moslem festival of Nebi Mussa, coinciding with Easter and Passover, provided a spark to ignite pent-up passions. Thousands of pilgrims started converging on Jerusalem on April 4, 1920; the crowd, inflamed by anti-Jewish diatribes, began attacking Jewish passers-by and looting Jewish stores. Soon, Jewish blood was shed and the mob rushed into the Jewish quarter to kill and to pillage. The Arab police either adopted a passive attitude or joined the rioters. The pogrom continued the next day, April 5. When order was restored, largely due to the Jabotinsky-led Jewish self-defense, five Jews and four Arabs were reported killed, and 211 Jews and 21 Arabs wounded; two Jewish girls were raped.[3]

At the military trials that followed, Haj Amin was charged before a military court with incitement to violence. His inflammatory articles in *Suriyah al-Janubiyah* were said to have touched off the riots. Since, absconding from his bail, he had meanwhile fled Western Palestine, he was tried in absentia and was sentenced to ten years imprisonment. (For organizing Jewish self-defense against the Arab onslaught, Vladimir Jabotinsky received a sentence of fifteen years penal servitude.) Hiding in Transjordan as fugitive from justice, Haj Amin was for a time forgotten in Jerusalem.

Pardoned by Herbert Samuel

The following year he was rescued from oblivion by one of those curious strokes of good fortune which so often marked his later career.

On July 1, 1920, the then Sir Herbert (later Viscount) Samuel, the first British High Commissioner for Palestine, assumed direction of Palestine affairs. Sir Herbert was a Jew, and he was British. He came to the country with an odd "impartiality complex," the specific brand of impartiality which Anatole France had once described as even-handed prohibition of both rich and poor from begging in the streets. Haunted by the fear of appearing too pro-Jewish, he became the first post-World War I appeaser.

One of the early acts of the new High Commissioner was to proclaim, on July 7, full amnesty for all prisoners sentenced by military courts. This act of mercy had specifically excluded the fugitive Haj Amin. But seven weeks later, Sir Herbert changed his mind. Addressing in Amman, capital of Transjordan, a group of local Arab notables, he—allegedly on the petition of the Transjordan sheikhs—announced a special pardon to Haj Amin.[4] Relates John Gunther in his *Inside Asia:* " 'Let Haj Amin come to Jerusalem; he will not be molested; we have pardoned him,' said the High Commissioner. There was a movement in the crowd, and, to the amazement of the British, Haj Amin proceeded to appear, lifted on the shoulders of the Arabs. He had been hiding—in a good enough place."[5]

So dramatically singled out for special treatment, Haj Amin, a few months later, returned to Jerusalem as a public figure, with a record of action, a man whose importance the British administration had publicly acknowledged.

Appointed Mufti of Jerusalem

Moreover, the same administration had very soon engineered his spectacular rise to power.

The two principal Arab families in Jerusalem were the Husseinis and the Nashashibis, and Arab political life in Palestine was largely conditioned by the rivalry between them. At the time of the capture of Jerusalem by the British Army, a Husseini had been mayor of Jerusalem, but he had subsequently been removed by the military administration, and a Nashashibi appointed in his stead. In March 1921, the Mufti of Jerusalem, Kamal el-Husseini (Amin's half-brother), died. The High Commissioner, considering it desirable to balance a Nashashibi mayor by a Husseini mufti, was eager to secure the appointment of Haj Amin to the vacant position. The electoral college consisted of the following three groups, according to the Turkish law, which was still valid in Palestine: (1) The scholars (*Ulama*), actually engaged in educational work in schools; (2) The readers of prayers (*Imams*) and the preachers (*Hatibs*) of the largest mosques of the town; (3) The Mohammedan members of the municipal council (*Baladiah*) and of the administrative council of the local government (*Idarah*).

They had to appear before the administrative council of the government and be instructed to nominate for the post of mufti three candidates "who deserve the trust and confidence of the public, and who are able to give a right answer to the questions brought before them."

The votes were to be handed over in a sealed official statement to the *Wali* (provincial governor), who in his turn had to submit the result of the election, together with a report on the persons of the candidates, in an official document (*Mazbatah*) to the Sheikh El-Islam, the spiritual head of the Moslem communities of the Ottoman Empire, whose seat was in Istanbul. It was with him that the final decision rested. All these provisions were necessary because of the considerable authority vested in the mufti as a supreme legal adviser in questions of religious canon law, whose opinion was sought by judges, courts, and private individuals in difficult questions.

When the post of mufti became vacant, widespread propaganda was launched by the Husseini family in favor of Haj Amin. But the groups entitled to vote refused to include him in the list of candidates, because they denied him the qualifications prescribed by the regulations; especially because, as a student of the Azhar University in Cairo, he failed to pass his examination, and hence was not regarded as an appropriate candidate. It was only on the insistence of some British officials that Haj Amin was added to the list.*

Professor A. S. Yahuda of the New York School of Social Research, who was in Palestine lecturing to the Arabs just at the time when preparations were being made for the election of a mufti and was in close touch with many prominent Arab leaders, presented in a letter to *The New York Times* (January 2, 1944) the following picture of the election procedure:

According to my information from a reliable and well informed source, the result of the voting was as follows:

Sheikh Husam al-Din Jarallash, a member of the Religious Court, received eighteen votes .Sheikh Khalil al-Khaldi, then the acting President of the Religious Court [*Mahkama*], and one of the most prominent Mohammedan scholars in the Moslem world, received seventeen votes. Sheikh Musa al-Budeiri,

---

* Norman Bentwich relates in his autobiography that "when Kamal fell seriously ill, Amin hastily repaired to El Azhar, the Moslem university of Cairo, whence he returned to Jerusalem with a religious turban in place of the national tarbush." (*My 77 Years*, p. 73.) There is no evidence to support this piece of information.

the supervisor of the Omar mosque, twelve votes. Haj Amin el-Husseini, nine votes. Sheikh Suud al-Uri, the Kadi [Judge] of Jerusalem, three votes. Sheikh Amin al-Uri, a member of the Religious Court, two votes.

As the last three candidates, including Haj Amin, got the lowest vote, they should have been dropped from the list and only the three first submitted as legal candidates (all of them were Nashashibi-sponsored) for a final decision to the governor of Jerusalem, who in this case replaced the Turkish provincial governor. Haj Amin was thus outside the scope of eligibility.

Yet this did not prevent him from getting the nomination.

"Wishing to keep a balance between the parties in the civic and religious honors of Jerusalem," says Professor Paul L. Hanna, "[Sir Herbert] Samuel induced one of the Nashashibi candidates to retire":[6] Sheikh Husam al-Din, the man who topped the poll, declared that he did not want to be considered. Haj Amin was thus pushed to the third place on the list and thus came within the area of selection.* Sir Ronald Storrs, then governor of Jerusalem, immediately apointed him as mufti, a position which was, by custom, a life appointment. The 1937 report of the Royal Commission notes, without comment, the fact that "no letter informing him of his nomination as Mufti of Jerusalem was dispatched to him, nor was his appointment ever gazetted."[7]

Once established, the new mufti devoted himself to building up his position with a single-mindedness that has few parallels in recent history. Nothing was allowed to stand in his way. The title bestowed on Haj Amin was in itself of no major significance. There was a mufti for every

---

* "Some manipulation was required to bring him into the list," admits Norman Bentwich (loc. cit.).

Arab town, and Islam has no priesthood. But Haj Amin succeeded in enhancing the status of the mufti of Jerusalem to unprecedented authority. "His word among the illiterate eighty-five per cent of Moslems had oracular power," related Ernest Maine in 1937.[8]

President of Supreme Moslem Council

But another position created for him by Sir Herbert only a few months after his appointment as mufti of Jerusalem proved to be even more powerful. In pursuance of its policy of providing for complete communal autonomy in religious matters, the British administration, in December 1921, provided for the establishment of a Supreme Moslem Council with full control over all *Waqf* (religious trusts) and over the *Shariah* (Moslem religious courts), which had jurisdiction over Moslems in matters of personal status. (Similar arrangements were subsequently made for the establishment of a Jewish rabbinical council and rabbinical courts.) Haj Amin became the president of this body. The 1937 report of the Royal Commission notes, again without comment, that "the present President of the Supreme Moslem Council has never been elected by general election but only by a mere remnant of the secondary electors of the electoral college of the last Ottoman Parliament . . . the functions, status and precedence of the existing President have not been defined and there has therefore been no legal limitation to his power."[9]

The appointment to the presidency of the Supreme Moslem Council took place in March 1922, about eighteen months after Haj Amin's appointment as mufti. "There was no *a priori* reason why the two offices should have been combined and, from the British point of view, there was every reason why they should not have been combined," says John Marlowe.[10]

The accumulation of power that Haj Amin thus achieved was indeed considerable. As president of the Council, he had full control of the *Waqf* funds (which by 1936 amounted to £67,000 a year) and of orphan funds amounting to £50,000. This made him "the most influential Arab in Palestine."[11] Haj Amin was pressed many times to publish accounts of his expenditure of the *Waqf* funds. But this demand was never met. The *Waqf* income was intended for religious and educational purposes, and for social services to ameliorate the condition of depressed Arabs. But in all the fifteen years Haj Amin occupied the presidency—and he held this post until he fled to Lebanon in 1937—the amounts spent on education and social welfare are known to have been infinitesimal. The bulk of the money went toward the recruitment and maintenance of an army of paid propagandists, agitators, thugs, and gunmen, to carry out Haj Amin's designs, and, later, toward the purchase of arms. Only a court order could compel him to publish accounts of his expenditure of the *Waqf* funds. And no court would make such an order since the Supreme Moslem Council controlled the appointment of judges to the Moslem *Shariah* courts, and only Haj Amin's trusted men were appointed.

The Supreme Moslem Council had within its power the appointment of preachers to the Palestinian mosques. Haj Amin took full advantage of the absence of legal restrictions on his authority and used the unlimited right of appointment and dismissal to build up a personal countrywide religio-political machine. In the course of years he had consolidated his position as the most powerful political figure in the Palestine Arab community. The

Council's growing annual revenues were approaching £600,000 in 1936. The control of these funds furnished its president with an effective levy by which to bring into line with his political policies the officials of dependent religious establishments. Through them he was able to reach the illiterate *Fallahin* (Arab peasants) and arouse their religious fanaticism against Zionism and the policy of the mandatory power.[12] Many of the preachers had played their part in subsequent uprisings by urging their flock to "go out and murder the Jewish infidel in the name of the holy Koran"; or by declaring week in and week out that "he who kills a Jew is assured of a place in the next world."

Half of Haj Amin's salary was paid by the government of Palestine. (The other half came from the endowment funds.) He thus occupied the unique and unparalleled position of being in open conflict with the same government that was subsidizing him. When promoting his career, the mandatory administration was apparently counting on his repaying their patronage by being "a good boy in the future," wrote H. J. Simson in 1937, who had for years been in the service of the Palestine administration.[13] British high officials were treating him as their "fair-haired boy," and he was a frequent and favored guest at the High Commissioner's table. But they miscalculated. As John Marlowe put it: "The Administration had thought perhaps to remove him out of politics into religion; Haj Amin replied by bringing religion into politics."[14]

Appointed in 1921, the Supreme Moslem Council was merely a provisional body. It was to serve only for a term of five years, at the end of which new elections were to take place along democratic lines. But Haj Amin was not prepared to take chances. And despite the demand of many Arab elders and notables, no election took place, neither after five years, ten years, nor fifteen years. In 1928, a committee of six was appointed by the Palestine government, under the chairmanship of the Mufti himself, to make recommendations for the reform of the existing regulations governing the constitution of the Council. In December 1928, the majority of the Committee presented a draft of new regulations, which contained the provision that Haj Amin should continue to hold his office for a period of nine years; thereafter his term of office would automatically be extended for further periods of nine years, unless, at the end of such period, it was otherwise decided by a majority of two-thirds of the members of the General Moslem Assembly. This amounted practically to a lifetime job. One member of the Committee, it is true, presented a minority report recommending that the question of the election of the president of the Supreme Moslem Council should be left for the determination by the General Moslem Assembly. This dissenting report commanded the support of some Arab newspapers, which insisted that the Mufti was appropriating and misapplying public funds, and was making use of his patronage to appoint his relatives and friends to the more important and more lucrative religious posts under his control.[15] But the Palestine administration disregarded these charges and consistently backed Haj Amin in his powerful position.

From time to time, British high commissioners seemed to realize the abnormalcy and the danger of this situation. Lt. Col. F. H. Kisch, who was chairman of the Palestine Zionist Executive in 1923–1931, relates in his *Palestine Diary* that when—during Sir Herbert Samuel's farewell visit to the Moslem Supreme Council—the Mufti made a strong political speech attacking the policy of the government and advocating the full independence of the

Arabs along the lines of Iraq, Sir Herbert flatly declared that the Mufti was not supposed to concern himself with politics, and ironically added that it was easy to criticize an administration, "as the Mufti would know from the criticism which is prevalent as regards the Moslem Supreme Council." "Things would have been different today if this had been Samuel's official attitude during recent years," sadly commented Kisch in an entry dated July 1, 1925.[16] Four years later, Sir John Chancellor, the third High Commissioner for Palestine, came to a similar conclusion, that "the worst thing that had happened to this country was the grant of extraordinary powers to the President of the Moslem Supreme Council from which Haj Amin derived his strength."[17]

But all these belated and casual *lucida intervalla* never resulted in any practical steps. Haj Amin el-Husseini was never disturbed in his "extraordinary powers" as president of the Moslem Supreme Council, and in October 1951, the Council, in its personnel and constitution, was exactly the same as that appointed in 1921, with the Mufti as the all-powerful president.

The Pogrom of 1921

Haj Amin's appointment as mufti of Jerusalem took place in March 1921. The second Jewish pogrom occurred in May of the same year. It was preceded by publication in the Arab press of the spurious anti-Jewish "Protocols of Zion" and by vicious anti-Jewish propaganda among the masses. An opportunity for an "explosion" soon presented itself.

On May Day, an authorized Jewish labor demonstration and an illegal Communist demonstration parade clashed in the streets of Tel Aviv. The Communists, a small and unpopular group, were easily dispersed. But the Mufti's agitators were immediately busy fanning the flames of national antagonism in neighboring Jaffa, and before long an Arab mob was attacking and murdering Jews with the active or passive assistance of the predominantly Arab police. Before military reinforcements arrived, rioters had stormed the Jewish Immigration Center and massacred thirteen Jews. Order was restored in Jaffa in the late afternoon of May 1 by the use of British troops, and on the evening of the following day martial law was proclaimed.

Disorders, however, did not remain restricted to Jaffa alone. The Mufti's agents busily circulated rumors of Jewish attacks on Arabs, and on May 3 the Jewish colonies of Kfar Saba and Ain Hai were looted, while on May 5 several thousand armed Arabs in semi-military formation attacked the colony of Petach Tiqva. On May 6 Arabs besieged Hedera and attempted an attack on Rehovot.[18]

The local commission of inquiry, which the Palestine government appointed under the chairmanship of Chief Justice Sir Thomas W. Haycraft to investigate the pogrom of 1921, did not even attempt to look into the delicate question of the Mufti's responsibility for those bloody disturbances. The report of the commission admitted, it is true, that the Arabs were the aggressors, but placed the underlying blame upon the Jews and denounced Zionist statements calling for the speedy creation of a Jewish majority; it quoted in particular the head of the Political Department of the Zionist Commission, Dr. David Eder, as saying that there could be only one national home in Palestine.*

* The conclusions of the commission appear in *Parliamentary Papers* (Great Britain) 1921, Cmd 1540, pp. 43-60.

The Mufti had every reason to be satisfied with the Haycraft report. He was especially gratified when Sir Herbert Samuel, continuing his policy of appeasement, yielded to the Arab compaign of violence and at least temporarily conceded Arab demands for a cessation of Jewish immigration. The military authorities at Jaffa halted the landing of Jews, and on May 14 Samuel announced the complete suspension of immigration pending revision of the existing legislation. The ban on immigration was not removed until July, when much more rigid regulations had been issued under the Immigration Ordinance.[13]

The Mufti learned well the lesson of the 1921 pogrom. He realized (a) that it was possible to foment and direct a bloody pogrom against Jews and to get away with this undisturbed; (b) that the Palestine administration was easily impressed, intimidated, and driven into concessions; and (c) that all he had to do was to continue to apply the well-tested methods of 1921 as a highly successfull dress rehearsal for the main performance to come.

No Contacts with Jews

The rigid rule adopted by Haj Amin in his capacity as the religious head of the Palestine Moslems was never to mix with Jews and to avoid any contacts with the Jewish leaders. Colonel F. H. Kisch notes in his diary on December 14, 1923, that the Mufti categorically refused to meet him, even at a private house. On February 28, 1924, the High Commissioner arranged at the Government House a luncheon for two Arab princes, Emir Ali (the oldest son of King Hussein of Hedjaz), and Emir Abdallah of Transjordan. The Mufti could not refuse an invitation to such a ceremony, although he knew that Kisch would be present. At the table Kisch was seated "with the Mufti facing him, but carefully avoiding to meet his eyes." There was no possibility of approaching the fanatical Jew-hater. Repeated attempts to this effect in the years to come failed completely, and on September 10, 1929, Kisch, who was certainly not an "extreme" Zionist, frankly told the then High Commissioner, Sir John Chancellor, that "the Mufti himself was at present the chief obstacle to a restoration of normal relations between Jew and Arab." In March 1931, the projected meeting between Dr. Weizmann and Emir Abdallah of Transjordan did not take place, largely because "Abdallah was influenced by the great pressure brought to bear by the Mufti to stop him from seeing Weizmann."[20]

The Boycott of the Legislative Council

Hoping to appease the Arab leaders, the British government, on August 10, 1922, enacted a Palestine Order-in Council, announcing the creation of a Legislative Council with limited powers; provision was also made for an advisory committee on immigration.[21] To accompany this constitution, the Palestine Legislative Council Election Order was promulgated, providing for indirect elections conducted on the basis of separate representation for the various religious communities.[22]

This constitutional experiment was very ominous—to say the least—for the Jewish cause, since it sealed the Jewish minority status. For the Arabs it meant a promising beginning of an Arab majority rule. Nevertheless, the Jews accepted the Legislative Council and pledged their fullest cooperation in the elections. The Fifth Palestine

Arab Congress, on the contrary, following the Mufti's line, rejected the offered constitution and refused participation in the Legislative Council elections. The Palestine government tried to make an appeal to the Arab masses over the head of the Mufti, and early in 1923, proclamations designating February 20 and 28 as the period for primary elections, and outlining the election procedure, were issued in Palestine. The Mufti and the Arab Executive Committee launched, however, a determined boycott action. The Mufti let it be known that any Moslem participating in the elections would not be buried in a Moslem cemetery.[23] In combination with the natural apathy of the Arab peasantry, this propaganda resulted in such a wholesale abstention from voting that only 68 out of the 663 Moslem and 14 out of the 59 Christian secondary electors were chosen. An order extending the time for completing the primary elections to March 7 resulted in the nomination of only 107 Moslems and 19 Christians. Full complements of 79 Jewish and 8 Druze electors could not hide the fact that the atempt to secure Arab cooperation on the basis of restricted popular representation was blocked by the Mufti and the Arab Executive Committee, who had called an Arab general strike in celebration of the successful boycott of the Legislative Council Elecons.[24]

Herbert Samuel was apparently deeply impressed by this manifestation of the Mufti's power, and until the very end of his stay in office he never dared to challenge the latter's authority. Moreover, as late as 1938, when the Mufti already was a fugitive in Lebanon and a confirmed Axis agent, Samuel (who in the meantime became Viscount Samuel) found it proper to defend his nominee in the House of Lords. Speaking in the debate on Palestine on December 8, 1938, Viscount Samuel said:

May I say a word or two with regard to the Mufti Haj Amin al Husseini, whose personality has aroused great interest? I was responsible for his appointment, and, looking back over the circumstances of the case, I have no doubt that that appointment was a right one. If necessary, I shall give your Lordships the reason, but it would be going into too much detail and would take up too much of your time. During my High Commissionership, for some years, I never knew him to refuse his co-operation in maintaining law and order. On what has happened I have no first-hand knowledge and therefore cannot speak, but in any case I feel sure of this: that if the Mufti were not there to give his leadership, someone else would be there, for a movement always throws up its leader, and if it were not one individual, then it would be another.[25]

Baron Plumer Gives a Lesson

This odd, fatalistic philosophy was not shared by Baron Plumer, who, in 1925, succeeded Herbert Samuel as High Commissioner for Palestine. He proved that firmness and even harshness were capable of coping with the Mufti's intransigency. Plumer was an old soldier, with five years of colonial experience as governor of Malta, and he was not a Jew. Far from being a pro-Zionist, he considered it as his primary duty to maintain law and order in the country he was governing, and he was not prepared to be intimidated by threats. He made this unmistakably clear when the Mufti once told him that unless a scheduled Jewish demonstration in Jerusalem was prohibited he could give no guarantee on behalf of the Arabs that peace and order would be preserved.[26] According to Humphrey Bowman, a high official in the Palestine administration, Lord Plumer then "put his eyeglass in his eye in characteristic fashion, gave the Mufti an uncompromising stare and said: 'Your eminence, there is no need for you to be responsible. It is I who am responsible for the maintenance or order in Palestine.' "27

There was no disturbance. The Mufti chose not to challenge the old soldier's firm and dignified stand. He was realistic enough to know that the British Administration was sufficiently strong to prevent any disturbances, if it was determined to do so, and that he could not defy a Plumer. So he kept quiet. And he did so during all the three years of Plumer's tenure. The second High Commissioner, a gentile, succeeded in repairing a great part of the harm done by the first High Commissioner, a Jew, to Britain's prestige in the Middle East and won the respect of both Jew and Arab. These three years were for the Mufti an uneventful and "empty" period. Under Plumer there was little chance for successful and safe troublemaking.

The Wailing Wall Provocation

But in 1928, Plumer relinquished his office. His successor was Sir John Robert Chancellor, also a military man, who had served the Colonial Office in the West Indies and Africa, but who was a man of quite a different stature. The Mufti felt that the new setup was propitious to venture a showdown.

The issue he chose this time was typical of him, as it was of the Arab mind in general, which still moved in a strange borderland between a medieval religious outlook and the strident confusion of militant modern nationalism. It was a resurrected religious issue, to be used as counter in a national and political struggle.

The carefully chosen pretext was an incident at Jerusalem's Wailing Wall on September 24, 1928, when the

Jews, celebrating their Day of Atonement, had on the evening of the preceding day put up a portable screen in front of the Wall. The Mufti claimed that thereby they had violated customary practice and Islamic property.[28] Obviously determined to exploit this incident to the hilt, he presented on October 8 a memorandum to the administration, insinuating that the Jews intended to take possession of the Haram esh Sharif, the third holiest shrine of Islam. Even British officials refused to take seriously the veracity, and even the sincerity of this accusation. Later, Haj Amin produced before the Shaw commission, as "evidence of Jewish designs on the Holy Places," certain "pictorial representations," some of which depicted the Dome of the Rock or a structure resembling it, with inscriptions in Hebrew on the walls of the building. In the course of presenting his evidence the Mufti swore, with reference to these pictures, that he "thought that this is a description of what the Zionists intend to do in regard to our Holy Places." The Shaw commission summarily dismissed this piece of evidence with the statement that it "cannot believe that the Mufti or any educated Arab can genuinely have entertained any such idea."[29]

The Arab-Jewish controversy on the Wailing Wall continued, with changing success, until August 1929 when a bloody anti-Jewish pogrom took place; 132 Jews were killed or died from wounds, and 187 Jews were wounded.[30]

The Mufti's Responsibility for the 1929 Pogrom

The Palestine Zionist Executive officially charged that the August disturbances "were in a large measure the direct result of organization and incitement, the main responsibility for which must be attributed to the Mufti and the Palestine Arab Executive." This indictment was largely based on a British official document. On August 23, 1929, the first day of the pogrom, L. Harrington, district superintendent of police, Jerusalem District, sent to his subordinate, Abdin Bey Hushemi, a "black-list" of persons whose names were to be indicated on a map by flags. The list, which presumably was drawn up on the principle of a hierarchy of "blackness," was headed by the following three names: Haj Amin Husseini, Jamal el-Husseini, and Subhi Khadra.[31]

The commission of inquiry, appointed by the British Colonial Office on September 3, 1929, nevertheless treated the Mufti with exceptional consideration. His evidence was taken at his home on December 6 behind closed doors; press correspondents were barred and official communiqués were exceedingly brief, giving no precision as to the content of his testimony. From what had transpired through Arab channels, the Jewish Telegraphic Agency was able to establish that the Mufti firmly asserted his belief in the authenticity of the notorious "Protocols of the Elders of Zion," long exposed as an anti-Semitic fabrication; he also repeated the statement he had previously made to Pierre van Paassen, correspondent of the Jewish Telegraphic Agency, in which he claimed that Lord Melchett and Professor Albert Einstein had allegedly openly voiced the Jewish intention to rebuild the Temple of Solomon at the seat of the Mosque of Omar. The Mufti, of course, denied that he had incited the Arab population to riot, and insisted that, on the contrary, he did everything in his power to pacify the people. According to reports received by the Jewish Telegraphic Agency, his testimony had largely consisted of long, violently anti-Jewish, tirades, and Stocker, the counsel for the Arab

Higher Executive, fearing that this performance might harm the Arab cause, suggested to Sir Walter Shaw, the commission's chairman, to permit only direct and brief answers to questions addressed to the witness, without giving him the opportunity of indulging in long-winded speeches at every occasion.[32]

In the eight-page chapter of the report dealing with the Mufti, the majority of the commission gave him a clean bill of health. Haj Amin was absolved from any direct responsibility for the events of August 1929. The report stressed, on the contrary, that "after the disturbances had broken out, the Mufti co-operated with the government in their efforts both to restore peace and to prevent the extension of disorder."[33] Only one member of the commission, Harry Snell (later Lord Snell) stated in a carefully worded "note of reservation," that he "takes a more serious view than do his colleagues" of the Mufti's responsibility for the disturbances:

I have not the least doubt that he, [the Mufti] was aware of the nature of the anti-Zionist campaign which was conducted by some of his followers and that he realized the danger of disturbance which is never absent when religious propaganda of an exciting character is spread among a Moslem people. I therefore attribute to the Mufti a greater share in the responsibility for the disturbance that is attributed to him in the report. I am of the opinion that the Mufti must bear the blame for his failure to make any effort to control the character of an agitation conducted in the name of a religion of which in Palestine he was the head.[34]

A similar attitude was taken by Mr. Van Rees, vice-chairman of the League of Nations' Permanent Mandates Commission. Commenting on the Shaw commission's account of the causes of the 1929 disturbances, he expressed the following view of the Mufti's responsibility: "It was very difficult to believe that . . . the commission had been able to conclude that there had been no premeditation or organization of disturbances on the part of the Arab leaders. It was even more surprising that the commission should have extended this conclusion to cover the head of the Supreme Moslem Council, the Grand Mufti Haj Amin el Husseini, referred to in several quarters as one of the principal organizers of these disturbances."[35]

The British government did not take any cognizance of these accusations against the Mufti. They fully accepted the whitewashing conclusion of the majority of the Shaw commission. In addition to being in full command of the Arab nationalist movement, Haj Amin enjoyed the confidence and support of the mandatory power.

He also enjoyed—however incredible it may sound—a measure of recognition on the part of the violently anti-Zionist Communist Party of Palestine which assessed the Mufti-instigated bloody pogrom as a national revolutionary movement, whose anti-Jewish concomitant was inevitable. In October 1929, the following statement appeared in a Communist underground pamphlet *The Arab Revolutionary Movement and the Tasks of the Proletariat:* "In a country like Palestine a revolutionary movement without pogroms is impossible." Quoting this statement, Walter Z. Laqueur says in his comprehensive study, *Communism and Nationalism in the Middle East* (New York, 1956):

This, in a nutshell, was the new line. Could a real revolutionist argue that such a movement should be disapproved of and discouraged merely because of danger of pogroms? Of course not . . . And how did the Mufti succeed in dominating the revolutionary movement? Well, this was the responsibility of the social-fascists of the Jewish Federation of Labor [*Histadrut*].

The Communists even considered the Mufti "too moderate" in the struggle against Zionism. In the leaflets pub-

lished in August 1931, on the occasion of the second anniversary of the 1929 pogrom, and in an *Appeal to Arab
Youth* (November 1931), the Party Executive claimed
that he, as well as the other Arab national leaders, would
act only if they felt considerable pressure from below, and
they, the Communists, were to exert that pressure by
using the nationalist clubs.[36]*

Haj Amin's odd ties with the Moscow-directed Communist Party of Palestine gave rise to rumors that his position had been so undermined that he might be compelled
to resign in favor of his brother. Commenting on these
rumors, published by the Arab press in Baghdad, the
Haifa Arab newspaper *El Carmel* wrote: "Even if the
Mufti was indeed in contact with Moscow, this could not
be a crime from the viewpoint of the British Labor Government, which had renewed diplomatic relations with
the Soviet Government. If such relations are harmful,
then it is the Zionist Executive that has to be punished
first, because they had introduced the Bolsheviks into
Palestine. Should the Mufti resign his position, it will be
for the better, because then he shall be able to occupy his
place as the head of the Arab national movement."[37]

Building Up a Leading Position in the Moslem World

In 1931, Haj Amin, having carried for more than a decade the badge of his pilgrimage to Mecca, made a fresh
effort to enhance his position in the Moslem world and to
rally support for the Palestine Arab cause by convening in
Jerusalem an all-Islamic Congress. This attempt proved to

* Another source of the Mufti's power since 1933 was supplied by
Nazi Germany. In the files of the German High Command captured in
Flansburg at the war's end, was found a report stating: "Only through
funds made available by Germany to the Grand Mufti of Jerusalem was
it possible to carry out the revolt in Palestine."

be only partly successful. The important Moslem countries were not officially represented, and the bulk of the
delegates were appointed by the Mufti's personal invitations. The Congress met in December 1931, and Haj Amin
easily secured his nomination as president of the elected
Executive. Yet his evident desire to use the Congress for
personal aggrandizement provided his Palestinian opponents with an opportunity for a bitter attack upon his
character and policy.[38]

Later on, Haj Amin used some of the *Waqf* money and
government subsidy to finance his trip to India, Iran,
Afghanistan, and other Moslem lands to gain political
support and to make himself better known to the Moslem
world. In 1934, he made a bid to extend his influence by
journeying into Arabia in the hope of being chosen as
mediator in the quarrel between Ibn Saud and the Imam
of Yemen. But Ibn Saud made his own peace as he had
made his own war, and it became evident that at that
stage of the Mufti's career his political authority did not
extend very far beyond Palestine and, partly Transjordan.[39] Yet, as an able organizer and financier, he succeeded in establishing and fully controlling a substantial
religio-political fund largely derived from contributions
obtained from wealthy Moslems, principally in India,
with the avowed object of establishing a Moslem university in the Holy City of Jerusalem. Another source of income was levies, such as that imposed upon each case of
citrus fruit exported by Arabs from Palestine: in the
citrus season of 1936–1939 this income was estimated at
£60,000. The University project has never reached the
embryo stage. But the accumulated money represented a
source of great political and religious power.[40]

As politician and schemer Haj Amin proved himself a
past master. He knew the art of rousing the Arab masses

to religious fanaticism. Making the utmost use of the
funds at his disposal for political ends, he gradually
ousted all other Arab leaders and built for himself an un-
assailable position, almost a "government within a government" in the Arab community. After 1930, as the new
educated Arab youth appeared on the political scene, he
knew how to keep up with its new outlook, which tended
toward imitation of the Fascist youth movements, storm
troops, and armed uprisings of Europe, and he was busily
building up and encouraging underground insurrectionist
activities.[41]

The Source of the Mufti's Hatred

The major source of Haj Amin's deep-seated, inexorable
enmity toward the Jews and their penetration into Palestine must be sought not only in the purely nationalistic or
political convictions and feelings of a Moslem cleric but
possibly also in his general outlook. He hated the Jews
primarily as bearers of a modern European way of life,
diametrically opposed to his innermost sacred concepts.
In an interview he accorded to Ladislas Farago, he was
quite outspoken in this respect:

The Jews have changed the life of Palestine in such a way
that it must inevitably lead to the destruction of our race. We
are not accustomed to this haste and speed, and therefore we
are continually being driven into the background. They have
also spread here their customs and usages which are opposed
to our religion and to our whole way of life. Above all, our
youth is being morally shattered. The Jewish girls who run
around in shorts demoralize our youth by their mere presence.[42]

When Farago ventured to say that "running around in
shorts" is quite usual in all European countries and that,

besides, it was in full accordance with the climate of Palestine, the Mufti violently retorted:

It is not a matter of climatic conditions, but of tradition. This is foreign to our tradition. And it is dangerous, so radical, almost revolutionary to bring "the other world" before the eyes of the youth. Please don't forget that our generation is the first that no longer lives in the desert . . . Now there suddenly appears the town as if growing out of the earth, with all its distractions and pretended beauties, and finds an Arabic youth which is not prepared for it and which cannot distinguish the good from the evil.

The Mufti wanted Palestine to remain as it had been in the course of many centuries of Arab and Turkish domination: a backward country, with a way of life untouched by modern civilization. In this yearning he had the full sympathy of many Britishers, professing romantic love for the picturesque Orient. The narrow streets of the Arab cities, the veiled Moslem women, the stench of the Arab villages, the chanting voice of the muezzin from the minaret, the camel and donkey, the nomadic Bedouins, the filthy children playing in the mud and running after the tourist clamoring for *baksheesh*—all this exercised a strange fascination for certain British visitors and officials, who wholeheartedly endorsed the Mufti's ardent efforts not to let the Jews introduce a dissonance into that age-long peaceful picture of romance.[43]

Anti-Jewish and Anti-British

For over fifteen years Haj Amin was able to pursue his line under the benevolent eyes of the British administration. He succeeded in conveying to the British the conviction that he was not anti-British, but merely anti-Zionist or anti-Jewish. The British mandatory authorities did not mind too much this direction of the Mufti's animosity. As long as they believed that his orientation was merely anti-Zionist and not anti-British, they let him continue his activities unhampered, preserving his privileged position.

Haj Amin had very good reasons for denying being involved in any anti-British activities. He was after all a salaried official of the Palestine government. As *Reis al Ulema* he was receiving a fixed salary—a state of affairs strongly resented by the country's Jewish community. For he was paid out of a budget raised from the taxes which Jews and Arabs equally had to pay, and since the Jewish share of taxation was incomparably greater than that of the Arabs, Haj Amin's salary was largely provided by the Jews. "We are compelled to pay our greatest enemy," the latter bitterly told Farago in 1937.[44]

Eventually, however, Haj Amin turned against his British paymasters and supporters. He chose his time very carefully. The turnabout came in 1936, at a juncture when British weakness in the Mediterranean was so startlingly revealed in the Middle East. Mussolini's aggression in Abyssinia made a profound impression upon the Arabs. They closely followed the march of events: the futile opposition of the League of Nations and Great Britain, the unsuccessful attempt at sanctions against Fascist Italy, the change in Britian's attitude, the formation of the Berlin-Rome Axis, and the final collapse of Abyssinia's resistance. They observed some of these developments with their own eyes, since all Italian military transports had to pass through the Suez Canal, and it was Jerusalem that offered asylum to the Negus' exiled family. The long expected military defiance of Britain and her allies had finally taken place. The Mufti was sure he saw it all coming: the second world war, the defeat of Britain and of the democracies by the totalitarian states, a new "liberation of

the Arab lands from the yoke of the Franco-British imperialism," and himself in a position of power and influence.[45]

Then and there, Haj Amin decided to play the anti-British card. At the outset he still proceeded in a cautious
way, and the British officials were extremely slow in becoming aware of this change of policy. For nearly two
years they continued tolerating and placating the Mufti-
led rebellion.

The 1936 Rebellion

The zero hour struck on the afternoon of April 19, 1936,
when mobs in Jaffa, incited by Mufti-spread rumors that
Jews were murdering Arabs, fell upon Jews who had been
visiting Jaffa and killed three of them before the police
managed to disperse the assailants. This first open outbreak of violence was immediately utilized by the Mufti
and his acolytes. They intensified their campaign for
adoption of the aggressive tactics successfully employed
by Egyptian and Syrian Arab nationalists. For the first
time Haj Amin openly and officially headed this movement. When, on April 25, a ten-member Arab Higher
Committee had been created, including leaders of all six
existing Arab parties, he took over the presidency of this
new body. The Committee endorsed the general Arab
strike proclaimed five days earlier at Nablus and announced that the strike would continue until Jewish immigration was prohibited.

The Palestine government, on May 5, warned the members of the Higher Committee against perpetrating or encouraging illegal acts. The Mufti calmly ignored this
warning. Three days later, he convened in Jerusalem a

countrywide congress of delegates from the local Arab national committees which had sprung up in every city and town and in many of the villages. The congress unanimously adopted a call for civil disobedience in the form of nonpayment of taxes after May 15.[46] This flat challenge of the mandatory's authority was permitted to remain unpunished. Instead of reprimanding or deposing the Mufti, Sir Arthur Wauchope, the then British High Commissioner, continued parlaying. This only encouraged the Mufti-led Higher Committee in its militant policy. In May and June, the strike was made effective through both persuasion and intimidation. Jewish colonies became objects of persistent sniping; public roads became unsafe for travel, and armed bands of terrorists appeared in the hills.

The Palestine administration was compelled to take action. Under the Palestine (Defense) Order-in-Council the High Commissioner was provided with extensive emergency powers for the preservation of domestic peace, including deportation of undesirables and unusual privileges of arrest and search. More than sixty Arab agitators were, on May 22, detained and placed under police supervision.[47] In June, some of the more prominent leaders, including Auni Abdul Hadi, the secretary of the Higher Committee, were interned. But Haj Amin el-Husseini, the president of the same committee, remained undisturbed. The *New York Times* correspondent in Jerusalem reported on June 14, 1936, that the shrewd Mufti somehow succeeded "in convincing experienced high British civil servants that he is working for the government's interests"; he even succeeded "in convincing the High Commissioner it was in the interest of the government that he should also be president of the new Arab High Committee," so that "Haj Amin el-Husseini now enjoys the government's complete confidence as its unofficial adviser on the

Arab side of the situation . . . The government believes that he and he only is in a position to appease the Moslem masses; therefore it gives him every support while at the same time playing into his hands." Illustrative of the Mufti's cunning influence in governmental circles was the fact that by mid-June 1936 more than ninety per cent of the Arab agitators and political leaders banished to the concentration camp in the Sinai desert belonged to the rival Ragheb Bey Nahashibi's party, and the remaining ten per cent were members of other parties; not one of Haj Amin's followers had been deported. By sending into exile his political opponents, Haj Amin managed to have the political arena for himself, so that if any concessions would have been accorded to the Arabs he and he alone would receive the whole credit. He became the sole actual chief of the Arab rebellion. He even succeeded in securing the cooperation of the Palestine Communist Party which had as early as November 1935 announced that a new revolt was brewing; it called upon the Jewish masses to support the Arab revolutionary movement and denounced the "Zionist Fascists and chauvinists for waging war on the Arab people and killing *fellaheen*." On the eve of the riots, representatives of the party met the Mufti in order to hammer out a working agreement; on the basis of such an agreement two Communists were attached to the general staff in charge of preparing and coordinating the riots. One of them, Nimr 'Uda, became one of the "Intelligence" chiefs of the Arab military units, since he had useful contacts with Jews via the party; the second Communist representative, Fuad Nāsir, became deputy to 'Abdul Qādir Huseini, commander of the Arab guerrillas in the Hebron-Jerusalem region.[48]

The Mufti's main task was to mobilize "a real national army," to strengthen the small nucleus of full-time professional rebels in the field. In his *Mufti over the Middle East,* M. P. Waters describes some of the means employed for this purpose (pp. 14-15):

A section of his thug nucleus would descend on a wealthy isolated Arab village. They would call out the *Mukhtar,* or headman, and make their demands: "We want 50 men, 50 horses, rifles, clothing, food for three days." The alternative? We'll shoot up the village. They got their fifty men.

Once a *Mukhtar* was "foolish" enough to resist. He was buried quietly the same day. And the villagers paid up just the same. An Arab newspaper was sufficiently "unwise" to object to such activities. The editor was paid a visit by a body of gunmen the next day. The new editor was wiser. The paper changed its policy. A couple of gunmen called on a wealthy Arab land-owner, demanded £5,000 "for the cause." He saw the bulge of a revolver muzzle in the fold of their dress. He paid up. They paid another visit a fortnight later, demanded another "dona-tion." He refused. They departed. But he knew it was no use. Two days later, he was shot in an alley 20 yards from his home. He knew his assassins. His family and friends also knew who they were. But the murderers were never caught. They were never even looked for. Everyone knew they were the Mufti's hirelings. But everyone was in the grip of the Mufti terror. The police were powerless. In the Arab villages, the police were Arabs. It was as much as their lives were worth to take action against the terrorists. And so the Mufti's army was raised, equipped and maintained. Gun-running across the Transjordan and Syrian frontiers kept the rebels supplied with the latest types of German and Italian weapons. When food was scarce, the rebels simply billeted themselves on a village, requisitioned food, cattle, grain, clothing. The villagers were happy when they departed without taking their menfolk. Too often, their men went also, taken to fill gaps after any serious losses in the field.

The Christian Arabs, a minority among the Arab population, came in for a particularly bad time. In addition to having funds extorted from them at the pistol point, they were made, by the same method, to conform to certain Moslem conven-tions. They were forced to discard their traditional headgear, the tarbush, in favour of the Kefieh. The point seems trivial. But tradition was so strong that these Christian Arabs felt that they were somehow being forced to change their religion. Similarly, Christian women were compelled to adopt the veil, a strict Moslem custom which is entirely against the habits of Christian Arabs.

The terror bands were also augmented by mercenaries from Syria. The Mufti's recruiting agents went around offering the following terms to all willing to fight in his "Holy War": (1) Once the recruits have crossed the Palestine frontier they are to submit to the discipline of the local "command"; (2) Recruits to be guaranteed their food, clothing, "all other requirements" and £2 a month. Married men to receive a further £2 monthly allowance for their families; (3) A special place in Paradise would be reserved for any killed in this "Holy War." The first condition was satisfied. The local "commands" saw to that. Only half the second condition was fulfilled—food, clothing and "other requirements." But the recruits never received any wages, neither they nor their families. Their "two pounds a month" and family allowance would be paid, they were told, when the "Holy War" was over. And only those who qualified for the third condition ever found out how far the recruiting agents' promises were fulfilled.

Palestine paid a high price for this Mufti-sponsored practice. During the first six months following the outbreak of the disturbances in April 1936, nearly 300 Jews and Arabs were killed and over 1,100 were wounded; the direct cost to the taxpayers of Palestine was estimated at $17,500,000, and the cost to the Palestine treasury at $7,500,000.[49]

The Mufti's Role

John Marlowe is convinced that "there is every reason to believe that the rebellion was largely organized by the Mufti assisted by agents both inside and outside Palestine, who had at their disposal a certain amount of money obtained both from Italian sources, and from the religious funds under the control of the Mufti." Moreover, armed rebellion in the hills rather than the general strike was apparently Haj Amin's main concern. As president of the Higher Committee, he was, of course, cooperating in organizing and directing the strike and civil disobedience movement. The Higher Committee was composed of members of almost every Arab party (including two Christian Arabs) and the Mufti was quite prepared to combine with other groups for the purpose of the strike. But even if he thought that the strike "were to be successful beyond all expectations, he was not interested in an independent Arab Palestine in which he would share the reins of power with the Nashashibis and the various other interests represented on the Higher Committee." The strike merely "served as a shield behind which the rebel bands could become organized; it created the conditions of disorder in which the rebel bands could best function." While the over-all campaign of civil disobedience was conducted under the auspices of the all-party Higher Committee, "the rebellion was directed only by the Mufti and his satellites . . . the control of the revolt had almost completely passed out of the hands of the Higher Committee, as a whole, and had passed into those of the Mufti and his agents, who were working to a great extent independently of the Higher Committee."*

Their concerted and well-financed effort resulted in a considerable growth of the Mufti's rebel and terrorist

* A. M. Hyamson, who for the first fourteen years of the British mandate headed the Department of Immigration in the government of Palestine, rather naively believes that "after a time" the control of the Arab rebellion passed out of the hands of the Mufti and his Higher Committee "into that of the soldiers in the field." (*Palestine Under the Mandate, 1920–1948.* [London, 1950], pp. 137-38.) "Soldiers in the field" were acting under strict instructions from the Mufti.

forces. By the middle of 1937 there were, instead of small scattered rebel bands, two well defined guerrilla groups: one operating in the hills of Galilee and the other in Samaria. By the end of 1938 their combined strength was estimated at about 15,000 men under arms as compared with 5,000 in 1936. No less important than his military organization was the Mufti's terrorist organization, which was again divided into two branches: one for the south with its headqarters in Jerusalem, and the other for the north with its headquarters in Damascus. For a time the terrorists and the rebel bands had worked to a large extent independently, but later, signs of liaison between them became apparent. Individual terrorists appeared to be acting in conjunction with, or under the control of, the leaders of one or other of the armed rebel groups, who were themselves operating under the direction of the Mufti.[50]

The central place occupied by armed rebellion in the Mufti's strategy became even more accentuated when the general strike proclaimed by the Higher Committee started becoming economically ruinous for the Arab population and unpopular in the country. Neither the Mufti nor the Higher Committee were prepared to risk the consequence to their reputation if they called off the strike; but what was more important to the Mufti was that the strike was really intended to act primarily as a diversion to draw British attention away from the assembling of the insurgent bands in the hills of Samaria and Galilee. Both the Higher Committee and the Mufti had also realized that if they did not end it, the strike would most probably peter out; on the other hand, they did not want to take the responsibility for a withdrawal. The British administration for its part was convinced that all that was necessary was some face-saving formula to enable the Higher Committee to call off the strike. So, while the British appealed to Abdallah, of Transjordan, the Mufti appealed to the kings of Saudi Arabia and Iraq to provide the alibi for ending the strike. On October 8, 1936, the Higher Committee received from King Ibn Saud a telegram announcing that he and the rulers of Iraq, Yemen, and Transjordan had agreed upon a request that the Committee should end the strike and place their trust in "the good intentions of our friend Great Britain, who has declared that she will do justice." Three days later, the Mufti announced that, in response to the appeal, the strike would cease on October 12.[51]

Calling off the general strike was for the Mufti merely the prelude for more bloody forms of intervention. He calculated (correctly) that there would be no disposition on the part of the British administration to pursue energetically the rounding up of the armed bands in the hills, provided that the strike were called off and conditions on the surface restored to normal. The administration seemed to hold the view that the rebellion in the hills was subsidiary to and merely a result of the strike. It did not appear to realize that the strike had been little more than a diversion staged by the Mufti to cover the formation of a rebel army and to create conditions favorable to its development.[52] British military forces, which by the end of September numbered about 20,000 soldiers, were therefore not employed to their full capacity, and no concerted and effective effort was made to liquidate the rebel bands in the hills or to disarm the Arab population.[53]

Haj Amin Before the Royal Commission

On November 11, exactly one month after the termination of the strike, the British Royal Commission, to be known as the Peel commission after its chairman, Earl

Peel, arrived in Palestine to conduct an inquiry into the disturbances in the country. Prior to its arrival, on November 6, the Mufti and his Higher Committee announced that they would boycott the Commission and called upon the Arabs of Palestine to follow suit.

This tactical move proved to be highly unpopular in the Arab community. Influential Arab leaders, including some members of the Higher Committee, insisted that it was a mistake to refuse the opportunity to make a reasonable presentation of the Arab case. *Falastin,* the organ of the Nashashibi party, published on December 24 an article strongly criticizing the Mufti's boycott tactics. Identical notes were received from the rulers of Iraq and Saudi Arabia advising the Palestine Arabs to trust to the sense of justice of the great British nation. Publishing these notes on January 6, 1937, the Higher Committee announced that it had acceded to the wishes of the Arab princes and that the Arab case would be presented.

The star witness was the Mufti himself.[54] Speaking in Arabic, he complained about sinister "Jewish designs on the Moslem Holy Places." When Lord Peel and other members of the Commission asked for proof of such design, the Mufti promised to produce it later. Lord Peel then asked: "Do you think that the Mandatory Power would permit the Jews to destroy the Mosque of Omar and build on its place a Jewish temple?"

"Yes," the Mufti replied, "the Jews are capable of doing anything in Palestine."

While stating that in a future Palestine Arab state every right would be granted to the Jews, whose position would be the same as in Iraq, the Mufti asserted that there were already now "too many Jews" in the country: their number must be reduced from the present 400,000 to the prewar total of 80,000.

The Minutes of the Royal Commission reproduce the following exchange of questions and answers:

Lord Peel: Does His Eminence think that this country [Palestine] can assimilate and digest the 400,000 Jews now in the country?

The Mufti: No.

Lord Peel: Some of them would have to be removed by a process kindly or painful as the case may be?

The Mufti: We must leave all this to the future.

Lord Peel: You complain that there are too many Jews. Would they be safe in an Arab Palestine?

The Mufti: That would depend on the Arab Government.

Lord Peel: Would Jews trust the intentions of a future Arab Government?

The Mufti: I cannot tell the Jewish reply.

Lord Peel: I think I can tell you. (laughter)

The Verdict of the Royal Commission

The Royal Commission had unhesitatingly established the direct responsibility of the Mufti and of the Higher Arab Committee that he headed, for the increasing violence of the rebellion. The Commission's report stated:

At an early stage in its course the Mufti and the members of the committee were allowed to make a tour throughout Palestine. We were informed that one district had been quiet until the Mufti was given the permission and held conferences at which neither police nor officials were allowed to be present. From the date of the tour the strike has spread and stiffened. It is unquestionable that the committee was to a large extent responsible for maintaining and protracting the strike. They constituted in fact the headquarters of the Arab nationalist movement. The Mufti as president of the committee must bear his due share of responsibility.

The Royal Commission firmly rejected the claim that the Mufti exercised a moderating influence:

Whatever may have been the apparent moderation of the Mufti's attitude at the commencement, the manifestoes issued by the Higher Arab Committee under his chairmanship, endorsing the strike and urging the Arabs to continue it until certain political aims have been achieved were clearly prejudicial to law and order. Nor, as far as we are aware, did the Higher Arab Committee at any time condemn the acts of sabotage and terrorism which became more frequent as the strike continued, and the Mufti as chairman must, in our view, bear his full share of responsibility for these disorders.

The Mufti is, the Commission's report stated, "now such a power in the land that, supplemented by the National Committees in the different towns of Palestine, he may truthfully be described as the head of yet a third parallel government" [the first two being the mandatory administration and the Jewish Agency].[55]

It was the first time that a British commission of inquiry expressly asserted the Mufti's responsibility for disturbances in Palestine and assigned to him his full share of blame.

New Evidence

The Royal Commission's outspoken condemnation of the Mufti, however, left the Palestine administration unimpressed. It persisted in backing him and disregarded any evidence establishing his responsibility for continuing bloody disturbances.

In February 1937, the Palestine police had received information that material endangering public security was being prepared for publication in the Jerusalem office of the Mufti-led Arab Higher Committee, and that arms were kept in this office. An unexpected search was carried out, and two bombs and twenty-five rounds of ammunition were found at the office itself; two more bombs were discovered in a shop opposite. The owner of the shop and his employees were arrested, but neither the Mufti nor any of the Higher Committee members of its office staff had been detained.[56] Almost simultaneously, Emir Abdallah of Transjordan, a fervent opponent of the Mufti, submitted a memorandum to Sir Arthur Wauchope, the British High Commissioner, describing the Mufti's machinations and revealing that some weeks earlier the latter had endeavored to persuade Transjordanian Bedouin tribes to join a new mutiny in western Palestine which would be engineered should Arab demands not be met by the British government.[57] This memorandum was handed over to the High Commissioner a week before he departed on leave for London, so that the British government was fully informed on the Mufti's activities. Nevertheless, on March 17, 1937, William Ormsby-Gore, the secretary of state for the Colonies, assured the House of Commons that he was "quite satisfied that . . . murders of Arabs by Arabs and Jews by Arabs are done by local bands of local character," and that he was sure that "these murderers and gangs were not connected with the Arab Higher Committee." As sufficient evidence for this statement, the Colonial Secretary "was glad to note," that on the 10th of February "the Mufti and two other members of the Arab Higher Committee had expressed their abhorrence of these acts."[58] Several days later, Mr. Ormsby-Gore once again hopefully informed the House of Commons that "the Arab Higher Committee had issued a statement containing an appeal to avoid acts of violence," and, when asked by a conservative member of Parliament, A. C. Crossley, whether he had "any reason to suppose that the Mufti and the Arab Higher Committee do not wholly disapprove of this violence," the Colonial Secretary emphatically stated:

"The whole of evidence at my disposal goes to show that they do.[59]

At the 1937 annual conference of the British Labor Party at Bournemouth, Tom Williams, Labor member of Parliament, reminded the audience that whenever, within the past twelve months, he drew the attention of the Secretary of State for the Colonies to the fact that the "Grand Mufti" was "largely responsible, with a few feudal overlords, for organizing the destruction and desolation in Palestine, the Secretary of State resented any reference to the head of the Moslem religion."[60]

After his return from London, the High Commissioner received a delegation of the Arab Higher Committee, headed by the Mufti, and asked them "to use their utmost endeavors to bring about a maintenance of law and order" during the coming Nebi Musa festivals in Jerusalem. The delegation promised that "it would do what it could to keep the people quiet." Reporting on this meeting, the Jerusalem correspondent of the London *Jewish Chronicle* (April 9, 1937), made the following comment:

The very fact that General Wauchope found it necessary, in anticipation of a period when mob excitement and incitement traditionally flourishes in Jerusalem, to appeal to the Arab leaders to use their influence in the direction of pacification, is an indication that he takes it for granted, as does everyone else in this country, that the Arab Higher Committee knows a great deal more than it will openly admit about the sources of past (and present) violence. It seems, therefore, somewhat strange for him to be cajoling upon political grounds a body of people whom he knows or suspects to be responsible for seditious outbreaks.

The Palestine Government Acts at Last

This cajoling of the Mufti continued until autumn, 1937. Indicative of the administration's long blindness and belated awakening is the following entry in the autobiography of Norman Bentwich, a British Jew and registered Zionist, who from 1920 to 1931 served as attorney with the British mandatory government of Palestine:

The Mufti, though he never disguised his Arab nationalism, seemed for a time loyal to the Administration; but once entrenched in power, he showed himself the extreme nationalist-fanatical, inflexible in aim, unscrupulous in means, ruthless against his Arab rivals not less than against Jewish enterprise, and hostile equally to British policy and to the Jewish National Home. He was to cause infinite mischief to both. He became a modern Haman plotting the destruction of the Jews. I met him frequently in my official capacity, and for some years our personal relations were on the surface friendly. He no doubt hated me, and did what he could to make my office a burden. I thought him foxy, but did not a first recognize his great capacity for evil.[61]

As long as Haj Amin's bands confined themselves merely to murdering Jews and Arabs, the government was maintaining its policy of nonintervention. But on September 26, 1937, British blood was shed: L. Y. Andrews, district commissioner for Galilee, and his police escort, were assassinated at Nazareth.[62] This direct attack upon British authority awakened the administration to a belated policy of striking at the very roots of the rebellion.

Four days later, on September 30, the Palestine government, acting under emergency powers conferred in March 1937 by a new Defense Order-in-Council,[63] enacted regulations allowing the government to deport political detainees to any part of the British Empire and to dissolve

any association whose objectives might be regarded as
contrary to the administration's policy. Simultaneously,
announcement was made of the removal of Haj Amin el-
Husseini as head of the Supreme Moslem Council and of
the General Waqf Committee, as well as of the proscription of the Arab Higher Committee.[64] On the following
day, six members of the Committee were charged with
"moral responsibility" for recent acts of terrorism and violence; five were, on October 21, deported to the Seychelles Islands; the sixth, Jamal el-Husseini, succeeded in escaping to Syria.[65] Shortly thereafter the administration
formally notified Jamal and four other members of the
Higher Committee then out of the country that they
would be debarred from returning to Palestine until formal notice.

This energetic action on the part of the Palestine government did not arouse any violent outburst of Arab fury
in the country. The Jerusalem correspondent of the *New
York Times* related on October 3 that "no untoward incident was reported," although Arab shops in the old city of
Jerusalem, Jaffa, Nablus, and Jenin were closed in protest
against the government's action in exiling high Arab leaders. The Mufti himself had chosen to disregard the government's order discharging him from the presidency of
the Moslem Supreme Council and from the chairmanship
of the Waqf; he contended that the government had no
right to dismiss him from either of these posts since both
are related purely to Moslem religious institutions.
Blandly overlooking the fact that he owed these positions
not to free elections by competent Moslem bodies, but to
the government's pressure, he maintained that it rested
with the Moslems of the country to decide whether he
was to remain in office, and that this was possible only by
a general election by all the Moslems in Palestine.[66]

In the meantime, suspecting that he would be the next object of deportation proceeding, Haj Amin, accompanied by his Sudanese bodyguards, secluded himself within the sacred Mosque El Omar area. He was confident that the British would not dare to follow him there, fearing that invasion of such a hallowed Moslem sanctuary would cause an unpredictable explosion. From this safe abode he issued a manifesto to the Palestine Arabs in which he thanked them for their "courageous attitude" toward the government's action.[67] But his position was far from secure. He was surrounded in the Temple area, and had no channels of direct activity.

If the Palestine administration had efficiently maintained this state of siege and practically isolated Haj Amin from any contact with the outside world, they might well have finally succeded in liquidating his influence. As early as August 1930, Colonel Kisch, who had an excellent insight into the mentality of the administration, noted in his diary: "If the Government would only show a little courage and strip the Mufti of his powers which are used for agitation and to foment hatred of the Jews, the whole situation would change for the better within a relatively short time." "What I fear," he added, "is that the Government may adopt some half measures against the Mufti which will be sufficient to arouse his jackals to fury, but not sufficient to make it impossible for him to maintain his position.[68] Seven years later, Kisch's apprehensions were vindicated. The Palestine government stopped at the half measure of deposing Haj Amin from the presidency of the Supreme Moslem Council. They did not touch upon his position as mufti. And, as reported by the press, the government's stringent measures of October 1 "served only temporarily to frighten a few Arab terrorists, who for a moment believed that the Government meant business and would not tolerate any further disturbances of the peace. For two weeks the country was unusually quiet and calm, but, seeing that beyond the deportation of these leaders the Government did not take further stringent action, the terrorists resumed their activities."[69]

The final blow to the government's prestige was delivered by the Mufti's successful escape from his semi-captivity. On October 15 he failed to appear for midday prayers at his mosque hideaway. This spurred rumors that he had slipped out of the country. This was, however, "authoritatively denied."[70] The greater was the confusion, when these denied rumors proved to be true. Eluding the allegedly tight British police cordon, Haj Amin slipped out of the Harramesh Sharif, disguised as a beggar.[71] He went from Jerusalem to Gaza, where he boarded a sailboat that carried him to Ras el Nakoura on the Lebanese border.* Lebanese custom guards saw the sailboat moving toward shore and boarded the craft in the belief it might be carrying smugglers. After searching the boat, the agents questioned several passengers and found one of them to be Haj Amin el-Husseini, the mufti of Jerusalem. Haj Amin presented his passport to a customs officer. After the usual formalities, he proceeded to Beirut and from there to Damascus.[72]

---

* The Palestine Communist Party protested vigorously against the "deportation" of the Mufti; in November 1937 its Hebrew organ *Kol Ha 'Am* accused the Jewish leaders of not accepting the "very reasonable proposals of Haj Amin al-Husseini" (Walter Q. Laqueur, *Communism and Nationalism in the Middle East*, p. 99.)

2

Political Émigré in Lebanon
1937-1939

A Villa in Lebanon

THE FRENCH AUTHORITIES IN SYRIA WERE GREATLY DISCON-
certed by Haj Amin's arrival. Officials of the French Foreign Office, it was reported from Paris, debated whether
to permit him to remain in French-mandated territory or
to send him back to Palestine.[1] They had forbidden him to
stay in Damascus, and it was largely believed that he
would be either interned in some village or deported. Had
the British government at that time put the slightest pressure on their French allies, they would probably have
obtained his extradition or deportation. Yet, so relieved
must the Palestine government officials have been in getting rid of the embarrassing problem of what to do with
the Mufti, that for a long time they simply enjoyed his
absence and did not annoy the French by protesting his
presence in French-controlled territory. The French authorities had no defensible grounds to deal with the Mufti

more severely than the more immediately concerned British, and had no other choice than to allow Haj Amin to remain in Lebanon, although in a remote spot. The first time that the British Government "had drawn the attention of the French Government to the Mufti's recent political activities" was some time in February 1938, four months after his arrival in Lebanon.[2]

Haj Amin took up residence in the coastal village of al-Zug, north of Beirut. Though he had been confined to the vicinity of his little villa, his trusted aides could generally come and go at will. Through them he established contact with his exiled colleagues, and the outlawed Higher Committee was reconstituted with its seat at Damascus. Their activities were now beyond the reach of the Palestine government.

For a time, the Mufti's disappearance from the Palestine scene emboldened his long-terrorized political opponents and less extreme Arab leaders and encouraged them to come out in the open.

First to voice open disavowal was Fakhri Bey Nashashibi. In October 1938 he published a challenging letter to the High Commissioner of Palestine in which he asserted: (1) that the anti-Mufti Arabs comprise seventy-five percent of the Arabs in Palestine, whom the Mufti had sought to crush through terrorism; (2) that the Mufti had "used official position and the funds collected for the national cause to exterminate or impoverish the leaders opposed to him" in Palestine; and (3) that the British should realize that the Mufti does not represent the Arabs of Palestine, and that terrorism is encouraged by this wrong assumption.

"I accuse Haj Amin el-Husseini, the former Mufti of Jerusalem, of diverting the noble Arab revolt to his own selfish ends," solemnly declared Fakhri Bey. "Haj Amin's fifteen years' tenure of office in Jerusalem proved his destructive tendencies."

The publication of this challenging letter was a bold act. The Mufti's response came quickly. An attempt was made to assassinate a member of the Nashashibi faction the very next day. Five other members of the Nashashibi family were murdered or attacked shortly thereafter. Nevertheless, Fakhri Bey had the courage to remain in Jerusalem, the only moderate Arab who had dared it. A month later, Nashashibi published a pamphlet in Arabic in which he was even more outspoken:

When Haj Amin was deprived of his office of President of the Supreme Moslem Council, and escaped and sought refuge in Beirut, he was joined by a group of his followers who had built up their careers with the money of the poor, the needy and the orphaned. There and then they began their campaign of terror and murder, there and then they launched their work of destruction, making shameful use of the well-meaning, and sweeping the country into an ocean of blood and evil. . . .

Those who work for Haj Amin are but creatures whose task it was formerly to stand up in mosques and make slanderous accusations and for whom the coffers of the Waqf were opened. Let their payment cease for a day and we shall soon see them forsake and overthrow their master. I could name them, one by one, and produce evidence as to how much remuneration each is getting. Suffice it to say that Haj Amin would not publish an account of the funds he received in 1936, because he dare not speak the truth about them. . . .

When he realized that he could not establish himself securely enough without money, he did not hesitate to spend the funds of the Waqf on a group of adherents and supporters who would build up a large following for him.

And when the funds of the Waqf did not suffice, he appealed to Moslems abroad, and they contributed generously, unaware of how the money would be spent. And when income even from this source began to dwindle, after the Moslems had begun to realize what had become of their gifts, then he offered the country at public auction on foreign markets. Soon a document was discovered to the effect that he was working on behalf of foreign countries. When the fact was made known he thundered and filled the earth with threats, with the object of dissociating himself from the document, but the noise was short-lived, and in the end he contented himself with the discharge of employees of the Supreme Moslem Council whom he accused of the theft of his personal papers. . . .

Nothing has moved me to make this declaration but the state of misery into which the country has drifted and the dastardly crimes that have been committed. Loyal Arabs and their families are being victimized every day, and their property wantonly burned and destroyed for no other crime of their commiting than that they are opponents of the Mufti. Why need he murder, torture and destroy if he is truly such a beloved leader as he claims to be?[3]

Nashashibi's bold challenge encouraged minor Arab politicians who for years did not dare to raise their voice against the Mufti's overbearance and his terrorist anti-Jewish campaign. Issa Effendi Bandak, editor of *Sowt esh-Shaab* (Voice of the People), an Arabic weekly issued at Bethlehem of which he was the mayor, editorially urged the British government to bring the Jews and Arabs together at a round-table conference. Sheikh Taji el-Faruq, the editor of *Al Jamia Al-Islamia* (Pan-Islam), declared that Arab policy must cease to be purely negative, and inveighed against terrorist methods and acts of violence, pointing out that their continuance merely led to the innocent being punished with the guilty and was doing great damage to the Arab movement. On November 30, 1938, twenty-five local Arab leaders who claimed to represent forty-five villages in the Jerusalem-Ramallah-Hebron areas, with a population of some 70,000, gathered secretly by night at Fakhri Bey's house to assure him of their support for his campaign against the Mufti forces. According to press reports, there were among them "bearded and turbaned Sheikhs, typical young countrymen, and a youth whom the murder by rebels of his father

The Grand Mufti of Jerusalem (center), in his home near the palace of King Farouk of Egypt. His guest is a representative from Yemen.   (Zionist Archives and Library)

The Grand Mufti meets with Adolf Hitler.

Mufti Haj Amin el-Husseini (right), and another exiled leader, Emir Abd el Krim (left), meet in Cairo following World War II. (Wide World Photos)

and uncle left head of his family." While addressing representatives of the press, these Mufti antagonists "constantly reiterated their fear of death if their names became known, and admitted that they would have to pretend to support the Mufti when, as often happened, armed men came to force them to sign up. Most of the men had suffered personally from terrorization, having lost some sons or relatives. They maintained that though they represented seventy per cent of the people they remained silent in face of armed threats.[4]

By mid-December these forces of opposition came into the open. In the presence of the British district commissioner of Hebron, Edward Keith-Roach; Maj. Gen. Richard Nugent O'Connor, military commander of the Southern district; and other high British officials, more than 2000 Arabs, including many notables, gathered on a hillside near Yatta, a village south of Hebron, and vigorously denounced the Mufti and his tactics.[5] The sheikh of Yatta, Khalil es Shariff, speaking on behalf of the gathering and claiming to represent 60,000 Arabs in that vicinity, declared:

Palestine Arab newspapers, whose proprietors have been compelled through terrorism to leave the country, and which are today published under the supervision of the terrorists, convey to the inhabitants nothing but falsehood and hypocrisies. . . .

The Arab Press has built up barriers of deceit and error in order to conceal the truth. If the Press has the intention to work for the interests of the nation and the prosperity of the country, it must destroy these barriers, and convey to the people the naked truth. . . .

A wave of terrorism has loosed destruction on the country, ruining the villages and their inhabitants through murder, looting and destruction, carried out by men who were given instructions to strike terror into the hearts of the Arabs in order to gain support for certain personal interests. . . .

At the head of these criminals was placed a man who has

nominated himself Commmander-in-Chief of the Rebellion in
Palestine, this man being Aref Abdul Razzik. . . .

By his campaign he has killed on the orders of his colleagues, both of Beirut and Damascus, more than 200 Arabs,
the anguish of whose widows and children still rings in our
ears. . . .

We place the responsibility for the crimes of murder and the
destruction of property on Haj Amin el-Husseini, now in
Beirut, and the men who have surrounded him.[6]

By far not all of the Mufti's opponents had the courage
to remain in Palestine and to face the constant menace of
being murdered by his henchmen. Many sought refuge in
neighboring Egypt. But once there, they did not remain
silent. The Cairo correspondent of the London *Times*
cabled to his paper (December 6, 1938) that fifty prominent Palestine Arab exiles in Egypt, who met in the house
of Sheikh Ali Shahine, "decided to protest against the
murders committed in Palestine by partisans of the Mufti
of Jerusalem, to send a telegram to Fakhri Bey Nashashibi
approving of his recent action in opposing the Mufti, and
to send a telegram to the High Commissioner for Palestine
declaring their disapproval of acts of terrorism and the
policy of the Mufti."

Even some of Haj Amin's own associates, who were at
first attracted by the "noble and religious appeal" of the
Mufti's cause, began to see the light. Early in 1939, eight
former "regional commanders" of the Mufti-led rebellion,
who had fled to Syria, published a manifesto condemning
the campaign of terror, and accusing the Mufti of receiving large sums of money from "foreign sources" and
spending it on his personal cause. Written in picturesque
and somewhat quaint Arabic, the manifesto began as follows:

"In order that the Moslem and Arab worlds should
know the truth about these matters, it would be sufficient

to give the names and description of some of the commanders, who were relied upon by Haj Amin el-Husseini and his faction in Palestine to carry out acts of destruction and sabotage in Arab property and to murder the best of Arab patriots and the most truthful to the country who had the interest of the people at heart."[7]

Citing numerous compromising details about several Mufti-appointed commanders of the terrorist bands, describing them as vulgar thieves, robbers, and killers, the document went on:

Those and many other similar persons are the commanders in whom Haj Amin Eff. has exclusive trust. It is they who have desecrated the holy rebellion by exploiting it for Haj Amin's selfish aims.

Now it is time to say who Haj Amin is: he is a member of one of the noblest families in Jerusalem. Nobody denies him that, but his education was ordinary. After staying in Egypt for eight months, he was appointed as acting Mufti in Jerusalem. He lost in the elections, but the High Commissioner Sir Herbert Samuel appointed him president of the Supreme Moslem Council, in exploitation of the rebellion of 1921-22 [?].

His activities in the Supreme Moslem Council during eighteen [?] years may be summed up in that he received as proceeds from the Waqf property something like *one million pounds*. For the Syrian rebellion, the disturbances of 1929, the reconstruction of the Aqsa Mosque, the Wailing Wall, the relief of the distressed in 1929, 1933 and 1936, and finally for the present rebellion in Palestine, he collected as contributions from Arab countries, America and India not less than *two million pounds*. This is in addition to the sums of money which he collected for the Aqsa Mosque, and the Moslem Congress and the inestimable sums of money received from foreign powers. These are millions of pounds, but can Haj Amin point to at least a single mosque, a school or a hospital he erected during this period? Did he build a shelter or an asylum or a charity cistern from which poor tramps could drink?

There are in the country about 20,000 orphans and sufferers. Will His Eminence, or his responsible adherents point out to us one orphan or one distressed person who had received even one piastre from the relief funds? Can His Eminence or his henchmen say that one piastre has been paid in compensation for the property demolished or blown up by the troops or for the houses and orchards damaged? Can His Eminence publish a statement showing the manner in which these funds were spent? And, finally, can he publish a statement on the latest contributions which have been collected by the Arab Delegation to the U.S.A.? Can he explain where and how these contributions were spent at the time when we, the *Mujahidin,* cannot find anything with which to maintain ourselves except through begging? Is His Eminence aware that the majority of the *Mujahidin,* now dispersed in Syria and Lebanon, are homeless and go to sleep hungry while His Eminence's friends, supporters and relatives live in luxury, receive large monthly salaries from the relief funds of orphans and spend their nights in cabarets, live with dancers, and each one of them has a number of stray girls?

Not every word in this bitter and acrimonious indictment, with its minor inaccuracies and clearly distinguishable undertone of envy by those out of favor with the Mufti against those still enjoying his bounty, has to be taken at its face value. But there can hardly be any doubt that the brunt of it, coming as it did from recent partisans and "inside men," reflected the true state of affairs in the Mufti camp.

British Complacency and French Uneasiness

These scattered manifestations of anti-Mufti trends however, remained spordic and unorganized. The British administration "never attempted wholeheartedly either to discredit Haj Amin or to back any of his political rivals."[8] The Mufti legend grew unopposed. Shortly after his flight to Lebanon, the Palestine administration made a half-hearted attempt to put an end to his advertising in the local press, and the official *Palestine Gazette* (October 8, 1937) announced a ban on literature relating to or written by the Mufti, as well as on all pictures of him. But no systematic anti-Mufti campaign was conducted or favored.* Haj Amin and his followers remained practically unchallenged in the propaganda field, and his popularity was steadily growing. The Mufti's "spiritual influence has only been increased by his voluntary exile," wrote Margaret Boveri in 1939, and he was considered a serious candidate for the Caliphate. "In the person of the Mufti the religious merges into the nationalist movement; he unites the ideals of pan-Islamism and pan-Arabism in his own person."[9] The British government was watching Haj Amin's activities, directed from his Lebanese villa, with a truly philosophical equanimity. In March 1938, the Liberal member of Parliament, Geoffrey Mander, asked the colonial secretary, William Ormsby-Gore, if he would state the present position with regard to the Mufti; whether he was aware that the Mufti was receiving a substantial monthly subsidy from foreign sources and was now directing terrorist operations from French Syria; and what representations had been made to the French government on the subject.

Mr. Ormsby-Gore replied: "I understand that Haj Amin is kept under surveillance by the French authorities in Syria. The High Commissioner for Palestine has received

---

* After Haj Amin's dismissal from his official position, the Supreme Moslem Council and the Waqf funds were put under the direct control of the British administration. Investigation proved what had long been apparent, namely that Haj Amin had for some time been diverting a substantial part of the funds at his disposal from their legitimate objects to the purposes of the rebellion. The maintenance of mosques and the general interests of the Moslem religion in Palestine had been grossly neglected. The administration, however, did not see fit to give more publicity than it did to this aspect of the Mufti's activities. (John Marlowe, *Rebellion*, p. 187.)

information from time to time regarding alleged political activities on the part of the Mufti, and this matter is engaging the attention of His Majesty's Government in close consultation with the French authorities both in Paris and Damascus."

Then followed a brief exchange of questions and answers:

Mander: "Is the Colonial Secretary satisfied that no money is reaching the Mufti from foreign sources."

Ormsby-Gore: "It cannot be that, because he is not living in territory under British control. All we can do is to make representations to the Government in France and through our Consul."

Mander: "Can I ask whether this is one of the matters that is being discussed with the French Government?"

Mr. Ormsby-Gore did not reply to the last question.[10] Nine months later, Ormsby-Gore, who was in the meantime elevated to the peerage and took his seat as Lord Harlech, said during a debate in the House of Lords December 8, 1938:

The Mufti . . . is playing his own dynastic game, and that game undoubtedly is to become not merely the sovereign of Palestine, not merely the crowned or uncrowned King of Palestine, but first head of Palestine, then of Palestine and Transjordan combined, and then of the whole of Syria, and, of course, in that position to be regarded as the leader of the Sunni world [Sunni is one of the two main Moslem sects]. . . . He is a man of quite unlimited political ambitions. He was a Turkish Staff Officer—and incidentally a Turk who knew him thought he was the blackest-hearted man in the Middle East. . . . He is a deepseated enemy of Great Britain . . . (he) uses for his own ends the private murder of Arabs in Palestine not friendly to his dynastic ambitions. Members of other leading families have been foully murdered. . . . The man stands condemned in the Arab world.[11]

The French themselves felt uneasy because of the Mufti's presence in Lebanon. The Radical Socialist *La Republique* devoted an alarming article to the Mufti-led pan-Arab, or rather pan-Islamic, movement. In May 1938, Robert Dreux, a noted Catholic clergyman, published an article in *L'Ordre*, a Paris conservative daily, charging that the Mufti was abusing the hospitality granted to him by the French authorities in Lebanon: his subversive activity was extending not only to the countries of the Near East but also to North Africa. "Frequent secret meetings," wrote Mr. Dreux, "are held at the Mufti's. There, the pan-Arab leaders and agitators come to take their orders; thence the emissaries depart. Since the principal person there has no scruples and is not in the least fastidious in the choice of his means, it would be useful to establish the origin of funds at his disposal." The main target was neighboring Palestine:

The executors of the high-handed terrorist activities, the incendiaries, assassins, and agitators, charged with the fomenting of trouble, all go out from the Lebanese residence of the Mufti. It is through his hands that the money awarded to them passes. It is his services that supervise the smuggling of arms shipments, which do not cease to be poured into Palestine; arms to a large extent of German origin.

Emphasizing that the activities of the Mufti constituted a source of danger to international stability, Dreux asked whether it were not possible to put an end to this state of affairs by removing the Mufti from Lebanon and offering him hospitality elsewhere in the French colonial empire, with the exception of the Near East and North Africa: Haj Amin had cynically abused the right of refuge, and no moral or international law could oblige France to tolerate him within her frontiers, or to permit his propaganda to be extended across the nervous center of the Near East.[12]

The French government apparently shared many of those apprehensions. But action had been easily foiled by colonial and military circles which had long been pandering to the Arabs in the Middle East, lest any trouble there should affect the recruiting and loyalty of their Arab and Moorish auxiliaries in North Africa, and incline them to look henceforth to Italy for sympathy and support. No action was taken, and the Beirut correspondent of the London *Times* complained on October 10,1938, that "the control upon the visitors who resort to the Mufti is regrettably ineffective, and he is free to carry on his intrigues from his Lebanon villa as much as he pleases. Of this laxity he is making full use."

In fact, the British government itself was hardly making any determined effort to induce the French mandatory power to curb the Mufti's diversionist activities. A very instructive brief discussion on this subject took place in the House of Commons on May 10, 1939, over a year and a half after Haj Amin's escape from Palestine. Geoffrey Mander asked the secretary of state for the Colonies Malcolm MacDonald whether he would consider the advisability of taking action to prevent the ex-Mufti from continuing his anti-British activities by staying in Syria and organizing outrages in Palestine:

MacDonald: His Majesty's Government are in close touch with the French Government on this matter.

Mander: Is there the slightest doubt that the ex-Mufti has been carrying on his propaganda for a long time, encouraging outrages in Palestine? Can the Minister say nothing more than that he is in close touch with the French Government? Are they not going to do anything about it?

MacDonald: We have made it perfectly clear from time to time what is our view of the activities carried on by the Mufti of Jerusalem, and we have not altered our opinion with regard to that matter.

Mander: What is the good of the Government having an opinion unless they do domething about it? Are they not prepared to bring pressure upon our friend and ally, France, to put an end to these activities of the ex-Mufti?

Lt. Comdr. Fletcher: For how many years have the Colonial Office been in close touch with France on this subject? Have they received a direct refusal from the French Government to take any action in the matter?

MacDonald: Our information is that in recent times the surveillance over the activities of the Mufti of Jerusalem has been stricter than it was some time ago.

Fletcher: Has it checked them?[13]

The question remained unanswered. As a matter of fact, Haj Amin continued his activities rather under the protection than under the surveillance of the French authorities in Lebanon. Roger Courtney, a member of the Palestine police force, saw him in Beirut when he was coming down the steps of his hotel to his car, accompanied by plain-clothes men from the *Sûreté.* "As I watched him," wrote Courtney, "I thought how contrary he was to one's idea of a Holy Man, which as the great Moslem leader he was supposed to be. . . . He had a mysterious air about him. The lower part of his face was concealed by a carefully arranged sweep of the turban cloth in which his fez was set. He wore dark blue spectacles."[14]

The Long Hand of the Mufti

Undisturbed by either British or French, Haj Amin continued planning and plotting and directing terrorist activities in Palestine. In 1938, 297 Jews were killed and 427 wounded by his bands.[15] At the same time, an extermination campaign against Arab opponents of the Mufti continued unabated. On October 15, 1938, the Jerusalem correspondent of the *New York Times* reported that extremist Arab followers of the Mufti . . . are rapidly achieving their aims by eliminating political opponents in Palestine who are inclined toward moderation. More than 90 per cent of the total casualties in the past few days have been inflicted by Arab terrorists on Arabs. Two categories of Arabs are being "liquidated" or forced to flee the country. First, there are politicians who oppose the policy of the Mufti and disagree with the terrorist activities . . . Other victims of the terror are less important Arabs who are suspected of being police informers, sympathizers with leaders in opposition to the Mufti, or brokers selling land to Jews. In this last category the danger of assassination appears to apply only to such brokers who openly disagree with the Mufti.

Admon Nashashibi, the nephew of Ragheb Bey Nashashibi, leader of the anti-Mufti Arab National Defense Party, was shot on March 4, 1938. Sheikh Mahmoud Ansari, member of a prominent Arab family that for generations had held the hereditary right for one of its members to serve as curator of the Mosque of Omar, was shot on December 15, because his family had opposed the Mufti. Two days later, another official of the Mosque of Omar, Sheikh Said al Khatib, was shot dead; he was the second victim in his family, Sheikh Abdul Rahman al Khatib having been fatally shot just a month before.[16] "Week after week," wrote the Jerusalem correspondent of the London *New Judaea* toward the end of 1938, "Arab Mayors and Mukhtars, Sheikhs and ulemas have been attacked, many of them assassinated, many more wounded and compelled to flee from the country. There is hardly any Arab of wealth or distinction left in Palestine. Egypt and Lebanon are crowded with the victims of the Terror. The few who have remained either bow their heads to the terrorists, as demonstrated by the stereotyped disavowels of Fakhri Nashashibi, or, if they refuse to do so, are extirpated with ruthless precision.[17]

But it was Fakhri Bey Nashashibi himself whom the Mufti regarded as the most dangerous of his political opponents. The latter, accordingly, was particularly eager to see this arch-enemy of his speedily liquidated, to make an example for others. He ordered his preferred henchman Aref Abdul Razzik to issue a death warrant against Fakhri Bey, calling on every Arab "in the name of God" to shoot this "traitor" on sight. The full text of this death warrant was published in the Damascus paper *Al Istiqlal al Arabi* (Arab Independence):

IN THE NAME OF GOD, THE MERCIFUL, THE COMPASSIONATE . . .
Tribunal of the Great Arab Revolution—
Southern Syria—Palestine
To The General Public

WHEREAS FAKHRI NASHASHIBI, a member of the Defense Party, has joined himself with the enemy in his memorandum, which is a disparagement of the country's rights;

AND WHEREAS he has made pretenses to which he is not entitled, and has put himself in a position, vis-a-vis the nation generally, of coming to terms with the British Government and the Zionists;

NOW THEREFORE the Tribunal of the Great Arab Revolution considers him to have committed the crime of High Treason, and passes sentence of death upon him. His blood and his property are now held forfeit. Every Arab is to carry out this sentence if he finds a way to do so.

The Tribunal of the Great Arab Revolution hereby also declares that the blood and property of anyone who joins himself with Fakhri Nashashibi is likewise forfeit, for such persons thereby oppose national unity.

The National Cause shows no mercy on intriguers and conspirators, for the Fatherland is above all. Trusting in God.
AREF ABDUL RAZZIK[18]

For a long time the death warrant remained a dead letter. Fakhri Bey Nashashibi stayed alive, and defied the Mufti's henchmen. But finally the long hand of Haj Amin found its victim. On November 9, 1941, while Fakhri Bey was walking through the streets of Baghdad, an Arab rode past on a bicycle and shot him dead. The assassin was a Palestinian, and his connection with the Mufti's organization has been proved beyond any doubt.[19]

The Mufti's Axis Ties

The "manifesto" of the former commanders, the French press, and interpolations in the British House of Commons unanimously referred to funds the Mufti was receiving from "foreign powers."[20] The source of these funds was not specified. But Haj Amin's ties with the Axis were by that time a matter of common knowledge.

Hitler's rise to power had early attracted Haj Amin's interest. He speedily made contact with Berlin, and it was not long before Arab students were going from Palestine to Germany. In the same way he sought the good offices of the other end of the Axis and began to receive financial assistance from both Berlin and Rome. It was well known in the Arab countries that the Mufti was in close touch with Emir Shakhib Arslan, an avowed supporter of Italy's action in Abyssinia. A letter from Arslan to the Mufti, published in the Arab Press early in 1935 and hinting at secret dealings with Italian agents, created a sensation. The Mufti's organ, while attempting to question the authenticity of the letter, did not conceal sympathy for Italy. *El Jamia el-Arabia* wrote openly of the value of Italy's sympathy with the Arabs.

Many Palestine Arabs frankly admitted that Italy had been "fanning the flames of Arab lawlessness," reported the Jerusalem correspondent of *The New York Times* on January 30, 1937. "We are fighting Zionism in Palestine, which is supported by Britain," they argued. "What do we care who backs us so long as it helps us to attain our goal?" Douglas W. Duff, who was in an excellent position to observe the reactions of the Arab extremists in Palestine, described in 1938 a discussion in an Arab coffee house, during which a young, fanatical-looking Arab exclaimed.

The true patriot is my noble chief, Haj Amin el-Husseini, Grand Mufti of Jerusalem, spiritual head of all Palestine's Moslems, the man who will some day be Caliph of Islam and Commander of the Faithful. . . . He knows that the day of the *Ingliz* is done, and their arm is paralysed. . . . All of you have heard the radio from Bari. The *Ingliz* are badly frightened of the growing might of the *Italiani*. Has not the noble Mussolini been proclaimed Protector and friend of Islam?.[21]

The link with Nazi Germany proved to be even more powerful and lasting.

Dr. Franz Reichert, director of the Palestine branch of Deutsches Nachrichten Büro from 1933 to 1938, had established a well-organized network of Arab contacts. But it was the Mufti who took the initiative of directly approaching the rulers of the Third Reich with an offer of Arab-German cooperation. As can be seen from a selection of captured Nazi documents, published in 1953 by the United States State Department under the supervision of a Franco-British-American editorial board, the Reich was for a time markedly cautious and reluctant to respond to the Mufti's overtures.[22]

Document 566 (pp. 756-56) in this collection established that on July 21, 1937, the Mufti paid a visit to the German Consul General Doehle in Jerusalem. He wanted to know to what extent the Third Reich was prepared to support the Arab movement against the Jews, and announced that he was sending a confidential agent to Ber-

lin for discussions with the German government. Those
responsible for the Reich's foreign policy were, however,
just at that time, not at all prepared to make the Palestine
issue a subject of possible conflict with Great Britain,
which, they believed, was earnestly advocating partition
and establishment of a Jewish State on the basis of the
report of the Peel commission. They also did not feel that
articulate opposition to such a solution of the Palestine
problem was very strong among Arab leaders. On July 29,
Senior Counselor Otto von Henting, head of the Middle
East Division of the German Foreign Office, circulated a
memorandum, "The Palestine Question" (Document 569),
asserting that the only strong protests against partition
had come from the Mufti and from the Iraqi government; all other Arab and Moslem countries, though opposed to "permitting the Jewish State to come into being,"
were "not in the least inclined to quarrel with England
over this question." Nor was the Reich prepared to do so
(pp. 758-59). Two weeks after Henting's memorandum,
a document on the same question, prepared on State Secretary Otto von Weizsaecker's request, insisted that "in
view of the development of Anglo-German relations, a decision to support the Arab world with money and arms is
out of the question." (Document 570, pp. 760-62). A further memorandum (Document 571) circulated on the
same day instructed the German missions that in their
diplomatic steps in connection with Palestine they must
observe that the Reich's "relations with England must
under no circumstances be placed under unnecessary
strain" and that they must not overlook "the notorious
political unreliability of the Arabs" (pp. 762-65).

The German consul in Jersalem was accordingly advised to discourage the Mufti from sending an agent to
Berlin. But it was too late. The agent was already on his

way (Document 572,p. 766). Contact was established in
Berlin toward the end of August. A note from Consul-
General Doehle giving the password of the Mufti agent
carries a remark by Henting, dated August 26: "Musa
Alami, staying at present in Karlsbad, is announced for
today with an English-speaking person, Husseini, from Jerusalem." But no record of the interview was found, and
apparently no active German support was enlisted.

Nevertheless, on the advice of Dr. Franz Reichert,
Chief of the Security Police Reinhard Heydrich in September 1937 assigned two young S.S. men, Hauptschar-
führer Carl Adolf Eichmann and Oberscharführer Herbert Hagen, to make a study trip to Palestine. At the trial
in Jerusalem, chief-prosecutor Gideon Hausner asked
Eichmann: "Is it true that one of the trip's main objectives
was to establish contact with Haj Amin el-Husseini?"
Eichmann first tried to evade the issue: "The objective
was to get acquainted with the country and the life and to
establish contact with people," he said. "Especially with
el-Husseini?" pressed the prosecutor. "Yes, with him too,"
was the reluctant answer.[23]

If this was indeed the main purpose of the mission, it
failed. Though Eichmann and Hagen were in possession
of valid tourist visas, the British authorities, apparently
advised of their identity and purpose, limited their sojourn to forty-eight hours. They also could not have met
the Mufti, who by that time had already fled Palestine.
Nothing more happened on this front until the end of the
year. Then, on December 14, 1937 (when the Mufti was
already living in Lebanon), the Reich Propaganda Ministry sent a batch of papers to the Foreign Office and the
War Ministry (Document 576) containing an introduction of another confidential agent, Dr. Said Imam from
Damascus, and a draft agreement between the German

government and "the Grand Mufti of Palestine"—presumably brought by Dr. Imam (pp. 777-79). In this the Mufti undertook, in return for Germany's ideological and material help, to support the Third Reich by (1) promoting German trade in the Arabic-Islamic world; (2) preparing a sympathetic atmosphere for Germany which would make itself felt in case of war; (3) continuing acts of terrorism in all French colonial and mandated territories inhabited by Arabs or Mohammedans (reckoning with the Reich's reluctance to be involved at that time in a conflict with England, the Mufti abstained from mentioning British colonial and mandated territories); (4) disseminating German culture in the Arab-Islamic countries; (5) willingness, in case of success of the Arab independence movement, to use only German capital and intellectual resources.

The Mufti's offer was ignored. The time was not propitious for active cooperation between the Mufti, for whom Jewish immigration into Palestine was anathema, and the Hitler regime which in 1937 still favored Jewish emigration from the Reich, even to Palestine, and even if it was against Arab wishes.

The Mufti's prospects in 1938–39 seemed, for a while, to have been more promising. The German Foreign Office was by that time aware that the British government had, after the report of the Woodhead commission, definitely dropped the partition plan and was veering toward a pro-Arab policy. When, on August 23, 1938, Fuad Bey Hamza, King Ibn Saud's deputy foreign minister, arrived in Berlin (Document 582), he was well received by Henting, who put him in touch with Vice-Admiral Canaris, head of the German Military Intelligence Service. Hamza successfully negotiated with the Supreme Command of the German Armed Forces an arms shipment which was to reach the Mufti via Saudi Arabia (Document 509, pp. 789-91). The ship was ready to sail from Hamburg when the blow fell: Henting received "absolutely definite information" that Fuad Hamza, who had been working with the German Military Intelligence, "was in British service." Consequently the shipment was stopped. So was a second, via Iraq.[24]

The arms deal fell through. But the Nazi Reich found many other ways and means of assisting the Arab anti-Jewish crusade, and the Mufti apparently made good his offer to "prepare a sympathetic understanding for Germany," whose image excercised an ever growing attraction in the Arab world.

Harold Callender, the *New York Times* correspondent in London, wrote on October 16, 1938: "It was no accident that the Arabs began issuing ultimatums a fortnight after Adolf Hitler did so in Europe, or that in two of Hitler's three recent big speeches he made caustic allusions to Palestine; or that the Nazi press this week gave vent to an outburst of sympathy for the Arabs in Palestine who were reported to be forming a 'free corps' on the Sudeten German model, in order to 'fight against Judaism.'" Hitler's two chief newspapers, the *Voelkischer Beobachter* and the *Angriff*, devoted their first pages to praising the Arabs and depicting Britain as powerless in Palestine.

In October 1938, the influential London *Quarterly Review* (p. 209) published a revealing editorial on "The Nazi International," stating: "That Germany has played a part in assisting the Arab revolt in Palestine and is exploiting both Pan-Islamism and anti-Zionism is by no means only a rumour." The Jerusalem police intercepted documents in 1936 proving that the Arab leaders received £50,000 from Germany and £20,000 from Italy for the purpose of strengthening their resistance.[25] The *Palestine Post* reported that the editor of the extremist Arab daily *Al Difa'a* visited Cairo to meet a "prominent German personage" and returned suddenly to expand its pages and greatly extend its news and pictorial services.[26] The swastika had appeared in Arab leaflets, and German rifles had been captured more than once from Arab terrorists.[27]

A *Quarterly Review* editorial of May 22, 1939, was quoted in the House of Commons by Noel Baker, who added that "money, arms officers, organizers, everything [for the Arab rebels] came from Italy and Germany" and that "we know that British officers in Palestine talk freely of the German and Italian arms and money that the [Arab] terrorists have received."[28]

Also instructive in this respect were reports published in the autumn of 1938 by the well-informed French democratic weekly *Marianne*. André Palert, special correspondent of the paper in Jerusalem, who had a conversation with the Mufti at his refuge in the Mosque of Omar a few days before the latter's flight—it was the last interview granted by the Mufti in Palestine to a foreign journalist—found out that the Mufti was sent £60,000 from Rome. This transaction was revealed because the intermediary deemed it advisable to retain half of the sum. The Mufti complained to Rome, and "a young man from Italy connected with the transaction had to abandon every hope of making a brilliant career and depart to a lost town in Central America." In spite of this misunderstanding, the Italian source of supply did not dry up, as evidenced by the arms, largely of Italian origin, found on the Arab rebels in Palestine.

Another, even more important, source of supply for the Mufti-guided rebel bands was Nazi Germany. According to *Marianne*, the arms employed by the Palestine Arab nationalists were, for the greater part, supplied by the works of Suhl and Erfurter Gewehrfabrik in Germany. These firms delivered, in particular, rifles and portable machine-guns.

The French frontier police often detain camel caravans which are trying to smuggle arms from Syria into Palestine. The most important traffic is to be found, however, on the frontier between Palestine and Transjordan. Every night numerous natives swim across the Jordan, delivering to their brethren in the Holy Land rifles and munitions. The arms coming from Transjordan are always of German origin. Indeed, Transjordan is free to buy arms where she pleases. She has signed a contract with the Krupp works at Essen which runs till the spring of 1938.

The chief of the arms merchants in Palestine is a German, who hails from Westphalia, and who has traversed in the past the whole of Asia as a member of a scientific expedition. He has lived in Palestine since 1920 and plays a part rather resembling that of Colonel Lawrence.

Marianne also quoted several examples of the Nazist "spiritual influence" among the Palestinian Arabs, whose mouthpiece Haj Amin claimed to be:

At Nablus, the Arab Population recently received the British troops with shouts of "Heil Hitler!"

A certain German garage, at Jerusalem, employs only Arab Nazis, who are made to wear the swastika over their buttonholes.

The Arab journals *Falastin* and *Al Difa'a* publish every week articles with a racial tendency and frequently reproduce large portraits of various leaders of the Third Reich. They do not even try to conceal the fact that they have become pupils of the Ministry of Propaganda in Berlin.

Doctor Canaan, a well-known Arab physician, has just submitted to the British authorities a strictly confidential pamphlet proposing to solve the Palestinian problem on "racial" lines. As it happens, Dr. Canaan has a German wife and is employed at the German Evangelical Hospital in Haifa.

The British authorities have just expelled twenty-seven Nazi tourists who came to "visit the Holy City" in order to establish themselves later in a German colony near Bethlehem. . . .
It was high time!

The Greatest Arab Hero

The Mufti's Palestine Arabs were not alone in their admiration for Hitler's Germany and Mussolini's Italy. This attitude was shared by most Arab countries of the Middle East which regarded the Axis leaders as their natural allies and protectors. Hitler pointedly invited Arabs to Germany as honored guests, and in the 1938 Nuremberg address he spoke about the "defenseless Arabs in Palestine, left in the lurch." An Arab spokesman in Jerusalem reacted promptly: "Now we are not without friends in Europe; our ultimate success as a nation lies in the hands of Hitler and Mussolini." Reported John Gunther in *Inside Asia:* "Hitler is highly popular with many Arabs. . . . The greatest contemporary Arab hero is probably Hitler."[29]

Admiration for Nazi Germany was particularly widespread among the Syrian Arabs. Raoul Aglion, chief of the Propaganda Office of the Free French, related in his very pro-Arab book, *The Fighting French*, that "mass demonstrations and riots were instigated in Damascus, Homs, Aleppo, and elsewhere." In the streets a new song was heard:

> *Bala Missou, bala Mister,*
> *Bissama Allah, oria alard Hitler.*
> (No more Monsieur, no more Mister,
> In heaven Allah, on earth Hitler.)[30]

In the semi-official organ of the British Colonial Office, *Great Britain and the East* (May 8, 1941), Shirdar Telkaz described in detail the pro-German activities of the Arab nationalists in Syria:

There are Arab Nazi organizations which operate from Damascus, Aleppo and Beirut. The Nadi El Arabi is the most dangerous Nazi propaganda machine. Its members are a group of fanatical Arabs turned Nazis at German universities and schools. One often sees in a Syrian market place posters prominently displayed. On them are inscribed in huge Arabic letters: "In heaven Allah is thy ruler; on earth Adolph Hitler." Dr. Gronau, head of the German intelligence system in the Near East, supervises the Syrian organization. . . .

Carl Raswan, a noted German-born traveler in Arab countries and possessing numerous personal friends among the Arabs, reported in his book *Escape from Baghdad* (London, 1938) intense pro-Axis, particularly pro-German, feelings he encountered among the Arabs of Transjordan during his trip to Palestine in 1939. The chief of an Arab tribe, which was a mixture of Huwaita and Beni Atiye, explained that the guns the tribe was armed with were of German origin: "The Germans help us to smuggle parts of the guns in tin cans and rice bags through Turkey and Iraq. We fashion the shafts of the rifles from ghada wood of the desert." In a tailor's shop in Mudawara, a customer, an Arab from the little town of Zerka, suddenly accused Raswan and his young fellow-traveler of being Jews. Raswan answered: "'And if we *were* Jews?' 'Then I have something on me that is German,'" the Arab answered, and drew, with an insolent gesture, both his hands over hips which bulged with two pistols. "I guessed that they might be parabellums, ten-shot German automatic guns. The man's eyes glittered with a fanatic light, and he seemed to feel sure that he had scared me thoroughly. 'Friend,' I said, 'I have something German not only on me but within me; I was born in that country.' I rose, but he roughly pushed me back on the bench. In an excited whisper he asked: 'Hast thou German ammunition for sale?' 'No. I am not here to help murder.' The Arab was restive and interrupted: 'I am a friend of the Germans but not of the German Jews, and it seems thou art one . . .' 'We are educating our youth to change things. We are learning from Mussolini and Hitler.'"[31]

Raswan was struck by the fact that in the eyes of all Arabs he met, only "Italy and Germany were strong, and England and the whole British Empire existed only by the Grace of Mussolini and Hitler."

By Remote Control

Throughout the two years of his self-imposed political exile in Lebanon, Haj Amin had not only maintained his grip over Arab policy on Palestine, but even solidified it. From his distant coastal village of al-Zug he both directed the continuing rebellion in Palestine and masterminded the political line of the Palestine Arab nationalists in their dealings with Great Britain.

A telling example of his ability to determine Arab policy by remote control is offered by the part he played in the abortive St. James conference.

After the British government had abandoned the partition scheme submitted by the Royal Commission in 1937, Colonial Secretary Malcolm MacDonald announced, on November 10, 1938, in the House of Commons, that the Jewish Agency for Palestine and representatives from Egypt, Iraq, Saudi Arabia, Yemen, Transjordan, and Palestine would be invited to London to discuss the settlement of the Palestine problem; he specified that the government would refuse to receive the Mufti as one of the delegates.[32] Jewish representatives and those from the Arab states were nominated fairly promptly. The choice of the Palestine delegation, however, proved a source of friction and vexatious delays. In the absence of any recognized body representative of the Palestine Arab community, the delegation necessarily had to be self-appointive and a bitter quarrel developed between the Mufti forces and those of the Nashashibi's National Defense Party.

On Novermber 15, a letter sent to the High Commissioner of Palestine by Fakhri Bey Nashashibi was published disputing the Mufti's claim to represent Arab opinion in Palestine and asserting that the National Defense Party represented fifty per cent of Arab opinion in the country and seventy-five per cent of propertied interest. Ragheb Bey Nashashibi, the titular head of the party, who was in Cairo, having left Palestine in order to escape the attention of the Mufti's henchmen, also launched a campaign for strong representation of his party.[33] On his part, the Mufti issued from Beirut a manifesto asserting: "There is no individual or body in Palestine, apart from the Higher Committee, which can accept the [mandatory's] invitation." The manifesto went on to claim that the Committee was representative of all but a minute faction of Arab opinion and should have the sole right to speak in its name.[34]

The British government would no doubt have preferred to deal with the more moderate delegates of the Nashashibi party rather than with representatives of the Mufti's Higher Committee. But, as usual, it yielded to the Mufti's intransigence. On November 23, the Colonial Secretary announced in the House of Commons that facilities at the Conference would be given to former members of the

Arab Higher Committee deported to the Seychelles.[35] He again stated that the Mufti himself would not be acceptable as a delegate, and when a pro-Arab member of the House of Commons asked, on December 14, 1938, whether "in view of the fact that the Grand Mufti is regarded by the majority of the Muslim people of Palestine not only as a leader but a prophet, [he would] reconsider the desirability of inviting him to the forthcoming conference," Mr. MacDonald's answer was another firm "No."[36]

"It soon became clear," says John Marlowe, "that the British Government's decision that the Mufti should not attend the conference was simply a piece of face-saving." On December 19, the ex-members of the Higher Committee left the Seychelles en route for Egypt. Shortly after their arrival in Cairo, London announced that Great Britain had no objection to their consulting with the Mufti before deciding on the composition of the Palestine delegation. Together with Jamal el-Husseini, who had met them in Cairo, the liberated deportees proceeded to the Mufti's retreat in Lebanon. Their original consensus of opinion was that all Nashashibi partisans be eliminated from the delegation. Through British pressure and more moderate counsels of the Arab states delegates assembled in Cairo, the Mufti was persuaded to admit two Nashashibi representatives—provided they would be chosen by the Higher Committee.[37] But when their names were announced, it was discovered that one was too ill to travel and the second had recently withdrawn from the Defense Party to join the Husseinis. Feeling that insult was thus added to injury, Ragheb Nashashibi rejected the offered "compromise" and demanded that half the Palestine delegates be appointees of his party. Failing to secure assent to this, he announced on February 1 that a separate delegation of three members and an adviser would be sent to London. The British government was perforce obliged to agree to receive it.[38]

The Mufti was now free to appoint a four-member delegation to his taste. They were all members of the old Higher Committee, though, with the exception of Jamal Husseini, who led the delegation, they were not going to London as the direct representatives of the Mufti. Says John Marlowe:

> The attitude of the British government had put the Mufti in a favorable position. He could see that his views were represented at the Conference, he could ensure that no settlement would be agreed to at the conference without his approval, and at the same time he bore no responsibility for the results of the conference, and was in a position to repudiate the delegates to the conference if he wished to do so. . . . How far the views of the Mufti coincided with those of the majority of the delegation is uncertain, but it is probable that an agreement was reached to pitch the Arab demands as high as possible.[39]

The Conference, which began in St. James Palace on February 7, 1939, gave little promise of success. The Arabs declined to sit with the Jews, while the Mufti's partisans refused to meet the Nashashibi representatives. No progress toward any agreed solution was noticeable. The Mufti's shadow hung over the proceedings, preventing the Arab representatives from making even the slightest concession. At one session of the Conference the British Secretary for the Colonies was reported to have scored a great success with the Arabs by saying: "I shall have to consult my Mufti—the Prime Minister" (*Palestine,* London, April 5, 1939). This was an admission that the Mufti, two thousand miles away, was as much the master of the Arab delegation as the prime minister at Downing Street was of the British delegation. On March 6, in a last attempt to save the Conference, the Egyptian undersecretary for foreign affairs flew from Cairo to Beirut to see the

Mufti in order to obtain his sanction to minor concessions envisaged by the Arab delegation. The last shred of pretense that the British government was not negotiating with the Mufti was thereby exposed.*[40] In actual fact, the Arab delegates were, willy-nilly, nothing more than the mouthpieces of the absent Mufti. But the Egyptian attempt failed. The Mufti was not prepared to be bound by any agreement the Arab delegations might come to. No settlement, however anti-Jewish, was of any use to him that did not carry with it immediate independence of Palestine, which would enable him to become master of the country. Any partial satisfaction of Arab grievances, he felt, would merely have the effect of depriving him of a weapon which he had been using for the furtherance of his own ends. And no Arab delegate was prepared to defy the Mufti's veto.

The St. James Conference came to an inglorious end on March 17, 1939.

The Aftermath

The failure of the St. James Conference had apparently convinced the British that it was impossible to bring about any settlement of the Palestine controversy against the Mufti's wishes. He was not placated even by the White Paper of May 1939, which was so far-reaching in its concessions to Arab nationalism and so devastating to Zionist aspirations. As late as November 1939 British representatives in the Middle East, assisted by the Egyptian

* There was no "letting up" on the terrorist campaign even during the London Conference. Right up to and including the Conference, the Mufti-led rebellion continued unabated: in February alone, no fewer than 113 people were killed and 153 wounded (John Marlowe, *Rebellion in Palestine*, pp. 213, 217).

and Iraqi prime ministers, were reported negotiating with the Mufti, then in Baghdad, with a view of securing his public endorsement of the White Paper and of the Allied cause. Yet even the strictest enforcement of the White Paper restrictions of Jewish immigration failed to win Haj Amin over to the British side. He only stepped up his anti-British agitation through personal agents left behind. It was not before the summer of 1940 that the British had abandoned all hope of obtaining the Mufti's cooperation during the war.[41]

In the absence of any active opposition, the Mufti in exile came to exercise supreme political authority in the Palestine Arab community. He "still commanded the loyalty of the majority of the Palestine Arab nationalists. In their eyes his practice of forcibly removing his political foes was outweighed by his nationalist achievements. More that any other local leader, the Mufti could boast of having focused nationalist attention everywhere in the Arab countries on Palestine." Small bands of local Palestine recruits, collected in the hill districts of the northern and central parts of the country, were still active as the Husseini's military arm. Describing their composition, J. C. Hurewitz says in his Struggle for Palestine: "Most of them were genuine patriots, who found their inspiration in the Mufti; others were paying off old family vendettas and personal scores; others again were professional bandits."[42]

But little by little the Mufti-instigated rebellion was fizzling out. The Arab population grew tired of murder, strain, and intimidation. By mid-1939 the peace of exhaustion had crept over Palestine. Gradually, some semblance of normal life began to return. The bazaars began to buzz. The crack of rifles was no longer heard.

Commercial and private relations between Jews and Arabs were hesitatingly resumed. The situation was still far from being normal, but the unbearable tension of the previous three years lessened somewhat.

Annoyance and Frustration

This even relative normalization of the Palestine scene was obviously bound to disturb the Mufti, confined as he was to his Lebanese exile. In addition, in the last few months preceding the outbreak of World War II, the French mandatory administration began to intensify its surveillance of Haj Amin's activities. Annoyed and frustrated, he reportedly sought as early as May 1939 to transfer his base of operations from Lebanon to Iraq. His apprehension must have deepened after the start of the European war, when he saw how the screw was suddenly being turned on all groups, including his own numerous followers, suspected of sympathizing with the enemy. He was understandably anxious to avoid possible imprisonment, which he had good reason to expect would be his fate if the fortunes of war went against the Allies while he was still in Lebanon. The emergency created by the war also made an early renewal of the revolt in Palestine increasingly unlikely. Haj Amin was looking for a new, more secure and promising base of operations—for new headquarters in an independent Arab country such as Iraq.

In the meantime, however, to cover up his intentions, he wrote, in September 1939, to Gabriel Preaux, the French High Commissioner for the Levant States, and General Maxime Weygand, the commander of the French forces of the Near East, thanking them personally and in the name of the Arab Higher Committee for the asylum offered the Palestine émigrés. He assured his hosts that the Palestine Arabs, who were merely "defending their rights and liberties [had] no relation with any foreign power" and would refrain from any activities detrimental to French interests. Less than a month later, Haj Amin showed up in Baghdad, whither his automobile and personal effects were forwarded by the French military and police authorities at their own expense.[43]

French cooperation in the Mufti's "escape" to Iraq—to the extent of defraying part of the costs—is easily explainable. They were not at all eager to harbor, even in forced residence, a widely venerated Arab national leader and martyr such as the Mufti. France had already incurred violent Arab hostility by the failure to ratify the treaties of 1936, which provided for the independence of Lebanon and Syria within three years; she was understandably reluctant to add to her difficulties by arousing an outbreak of Moslem fanaticism, which Haj Amin's arrest would have invited. The French mandatory administration was already sufficiently alarmed by frequent Nazi broadcasts to the Middle East, which were portraying "in lurid colors the alleged ill-treatment of the Mufti in Lebanon."[44]

Years later, in the fall of 1946, when Haj Amin had nearly completed the cycle of his escapes, he told an American journalist, M. J. J. Sargint: "When the war broke out the British pressed the French authorities in Lebanon to hand me over, so I left for Iraq."[45] There is not the slightest evidence in support of this allegation. In 1939 as much as later, the British government was anything but eager to have the Mufti "handed over" to them. On the contrary, if the French were content with the convenient way of getting rid of the Mufti's embarrassing presence in the territory under their mandate, the British for their part were not less pleased by his choosing Iraq as his new residence. J. C. Hurewitz explains that they

> still appeared to be eager to convince the Mufti that it was in his own interest to support the Allies. They felt that if the one Arab leader who enjoyed the confidence of the Palestine Arab community could be persuaded voluntarily to come over to the British side, the Palestine Government would enjoy the backing of both the Jewish and the Arab sections of the population and would be able to fully devote itself to the war effort. Since the Prime Minister of Iraq at the time was the staunchly pro-British Nuri Said Pasha who could be enlisted to mediate with the Mufti, the British had no objections to Haj Amin's going to Baghdad.[46]

Nuri Said was apparently willing to play the role of a matchmaker. His biographer, Lord Birdwood, believes that his "motive, with so controversial a figure in Baghdad, was most certainly to influence him towards a more cooperative spirit in relation to Arab unity in Palestine and accommodation with Britain, the Mandatory Power." "If so," dryly comments Lord Birdwood, "a miscalculation would seem to have been made. The Mufti . . . remained an embarrassment to his hosts not less than to British officials in the [Iraqi] capital."[47] As we shall see later, Nuri Said, who was being accused by Iraqi nationalistic and military circles of serving as a British stooge, also miscalculated in his hope of strengthening his own position by welcoming and befriending the popular Mufti. He demanded and received from his guest the promise "not to indulge in undesirable activities," but this turned out to be an empty pledge. For a time, until he got his bearings, Haj Amin refrained from active participation in Iraqi politics. But this restraint was of short duration.

3

Mufti Over Iraq
1939–1941

Lionized by Government and Public

ASKED IN THE HOUSE OF COMMONS "WHETHER HIS MAJESTY'S
Government was consulted by the Government of Iraq
with regard to the admission to Baghdad of the former
Mufti of Jerusalem," Mr. Butler, Under Secretary of State
for Foreign Affairs, replied on October 25: "No, Sir. There
was no opportunity for consultation since I understand
that the Mufti entered Iraq without having obtained permission to do so from the competent Iraq authorities, and
that he crossed the frontier undetected."[1]

As can be seen from the preceding chapter, this answer
was a complete distortion of the actual situation. The
Mufti entered Iraq not as an undesirable "illegal immi-
grant" or as a refugee, and the British government must
have been fully apprised of the true state of affairs by its
own Intelligence. An extensive G.S.I. (General Service of
Intelligence) report on "The Ex-Mufti's Role in the Iraqi
Revolt," dated December 1, 1941, gives a detailed descrip-

tion of the reception accorded to him by both the Iraqi
government and the local nationalistic politicians:

As soon as he [Haj Amin] arrived, he was generally ac-
claimed as an Arab national hero and parties were given in his
honor by every leading personality in the Capital, from the
Prime Minister downwards, as well as by all Nationalist Clubs
and Societies. To these parties were invited other well known
Syrian and Palestinian political refugees as well as Iraq's own
reactionary politicans and they became veritable demonstrations of Arab nationalist feeling and unity.

As the British were the cause of the "martyrdom" of Palestine, these parties allowed much ventilation of anti-British
propaganda and the ex-Mufti and his partisans indulged freely
in expressing not only their anti-British sentiments but in the
spreading of deliberate and scandalous lies about the British
and the Jews and about British and Zionist actions and policy
in Palestine. The Iraqis, ready to believe anything anti-British
and dreaming of Iraq as the nucleus round which a United
Arabia was to form, swallowed the propaganda as though it
were a wholesome diet, and these receptions and parties
greatly increased the ex-Mufti's prestige with the Iraqis, and
although the Prime Minister, Nuri Pasha, was promised that
the ex-Mufti had given an undertaking not to indulge in politics while in refuge in Iraq and that he would be closely
watched by the Government, the ex-Mufti commenced his political activities without check from the first day of his arrival
in the country. In these activities he was encouraged by the
reception he was accorded on all sides, including parties given
by responsible Ministers and Nuri Pasha, the Prime Minister
himself, which have already been referred to above.

The ex-Mufti soon had his old Palestine "Headquarters"
established and modified to suit the new conditions under
which he was working. Jamal al-Husaini was his Chief of Staff.
Shaikh Hassan abu Saud was the Islamic religious adviser and
expert. Musa bey al Alami was the legal adviser and critic on
occidental affairs and, with the authority of his background, he
spoke convincingly to responsible and willing listeners on the
"British injustices." Fawzi al Qaoukji was the militant member
and contacted the Iraqi Army, raising from this source arms

and ammunition and the facilities to train men for guerilla warfare. Salim Abdur Rahman was Press Officer and publicist. Ishaq, Munif, Musa and Tawfiq Saleh al Husaini, Emil Ghouri, Izzat Darwaza, Ibrahim Darwish, Izzudin ash Shawa and others formed the Foreign Relations committee who were responsible for propaganda, intrigue and subversive activities inside and outside Iraq.*

The ex-Mufti held the money bags and paid these, as well as many other refugees, their allowances as most had no other livelihood but what they were paid from this source. The ex-Mufti's funds for this purpose were considerable, and it is known that he was voted ID 18,000 [Iraqi dinar=Pound Sterling] by the Iraqi Parliament, was paid ID 1,000 a month from Iraqi secret service funds, was paid 2% of the salary of every Iraqi government official, including the Military and Police (all stopped at source), considerable sums raised by the Palestine Defense Society, by the Red Crescent Society and through public collections. In addition, authoritative sources now claim he was paid ID 60,000 by the Germans and ID 40,000 by the Italians; he also raised other monies from outside Iraq—including generous gifts from Ibn Sa'ud and Egypt. This money enabled him, his followers and even Syrian political reactionaries to live in affluence, many owning cars and keeping reasonable establishments. Several were beyond doubt also getting additional allowances from Axis sources.[2]

Well-organized political machinery and abundant funds "were unfortunately not all the implements at the command of the ex-Mufti in Iraq," the British intelligence source admits:

He had another valuable method of obtaining influence within the government and also money for those working for him. These he commanded by furnishing the Iraqi Government with Palestinian and Syrian nominees to fill essential government positions that Iraq's illiteracy prevents her from provid-

---

* Several leading Arab Communists, among them Fuad Nasir (who was later to become first secretary of the Communist Party in Jordan) and Nimr Uda, belonged to the Mufti's entourage in Baghdad (Walter Laqueur, *Communism and Nationalism in the Middle East* [New York, 1956], p. 182).

ing for herself. These include education experts, schoolmasters, doctors, dentists, etc., and were largely enlisted from political undesirables found in Syria and Palestine. Most of them would have obtained no livelihood in the countries of their origin. The ex-Mufti in Iraq could get these appointed, dismissed or promoted at will through his influence in Government Departments. . . . These officials were spread throughout the length and breadth of Iraq and nearly all were used, willy-nilly, as "cells" for the ex-Mufti's propaganda campaign.

Also, he "quickly won to his cause certain nationalist organizations . . . some of which had already benefitted by German support and money." The most important of these were the Muthana Club, the Moslem Guidance Society, the Rover's Society, the Teachers Club, and the Olympic Club. Through his influence in these quarters Haj Amin and his followers contacted many of the Iraqi officials and Army personalities. They concentrated mostly on police and army officials, schoolmasters, doctors, and those of the legal professions. The ex-Mufti was soon making each government department carry out his benefits. For example, passports were issued at his request, refugees from Palestine were not allowed to remain in Iraq unless he agreed they were genuine "nationalists," refugees' cars were admitted duty-free and paid no taxes, and the Press and Propaganda Department did not interfere with his papers—especially the *Istiqlal* paper whose editor, Osman Qassim, had been editor of the Mufti's paper *Al Liwa* in Palestine (which was subsidized by both Germany and the Iraqi government and was consistently pro-German, anti-British, and pan-Arab in complexion).

Throughout his stay in Iraq, Haj Amin was always made a special guest at state or public functions. He and his followers were, on such occasions, given special places of honor equal to those of ministers of state, "and seldom were the feelings of British officials attending such functions considered in allowing the ex-Mufti such considerate treatment," complained the British intelligence report. In his highly successful endeavor to insinuate himself on the government officials and the common people, Haj Amin was "no doubt . . . assisted by the respect and esteem in which he was held by the highest authorities in the land; each wished to become the Arab hero who solved the Arab problem in Palestine and in consequence basked in the sunshine of his grace full of hopefulness and expectancy."

In seeking the Mufti's political support, the pro-British Nuri Said Pasha unwittingly associated himself with the anti-Allied activities of his supporter.

Haj Amin's "political department" in Baghdad "maintained close contact with Germany's Middle Eastern oasis at Teheran. Part of the Propaganda Department's function was to send regular despatches to Yunis el-Bahri, the Arab 'Haw-Haw,' the Iraqi in Berlin responsible for Germany's Arab broadcasts." The Mufti and his followers openly "admitted their regular contact with Yunis el-Bahri in Berlin."[3]

The line of goods Haj Amin was selling in the political bazaars of Baghdad was the creation of a vast Arab Union to include Iraq, Saudi Arabia, Syria, Palestine, Transjordan, and, later, Egypt. This pan-Arab bloc, linked to a victorious Nazi Germany, would play the role in the Middle East which Japan would be playing in the Far East and Nazi Germany in the West. Worked over by the Mufti and Germany's agents in the Middle East, the scheme for a time caused some heated debate between the agents of Berlin and Rome, with Germany urging the unification of all Arab lands, and Italy objecting. But as in Europe, so in the Middle East Italy's viewpoint was largely dismissed, and the Mufti group was encouraged to proceed with the Arab bloc plan. Their task was to stir up disturbances over Arab countries, to destroy or immobilize Allied eastern lines of communication, and to assist Germany's invasion forces "when they arrive."[4]

The Berlin-Baghdad Axis

German influence in Iraq can be traced back as far as October 1936, when General Bakr al-Askari Sidki Pasha executed his *coup d'état*. It was accompanied by its usual concomitant, "anti-Jewish violence": the same month of October witnessed violent anti-Jewish riots in Baghdad, and several Jews were killed. Sidki Pasha bought airplanes from Italy, planned a visit to Berlin, and had dealings with the Germans in connection with the purchase of military supplies. When he was assassinated, on August 11, 1937, in Mosul, lucrative German arms contracts were reportedly found in his pockets.

The Axis positions had been systematically built up in Iraq through the efforts of Dr. Fritz Grobba, since 1932 German minister to Baghdad and one of Germany's ablest experts on Arab affairs. Notwithstanding the existing Anglo-Iraqi treaty of 1930, German and Italian influence began to replace the British in education, government, and particularly in the army. Trade with the Reich boomed under barter agreements.

At the outbreak of war, pro-British Prime Minister Nuri Said, in accordance with the Anglo-Iraqi treaty, broke diplomatic relations with Germany, took over German property, and interned all Germans who remained in Iraq. Axis affairs were then conducted by the Italian Legation, which launched an all-out anti-Allied propaganda campaign. "The Italian Legation," reveals the "Inside Story of

Rashid Ali's Treachery," published in *Great Britain and the East* (July 10,1941), "became the center of Axis intrigues and it was obvious to all that every order was coming from Germany, and that the [Anglo-Iraqi] Treaty of Alliance was being violated in the spirit and more deliberately." On May 24, the Italian minister in Baghdad reported to the Rome government that "he had a long talk" with the Mufti who told him that "he was rousing the Arabs to revolt against England wherever he could:"

In Palestine the uprising was in full swing. In Transjordan he was able to rely on the friendship of Talal, Emir Abdallah's son, and point to the fact that the Transjordan Arab troops in the meantime had refused to fight against their Iraq brothers. Ibn Sa'ud did not want to take a position against England but would be compelled, in the course of the present struggle, at least to manifest his solidarity, so as not to jeopardize his popularity. As regards Egypt, the Mufti was counting heavily on Ali Maher and his political friends, who were collaborating with Misr el Fattat and had the backing of the young King. The Mufti and Gaylani have sent messages to Imam Yahya, designed to raise revolts in the Aden area and revive his aspirations to acquire new emirates. The Mufti believes, however, that all this is only of limited value if the current uprising in Iraq, which in his opinion is the key to the situation, should fail. Because of this he had held back sending ammunition and arms to Palestine in order to have all strength and resources available for Iraq.[5]

Raoul Aglion and John Gunther complete the picture by relating that "money and arms poured into the country and provincial sheikhs organized groups of rebels" (*War in the Desert* p. 14) and that "the country was filled up with Axis agents and Fifth Columnists directed from the Italian Legation" (*Inside Asia*, pp. 564-65).

Another center of anti-Allied propaganda was the Japanese Legation set up in November 1939 with the professed object of developing a greater volume of trade with

Iraq; yet it very soon rivaled the Italins in pro-Axis drive. While maintaining contact with the Japanese, Haj Amin was increasingly associating himself with the Italian Legation, through which he was able to remain in direct communication with the upper strata of the German and Italian Foreign Offices.

As the *Wehrmacht* continued to win its impressive victories, the belief grew that Britain was bound to lose the war. Rumors were spread that Nuri had promised military aid to the Allies.

With this situation prevailing in the background, General Rashid Ali el-Gailani, a militant and ambitious Arab nationalist, well-situated with the pro-Axis military clique, and the so-called "Golden Square"—a group of powerful pro-German army leaders—were able to secure far-reaching control over state affairs. They placed in key positions handpicked officers, who began increasingly to interfere in state matters and assert their pro-Axis leanings. In the spring of 1940 Nuri Said resigned and on March 31 Rashid Ali took over the Prime Ministry.

Acting partially behind the scenes and partially as exponent of Axis interests, the Mufti played a major role in this new political set-up.* He established a kind of miniature government of his own, a "shadow cabinet." Baghdad had become the hub of a vast pan-Arab conspiracy. Strongly pro-Arab Miss Freya Stark, who during the first years of World War II served with the British government in the Middle East and was exceptionally well-versed in Arab politics, testified in her book *The Arab Islands* that the Mufti "was the source of perhaps more than half our [British] trouble in Iraq."[6]

---

* "In his young days, as an officer of the Turkish infantry, in Smyrna, he [Haj Amin] had made a close and lasting friendship with Mahmud Salman, later one of the generals of the Golden Square" (Freya Stark, *The Arab Islands*, p. 159).

When Italy entered the war in June 1940, Rashid Ali's cabinet refused to sever diplomatic relations with this new belligerent, though such a step was clearly called for by the Anglo-Iraqi treaty. According to Majid Khaddury, the Mufti and his pan-Arab circle were at that stage still advocating "strict neutrality so long as the issue of war was uncertain" and "advised the minimum fulfillment of Iraq's treaty obligations [toward England], always provided that this would not arouse undue Axis suspicion."[7] The new administration provided Haj Amin with an outright gift of £572,000 and a monthly stipend of £4,000. The Axis supplemented these funds with gifts reportedly totaling £400,000, some 60 per cent coming from Germany. With well-filled coffers, Haj Amin was now able to gather around him an estimated three hundred loyal followers by either placing them on his own payroll or obtaining employment for them in Iraqi government departments.[8] Before the end of 1940 the Mufti had become a towering figure in Iraq's domestic politics.[9]

Wooing Hitler

Haj Amin was, however, not prepared to limit himself to the local political scene. Following the course of the war from Baghdad, he apparently came to the firm conclusion that an Axis victory was both inevitable and impending, and was eager to establish, before the war's end, "priority with the likely victors by becoming the first Arab leader to join their camp." He must also have expected to obtain

from the Axis in World War II what the Sharif Husayn had not fully obtained from the Allies in World War I— independence everywhere in the Arab East. The victorious Axis, he could be sure, would promptly replace the pro-British Hashimi rulers of Transjordan and Iraq and would never permit the

French to regain a foothold in the Levant States. The Mufti could therefore hope that, as a reward for services rendered, he might be made ruler of an Arab realm stretching from the borders of Iran to the Mediterranean and from Saudi Arabia to Turkey.[10]

It was with this vision in mind that Haj Amin started conducting negotiations with Germany on his own.[11]

In June 1940, an official Iraqi delegation went to Ankara to "seek consultation with Turkey on the present momentous issues." One member of the delegation, Minister of Justice Naji Shawkat Bey, was, however, in addition to his official legitimation, also the bearer of a personal letter of introduction from the Mufti to Franz von Papen, German minister to Turkey. In the letter, dated June 21, 1940, the Mufti asked von Papen

to convey to his Excellency the Great Chief and Leader my sincerest felicitations on the occasion of the great political and military triumphs which he has just achieved. . . . I beg your Excellency to convey to him my regards and compliments, together with my best wishes for the undertaking entered upon to create a new order. I must also express to him my thanks for the interest and attention which he has never ceased in the past four years to give to the Arab question in general and Palestine in particular. The Arab nation everywhere feels the greatest joy and deepest gratification on the occasion of these great successes. Palestine, which has for the past four years been fighting the democracies and international Jewry, is ready at any time to assume an active role and redouble her efforts both at home and in the other Arab countries. The Arab people, slandered, maltreated, and deceived by our common enemies, confidently expect that the result of your final victory will be their independence and complete liberation, as well as the creation of their unity, when they will be linked to your country by a treaty of friendship and collaboration.

The Mufti asked von Papen "to discuss with my friend Naji Bey in detail the Arab question and the future of

Palestine and of Syria, as well as the program which your government may deem advisable to lay foundations for bringing collaboration between our two peoples."

Shawkat went to Istanbul and was received on July 5 by von Papen, whose attitude was both friendly and encouraging.

Meanwhile, Rashid Ali, in agreement with the Mufti, approached Luigi Gabrielli, the Italian Minister in Baghdad, who, with Count Ciano's consent, issued a written statement (July 7, 1940) assuring them that "Italy aims at ensuring the complete independence and the territorial integrity of Syria and Lebanon as well as Iraq and the countries under British mandate."

The Mufti and Rashid Ali then decided to negotiate directly with the German government. Uthman Kamal Haddad, the Mufti's private secretary, was delegated to Berlin via Turkey. He saw von Papen on August 6 in Ankara and informed him that an "Arab Committee" under the presidency of the Mufti had already been formed in Baghdad, composed of Iraqi, Syrian, and Palestinian leaders, which decided to establish contact with Germany. From Ankara, Haddad, under the name of "Max Müller," proceeded to Germany via Budapest. On August 26 he saw Dr. Grobba, former German minister in Baghdad, and, on the Mufti's instructions, told him that the rupture of relations between Iraq and Germany was condemned by the majority of the people and the leading politicians. After lengthy negotiations, a joint Italo-German declaration, endorsing a pro-Arab stand, was simultaneously broadcast in Arabic from Rome and Berlin on October 23, 1940. On his way back to Baghdad, Haddad took to the Mufti a letter from the Reich's foreign minister Joachim von Ribbentrop.

In January 1941 he was again sent to Berlin, armed with

a letter from the Mufti to Hitler himself (dated January 20), in which were stated Arab national aspirations and Rashid Ali's willingness to fight Britain if Germany would recognize the independence of Iraq and the other Arab countries:

Arabian nationalism owes our Excellency much gratitude and recognition for the fact that you raised the Palestinian question repeatedly in public addresses. . . . I should like to thank your Excellency again at this opportunity and to reassure you, your Excellency, of the feelings of friendship, sympathy and admiration which the Arabian people devote to your Excellency, Great Leader, and the courageous German people.

I take this opportunity to delegate my private secretary to the German Government so that—in the name of the strongest and largest Arabian organization as well as in my own name— he may initiate the negotiations necessary for a sincere and loyal collaboration in all spheres.[12]

Hitler's reply was conveyed in a letter by State Secretary Freiherr von Weizsaecker. The English text reproduced below in full is from the French translation found in the Mufti files in Germany, on which annotations in the Mufti's handwriting are discernible:

Secret
March 1941

Copy Pol. VII 188 g. Rs.

Eminence:

The Fuehrer received your letter dated January 20th sent through your private secretary. He took great interest in what you wrote him about the national struggle of the Arabs; and he took cognizance, with great interest and sympathy, of your report concerning the national struggle of the Arabs. He was pleased with the friendly words addressed to him in the name of Arab Nationalism and in your own name.

Your private secretary began the discussions which you in

your letter requested. In response to your desire to have a clarification of German policy toward the Arabs, I am empowered to state the following to you:

Germany has never occupied any Arab countries and has no ambitions whatsoever in Arab lands. Our view is that Arabs, who possess an ancient culture and have proved their administrative, judiciary and military maturity, are capable of self-government. Germany recognizes the full independence of the Arab countries, or where this has not yet been attained, their right to it.

The Germans and the Arabs have common enemies in England and the Jews; and are united in the fight against them. Germany, traditionally friendly to the Arabs, and in accordance with the desires expressed to your private secretary, is ready to cooperate with you and to give you all possible military and financial help required by your preparations to fight against the British for the realization of your people's aspirations. In order to enable the Arabs to begin the necessary preparations for their future war against the British, Germany is prepared to deliver to you immediately military material, if the means for transporting this material can be found.

In order to further develop the details of our friendly cooperation, I would like you to send your private secretary back to us; or, if he is unavailable, another emissary.

I request you to keep the contents of this communication secret. The Italian Government has been informed of its contents and subscribes to them.

I am sure your private secretary will inform you of his impressions of Germany; i.e. that the victory of the Axis is certain and Britain's downfall assured.

With best wishes for your personal well-being and for the further success of your vigorous undertakings in behalf of the Arab cause, I remain, your Eminence,

Very Devotedly
Freiherr von Weizsaecker

The Pro-Axis Coup

News of the behind-the-scenes negotiations between the Mufti and Hitler reached Nuri Said who, uneasy about the future of Iraq should the Axis powers win the war, was anxious to learn what promises the Mufti and Rashid Ali had obtained from Axis quarters. He approached a few of the Mufti's close associates and offered to work with them. Warmly supported by some of Haj Amin's advisers, this offer was rejected by Amin himself who contended that it had been made merely in order to find out what his plan was and then to pass it to the British authorities.[13]

Encouraged by German assurances and determined to force a decisive showdown, seven officers of the Iraqi division stationed at Baghdad in late January 1941 called on the Regent Abdul Ilah at eleven o'clock at night demanding that he sign an agreement with the Reich and that all pro-British political leaders in the country be interned. Faced with this ultimatum, the Regent, the boy King, and Nuri Said fled the capital the same night. The Iraqi parliament, however, took side with the royal family, and, on January 30, Rashid Ali was compelled to resign.

A new cabinet was formed on February 1 by Taha al-Hashimi, former president of the Iraqi Palestine Defense Society and a close friend of the Mufti as well as of Germany's number one Arab agent, Dr. Amin Ruwaiha.[14] Taha's announced policy was to preserve the position of Britain's "non-belligerent ally": "To ensure the safety of the State by refraining from any action which might result in Iraq being dragged into the conflict, and the continuation of all possible endeavors to ensure that Iraq will continue to enjoy peace."[15]

Taha's "neutral" cabinet proved to be short-lived. On April 12, Rashid Ali was returned to power, this time as a result of a well-prepared pronunciamento. "The rebel army officers who organized the coup d'état on April 7, 1941," testifies Raoul Aglion, "had been plotting for a long time and carried out their scheme only after they received specific orders from the German so-called 'commercial mission' of Syria."[16]

Gerald de Gaury, who in 1941 was British special Chargé d'Affaires with the Regent of Iraq, relates in his study, *Three Kings in Baghdad,* that the head of the United States' Office of Strategic Services (Intelligence arm of the U.S. Army, Navy, and Air Force), Colonel William Donovan (whom he describes as "the spendidly enthusiastic 'Fighting Bill'") "at this time visited Baghdad in passing." Donovan "asked to see the ex-Mufti and his followers among the politicians":

The Mufti . . . rather reluctantly, came to see him at the American Legation, but was alone, having concealed from his companions the invitation extended to them. Donovan explained to the Mufti that America, though she had not yet declared war, was already behind Britain and would resent the activities of persons working against her. The Mufti should look ahead and understand the consequences of actions which, being against the interest of Britain, were therefore against the interests of America herself. He asked him to explain the position to his friends.

"The Mufti agreed," reports De Gaury, "but never, it is believed, did so. On the contrary, he continued his intrigues against the [Iraqi] authorities and his dangerous plots."[17]

The Axis orientation of this second Rashid Ali cabinet was unmistakable. Pro-British Iraqi politicians fled the country. Egged on by the Germans and with German assistance, Rashid Ali seized British-controlled oil fields. Soon, clashes occurred between Iraqi and British soldiers. The Regent fled again.

The Mufti had every reason to be satisfied with the course of events. His influence and stature were tremendously enhanced. He threw himself wholeheartedly into the anti-Allied crusade.* On May 9, he broadcast over the Iraqi and Axis radios the following "*fatwa* announcing a *jihad* (holy war) against Britain" and urged every Moslem to join in the struggle against "the greatest foe of Islam":

In the name of Merciful and Almighty God.

I invite all my Moslem brothers throughout the whole world to join in the Holy War for God, for the defense of Islam and her lands against her enemy. O Faithful, obey and respond to my call.

O Moslems!

Proud Iraq has placed herself in the vanguard of this Holy

---

* In November 1946, Dr. Ahmed Bey Kadri, former private physician to King Feysal I of Iraq, in an obvious attempt to prove that the Mufti was not completely anti-British and pro-Nazi, related the following episode: At a time when the Axis forces were at the zenith of their successes and the Allies were badly in need of Arab support, pro-British Nuri Said Pasha, then Iraq's foreign minister, asked Dr. Kadri to contact the Mufti with a proposition of a "deal." The British would abolish the Palestine mandate, stop Jewish immigration, announce complete independence of Palestine and install there an Arab Government, and, in exchange, "the Arabs of Palestine, with the Grand Mufti at their head, would then support the Allies in their war against the Axis." Dr. Kadri had a "preliminary conversation" on the subject with Amin Bey Al-Faurmini, "a member of the Grand Mufti's suite." They reached an agreement on the text of a statement in which the Mufti would say that should the British government accept the above enumerated conditions, "I, as well as the Arab Higher Committee, and all the Arab population of Palestine, will not confine ourselves to support the Allies in their present war. We are prepared, as a price of the independence of our country and our freedom, to declare a Holy War [*jihad*] against the Axis Powers." This text was communicated to Nuri Said Pasha. No further action was apparently taken (*Middle East Opinion*, Cairo, November 11, 1946).

Struggle, and has thrown herself against the strongest enemy of Islam, certain that God will grant her victory.

The English have tried to seize this Arab-Moslem land, but she has risen, full of dignity and pride to defend her safety, to fight for her honor and to safeguard her integrity. Iraq fights the tyranny which has always had as its aim the destruction of Islam in every land. It is the duty of all Moslems to aid Iraq in her struggle and to seek every means to fight the enemy, the traditional traitor in every age and every situation.

Whoever knows the history of the East has everywhere seen the hand of the English working to destroy the Ottoman Empire and to divide the Arab countries. British politics toward the Arab people is masked under a veil of hypocrisy. The minute she sees her chance, England squeezes the prostrate country in her imperialist grasp, adding futile justifications. She creates discord and division within a country and while feeding it in secret openly she assumes the role of advisor and trusted friend. The time when England could deceive the peoples of the East is passed. The Arab Nation and the Moslem people have awakened to fight British domination. The English have overthrown the Ottoman Empire, have destroyed Moslem rule in India, inciting one community against another; they stifled the Egyptian awakening, the dream of Mohammed Ali, colonizing Egypt for half a century. They took advantage of the weakening of the Ottoman Empire to stretch out their hands and use every sort of trick to take possession of many Arab countries as happened to Aden, the 9 Districts, the Hadramut, Oman, Masqat and the Emirates of the Persian Gulf and Transjordania. The vivid proof of the imperialistic designs of the British is to be found in Moslem Palestine which, although promised by England to Sheriff Hussein, has had to submit to the outrageous infiltration of Jews, shameful politics designed to divide Arab-Moslem countries of Asia from those of Africa. In Palestine the English have committed unheard of barbarisms; among others, they have profaned the el-Aqsa Mosque and have declared the most unyielding war against Islam, both in deed and in word. The Prime Minister at that time told Parliament that the world would never see peace as long as the Koran existed. What hatred against Islam is stronger than that which publicly declares the Sacred Koran an enemy of human kind? Should such sacrilege go unpunished? After the dissolution of the Moslem Empire in India and of the Ottoman Caliphate, England, adhering to the policy of Gladstone, pursued her work of destruction to Islam, depriving many Islamic States both in the East and in the West of their freedom and independence. The number of Moslems who today live under the rule of England and invoke liberation from their terrible yoke exceeds 220,000,000.

Therefore I invite you, O Brothers, to join in the War for God to preserve Islam, your independence and your lands from English aggression. I invite you to bring all your weight to bear in helping Iraq that she may throw off the shame that torments her.

O Heroic Iraq, God is with Thee, the Arab Nation and the Moslem World are solidly with Thee in Thy Holy Struggle![18]

Abortive Attempt to Kidnap the Mufti

The entire British position in the Middle East was greatly jeopardized by the emergence of an openly pro-German regime in Iraq. In May, it came to an open armed conflict. Five to eight thousand Iraqi soldiers, with a liberal supply of artillery, armored cars, and about fifty first-line aircraft, besieged the R.A.F. air base at Habbainya, where the British colony found refuge.[19] British forces were greatly outnumbered. The arrival of German reinforcements was impending.

In this predicament, General Archibald Percival Wavell, commander of British forces in the Middle East, decided, among other countermeasures, to take advantage of the experience in guerrilla tactics acquired by the underground fighters of the *Irgun Zvai Leumi* (Jewish Military Organization) in Palestine. Since the outbreak of World War II the Irgun suspended its anti-British activities and offered to the Western democracies its cooperation in the

common struggle against Nazi Germany. Despite this declaration of loyalty, David Raziel, the commander of the
Irgun, and several of his comrades, were still imprisoned
in the spring of 1941. In the new critical situation, General Wavell ordered Raziel's release and suggested that
the Irgun launch a commando-type operation in Iraq,
aimed at (a) sabotaging oil stores in the vicinity of Baghdad which were expected to be used by German planes,
and (b) gathering information about the enemy's position. Raziel and his second-in-command, Yaakov Merridor, were inclined to accept the offer. They demanded,
however, that they be given authority to act independently and be permitted to add to the two assignments a
third, special operation, in which they were particularly
interested. When asked what that operation was, they
frankly admitted that their intention was to kidnap Haj
Amin el-Husseini who, they knew, had been in Baghdad
since October 1939. Recalling this episode twenty years
later, Merridor told a press reporter:

The British strongly opposed our demand when they learned
the nature of our operation. So we said to them: "O.K., no
Mufti—no operation!" In the end the British authorities hinted
that although they were not in agreement with our plan to
kidnap the Mufti, they were in fact completely disinterested in
any activity that we carried out after the destruction of the oil
tanks in Baghdad. We had no knowledge of the Mufti's address in Baghdad, but we had ways and means of finding out.
And then . . . (he stopped here for a while) and then we
would either have kidnapped him, or . . . how can I express it?
. . . or carried out his sentence on the spot.

Together with two Arabic-speaking young Irgun soldiers in civilian clothes, Raziel and Merridor boarded a
British military plane and arrived at Habbaniya on May
18, 1941. Informed of the task assigned to the group, the
British commander smiled pityingly and said to Raziel:

It appears that you do not know the state of affairs. We are surrounded, Sir, completely surrounded. The pro-British Iraqians outside have all been massacred, and those who are on our side are hiding themselves in the huts in these camps and don't dare to put their heads outside. So whom can I send with you on this operation?

Raziel suggested that he and his men be parachuted behind the enemy lines, east of Baghdad, near the entrance to the city. The answer was that no means for such an operation were available. Somewhat later, Raziel reconnoitered the flooded area around Baghdad, in the company of a British major and one of his companions. They were traveling in a small "Anglia" car when German planes started strafing them. Both Raziel and the British major were killed. The Irgun group lost its commander.[20]

The Tide Turned

In the meantime, the tide turned. German arms and aircraft requested by Rashid Ali did arrive by way of Syria, but in insufficient quantities to secure the success of the rebellion. The British reoccupied the lost positions, one after the other, and by the end of May both Rashid Ali and the Mufti fled from Baghdad. Haj Amin's Baghdad chapter came to an inglorious end.

The Jews were made the scapegoat of failure. The Mufti's sustained anti-Jewish incitement bore bloody fruits: on June 1 and 2, in the immediate wake of the lost rebellion, Arab mobs staged a Jewish pogrom. The police, far from trying to prevent the rioters from looting and killing, fired on Jewish homes and openly participated in the attack. The report of the official investigation commission appointed by the new government of Jamil al-Mifdai —moderate as it endeavored to be—established that 110

Jews were killed and 240 wounded; 86 Jewish enterprises were looted and 911 Jewish homes (inhabited by 2,985 families—with a total of 12,311 persons) destroyed. Unofficial accounts put the number of deaths at 150 and the number of wounded at more than 700, while the material damage was estimated at 750,000 dinars, or about three million dollars.[21] The causes of the disturbance were, in the opinion of the investigating committee, "Nazi propaganda emanating from the following sources: (1) the German League; (2) the Mufti of Jerusalem and his henchmen who followed him to Iraq. This man was accorded enthusiastic reception in Iraq and has turned it to his own use to disseminate many-sided Nazi propaganda. His influence on government and army circles became so strong that he could give orders to his group to set to work to spread anti-Jewish and anti-British propaganda among all classes of the population."

Even more devastating was the post-mortem of the Mufti's general activities in Iraq published on July 13, 1941, in the Baghdad daily *Al-Thagr* under the headline "The Crimes of the Fifth Column":

Iraq is well known for her hospitality. It is her theory that whoever has spent one night within her boundaries has become a genuine son of the country. Therefore the Mufti established himself in Iraq and soon hungry vagabonds gathered round him and every vagrant found in him the best means for spreading confusion and evading the law. . . . In addition to money lavishly bestowed upon him by the Nazis, a monthly subsidy of 1,000 Dinars was granted to him by the Iraqi treasury in order that he should arouse a revolt in Palestine and issue a *fetwa* prescribing a Holy War. He really issued a *fetwa* which, however, had greater influence in Iraq than in Palestine. It produced orphans and widows and tinged the ground with innocent blood. Then, snatching the mammon of the Nazis, he fled.

4

In Axis Service
1941–1945

Escape to Teheran

AFTER THE COLLAPSE OF THE IRAQI REVOLT, THE MUFTI AND
Rashid Ali fled Baghdad on May 29 and reached Teheran
two days later. On June 4, German State Secretary Weizsaecker despatched a "top secret" telegram to the German
Legation in Iran, stressing that "it is of great importance
to our policy in the Arab world that the impression does
not arise that we drop our friends as soon as they have
experienced a failure. . . . We are particularly interested in
convincing the Grand Mufti that we will continue to support him and the Arab fight for freedom; he can likewise
be promised further financial support."[1]

During their stay in Teheran, Rashid Ali and his entourage felt frustrated and preferred to live in isolation;
Haj Amin, on the contrary, remained active and maintained constant touch with German, Italian, and Japanese
legations.[2] His refuge and main base of operations was

the Japanese Legation, since the German Legation, about to be seized by British and Soviet military authorities, was not a suitable place for a marked pro-Axis Arab dignitary. Major Marrvede of the German *Abwehr* was assigned to his staff to facilitate further operations. On September 3, 1941, Major General Erwin Lahousen, one of the top officials of the *Abwehr*, whose secret diary was among the captured German documents, wrote: "The Grand Mufti, who left Iraq to go to Iran, is currently in connection with the *Abwehr* II [Sabotage division of the *Abwehr*]. According to reports from Teheran he is safe with the Japanese envoy."[3]

The Mufti found a fertile soil for his operations. Nazi influence in Iran was on the increase after 1936. In 1946, Arthur C. Millspaugh, who was administrator general of Iran's finances from 1922 to 1927, and again in 1943–1945, testified, "To all intents and purposes Reza Shah handed Persia over to Hitler. After Hitler's rise to power, some if not all the German experts became Nazi representatives in disguise, and when, in June 1941, the Nazis invaded Russia, their activity in Persia intensified."[4] Their agents played a leading role in the country, distributing Hitlerian propaganda in Russia. Dr. Schultz, German consul-general in Teheran, published a viciously anti-Jewish weekly, *Nabard* (Battle). Fearing a possible repetition of the bloody riots which took place in Baghdad during the Mufti's stay in Iraq, many Iranian Jews fled to Istanbul.

Haj Amin had every reason to be confident that he would be able to carry on his work without interference. The beginnings had been rather promising. Some knowledgeable observers of the Iranian scene were convinced that behind the ex-Shah Riza Pahlevi's passive but stubborn opposition to Britain, behind his stalling of action against the Germans in Iran following the British-Soviet requests, stood the Mufti surrounded by the Nazi agents. "The people were being told and indeed were believing that Hitler was a Moslem," testifies Lord Birdwood.[5]

But Haj Amin's time was short. The Allies struck swiftly. In September 1941, British troops entered Iran from the south and east, and Soviet troops from the north. The hope for a quick Axis drive into the Middle East vanished. Pahlevi was forced to abdicate, and his son Mohammed Riza ascended the throne on September 16. The Mufti's game was frustrated once again. He himself seemed trapped. His refuge was surrounded by the police. Both Haj Amin and Rashid Ali began to look for another country of refuge. They applied for admission to Turkey as political refugees, but only Rashid Ali's bid was granted. The Mufti was left to his own devices.

. . . and to Rome

The question on everyone's lips was: "Will he manage to escape once again?" The bets were predominantly in the Mufti's favor. Everybody remembered that he had already slipped through British fingers three times: in Jerusalem, in Lebanon, and in Iraq. Why shouldn't he succeed once more? And he did succeed, literally in accordance with the recipe described by "Beachcomber," the *Daily Express* humorous columnist:

Unofficial spokesmen, out of touch with authoritative sources, are saying that the elusive Mufti cheated. We hid our eyes, and counted up to a hundred, but the Mufti shouted: "Cockoo!" before we had reached forty-seven, and ran away for the fourth time.

British official circles naturally were disconcerted by this new fiasco after their widely advertised vigilance (a reward of £25,000 was offered for Haj Amin's capture). And for weeks there was complete silence regarding the Mufti's whereabouts. Then, late in October, it was announced that he had reached an airport in southern Italy and was safe under Mussolini's protection.

The Italian Interlude

Italian press reports revealed that after his escape from Teheran Haj Amin had reached "either Afghanistan or Turkey where he is known to have many friends"; the government-controlled Arabic World Agency in Rome added that in one of those two countries he was able to get a plane to Albania, "with the help of a foreign power that favored and protected his escape"; there, he boarded another plane, and, after what was described as "an adventurous flight," landed at a southern Italian airfield on October 24.[6]

Radio Bari solemnly announced this "great and happy event." The general tenor of the official comment was: "Italy, which knows [Haj Amin el-] Husseini's feeling of friendship and admiration for the Duce and the Fascisti, is glad to learn that he is safe and sound on her territory." On October 27, the Mufti arrived in Rome. The official *Tribuna* reported that "the Mufti will soon have important political colloquies with Islamic personalities in Europe and with outstanding personalities of the Italian capital; he will also visit Moslems in the Italian Empire."[7]

In fact, Il Duce, who still persisted in his claim to the title of "Protector of Islam," made much of his distinguished Moslem guest, welcomed him to "his spiritual home, the city of Fascism," and placed at his disposal a palatial house just outside Rome, which was to become

the Mufti's political headquarters. From there he conferred with Mussolini, Count Ciano (Mussolini's son-in-
law and foreign minister) and Dino Alfieri. He also got in
touch with Balkan Moslems under Italian rule in Yugoslavia and Albania.

Mussolini obviously had far-reaching plans for the
Mufti. He was determined to use him for purposes of his
own and was eager to keep him away from the other end
of the Axis. Reviewing, in retrospect, the relationship between the Mufti and the Fascist regime, Mussolini, on
May 13, 1943, stressed in a conversation in Rome with
Nazi Foreign Minister Joachim von Ribbentrop, in the
presence of Count Ciano (a memorandum of this conversation was published by the U.S. State Department on
July 12, 1946) that Italy "had been attempting, by extensive use of money, to induce the Grand Mufti to activity on the side of the Axis"; the latter had "already summoned the Arabs of the world to a holy war against the
English," and Mussolini "considered this action of considerable importance." The Mufti himself had, however,
different plans.

Pilgrimage to Berlin

Haj Amin had no intention of making Rome the base of
his operations. Italy had been, no doubt, very useful to
him in the matter of subsidies. Yet he preferred to deal
with principals and not with second-rate partners. And he
apparently concluded that it was time for a pilgrimage to
Berlin, to meet the "Big Boss" himself. After a twelve-day
sojourn in Rome he was off to Berlin where he arrived on
the night of November 6 and was greeted as a guest of
honor. A Wilhelmstrasse spokeman assured the world

that the fugitive Mufti would be accorded the "full honors due to his exalted rank." The Nazi press described him as "a great champion of Arab liberation and the most distinguished antagonist of England and of Jewry." He was assigned a villa in a western suburb of Berlin. Rashid Ali el-Gailani reached the Nazi capital two weeks later. At first he shared the Mufti's villa but was later provided with a separate residence.[8]

"From the time they set foot in Axis lands, the two pan-Arab leaders failed to cooperate," relates Majid Khaddury. "Competition for leadership, as well as personal jealousies aroused by the vested interests of their entourages prompted them to negotiate separately with the Axis authorities and each sought to secure recognition of leadership in activities in which he was personally most interested."[9] Count Ciano, the Italian foreign minister, noted in his diary: "The Mufti makes loud accusations against al Gailani; as was to be foreseen, the two quarrelled."[10] Both the Mufti and Rashid Ali later told Khaddury in separate private interviews that there was no disagreement between them over fundamental principles and that the differences were mainly on precedence and leadership.[11]

In this contest for leadership Haj Amin had several advantages over his rival. "While Rashid Ali led a relatively quiet life with his family, the Mufti, alone and restless, became very active," relates Khaddury. "Far more astute and persuasive than Rashid, the Mufti was looked upon as the leader of the pan-Arab community in exile." He "soon became the dominant figure in Arab affairs. As a religious leader who championed the cause of Islam, in addition to his pan-Arab activities, he exerted greater influence on personages such as von Weizsaecker [state secretary] and in particular on Himmler [Reichsführer S.S. and chief of the Gestapo]. He carried on end-less correspondence with Arab leaders in Europe such as Emir Chakib [Shakhib] Arslan, and others in Asia and North Africa: his influence may be said to have extended throughout the entire Moslem world. . . . In Rome the Mufti was still more influential and was able to make a great impression on Mussolini and Ciano, who regarded him as the future leader of the Moslem world." Majid Khaddury goes on to stress that "since Palestine was re-garded as falling in the Italian zone of influence, it was in the interest of Italy to cultivate the friendship of the Mufti and support his leadership over that of Rashid Ali. It was reported that the Mufti was to accompany Musso-lini on his well-prepared plan to enter Cairo after Rommel would have won the battle of Al-Alamayn."[12]

Received by Ribbentrop and Hitler

On November 20, the Mufti was received by von Rib-bentrop to whom he pointed out that Arab support for the Axis powers would be assured if the German government would recognize the independence of the Arab countries. Ribbentrop agreed but told the Mufti to take up the mat-ter with the Führer, whom he was to see the following day. John Eppler (alias Hussein Gâaffer),* who served as

* Eppler was born in Alexandria of a German mother and father and was registered at the German Consulate as a German child. After his father's death, the mother married a Moslem Egyptian lawyer, Saleh Gâaffer, who adopted him and converted him to Islam under the name of Hussein. The boy learned to speak Arabic from his nurses and German from his mother. In 1935 he went to Mecca. In 1938, while in Rome, he rediscovered his allegiance to Germandom and was recruited into Nazi service. He arrived in Berlin in 1939 with a German passport under his father's name, John Eppler. (Leonard Mosley, *The Cat and the Mice* [London, 1958]).

interpreter at this first meeting between Hitler and the Mufti (Hitler's usual interpreter, Dr. Schmidt, was also present), later told Leonard Mosley an amusing story of the initial stage of this encounter.

When he led the Mufti into Hitler's room in the Wilhelmstrasse,

the Mufti approached the Führer and held out his hand for Hitler to shake, and then, when he saw that no handshake was to be given, he drew it back and put his hand to his heart, in the Arabic way, and sat down. Hitler at once said to me: "Tell him that I welcome him here, and I am glad that the free people recognize that Germany has their interests at heart." I translated this, and the Mufti nodded. Hitler went on, "And now I will tell him my ideas of Pan-Arabism."

Instead of translating, I said: "My Führer, you have forgotten the coffee. . . . This is the Mufti of Jerusalem. . . . Even with minor dignitaries in Arabic countries, it is usual to start with coffee. It is the custom. We must not talk before coffee."

Hitler stared at me coolly: "I do not drink coffee" . . . sprang to his feet and made for the door shouting: "I will not have anyone—anyone, do you hear—drinking coffee in these headquarters."

. . . Five minutes later the door opened again and Hitler marched in, staring in morose irritation at his guest. Presently an S.S. man appeared with a tray in his hand and set it down on the table between the two men. On it were two glasses of lemon-barley water.

And as the Mufti began to sip at his, Hitler launched into a ninety-minute lecture on Pan-Arabism.[13]

The context of this meeting, which lasted from 4:30 P.M. until a few minutes after six, is recorded in the Mufti's diary in his own handwriting and is reproduced in full in the Appendix. It appears from this account that Hitler was markedly noncommittal. In reply to Haj Amin's plea for a formal recognition of the independence of the Arab countries, he stated that he was not ready to make long-term promises; the opportune time to make such a declaration would be when the German forces approached the borders of the Arab countries. Quoting the Mufti's *Memoirs,* Majid Khaddury says: "Despite the Mufti's disappointment he assured Hitler of Arab friendship and their willingness to collaborate with Germany."[14]

Rashid Ali's turn to be received came somewhat later. He saw Ribbentrop on December 16 and on December 19 obtained from him a letter recognizing his position as the Iraqi prime minister. An interview with Hitler was secured only in mid-July 1942, at the Führer's military headquarters in occupied Soviet territory. For his part Haj Amin sought to secure a letter addressed to him personally which would recognize the independence of the Arab countries. The desired letter from Ribbentrop came in January 1942. It contained the usual promise of recognition of such independence when the Arabs had won it. The Mufti was more successful in securing a pledge from the Italian government. To an application made jointly with Rashid Ali, Count Ciano answered on April 28, 1942, with a letter addressed to the Mufti, which contained a specific reference to Palestine. (The full text of the letter appears in the Appendix.)

Italy is . . . ready to grant to the Arab countries in the Near East, now suffering under British oppression, every possible aid in their fight for liberation; to recognize their sovereignty and independence; to agree to their federation if this is desired by the interested parties; as well as to the abolition of the National Jewish Homeland in Palestine. It is understood that the text and contents of this letter shall be held absolutely secret until such a time as we together decide otherwise.[19]

Their rivalry notwithstanding, the Mufti and Rashid Ali were united and vocal in their praise for the abortive Iraqi rebellion. They were the star speakers at an anniversary broadcast in Arabic beamed to the Arab world and relayed from Berlin Radio by radio stations of Zeissen and Athens.

Haj Amin said in his address:

Our celebration today is in honor of the glorious anniversary of the movement of the Iraq government, army and nation in the face of British aggression. Today we recall the martyrs who fell on the Iraqi front. Today we remember our patriots who made a stand before the tyrants.

Britain's attack on Iraq was not due to political mistakes on the part of Rashid Ali. It was made by the British as part of their plans to turn Iraq into a military base for themselves in the Near East. They wanted to secure their lines of communications and the oilfields, and to strengthen their military and political position. They also planned to penetrate into Persia. The plan was Wavell's, approved by the British government during the first year of war. Plots were hatched in the dark to fulfill it. Excuses and various tricks were devised to hide their true aims and shift the blame for their crimes on to other people. This has always been typical of British conduct. The British saw in the government of Rashid Ali and the Iraq army leaders an obstacle to their designs. They used their political methods to overcome it. But these Iraqi patriots refused to be misled by British tricks, and refused to play with the independence of Iraq. So the British resolved to get rid of them and brought up their armies to do so and to occupy the country. . . . Responsibility for the shedding of Iraq blood and for damage to the country falls on the neck of the British. . . . The Anglo-Iraq treaty was not the first to be violated by the British. Britain broke her promises to Egypt, India and other Islamic and Eastern countries. . . .

Today reminds us of those in concentration camps, prison and exile. This commemoration extends to those killed and injured in the Arab cause since the last war, and to the revolts in Iraq, Egypt, Syria, Palestine and other Arab countries. With this commemoration our determination is renewed to continue our struggle and to maintain patience whatever the difficulties. Victory is ours. The Arabs alone have carried the burden for many years, while the Jews and British have done as they liked. Today we oppose them at a time when they are being attacked by powerful friendly countries. Arab blood has not been shed in vain. It is a high price, but they who ask much must sacrifice much. The aims of our countries must be achieved. The Muslims will be victorious. The morning is not distant.

A week later Haj Amin was on the Axis air again, this time with a straight call to arms against the British and Allies. The occasion was the German announcement that three Iraqi military leaders, Sabbagh, Sa'id and Salman —members of the "Golden Square"—had been condemned to death by an Iraqi military court.

In a recorded program from Berlin, relayed to the Near and Middle East by the powerful Bari Radio at 1:00 P.M. on May 10, the Mufti said:

O Arabs, rise and avenge your martyrs. Avenge your honor. Fight for your independence. I, Mufti of Palestine, declare this war as a holy war against the British yoke of injustice, indecency and tyranny. We fear not death, if in death there is life and liberty.

The blood of these martyrs was shed for the cause of Islam and for an Arab country. They will remain immortal in the heart and history of the Arabs.

Rashid Ali was again in the same program.

Haj Amin also was at loggerheads with Fawzi Kaukji, former commander of Arab armed bands during the rebellion of 1936–1939. A pamphlet published after the war by anti-Mufti groups, devoted much attention to "the Mufti's intrigues against Kaukji":

Driven by Kaukji's military reputation to the fear that Hitler might place him rather than the Mufti in charge of the attempt to organize Arab resistance to the Allied Armies in the Middle East, Haj Amin constantly whispered into the ears of German intelligence officers that Kaukji was nothing but an English instigator whom the British had specially brought to Lebanon for this purpose from Turkey.

The pamphlet also claimed that the Mufti had intrigued against Kaukji during the 1936–1939 rebellion and that Kaukji had "only succeeded by a miracle in escaping his clutches in Palestine."[16]

Büro des Grossmufti

The center of Haj Amin's almost world-wide net was Germany. A special office, called *Büro des Grossmufti* was established in Berlin (and later in Oybin) with branches in other parts of Germany and in Italy. Its activities included: (1) radio propaganda, (2) espionage and fifth column activities in the Middle East (sabotage and parachutist expeditions), (3) organization of Moslems into military units in Axis-occupied countries and in North Africa and Russia, and (4) establishment of the Arab Legions and the Arab Brigade. To each of these fields Haj Amin devoted his truly extraordinary energy and dynamism.

Broadcasting

Since his arrival in Berlin, the Mufti was in charge of supervising Axis propaganda broadcasts to the Middle East. He himself went on the radio on several occasions and his broadcasts were among the most violent pro-Axis utterances ever produced. He had at his disposal no less than six "freedom stations" (Berlin, Zeissen, Bari, Rome, Tokyo, Athens), urging the Arabs of Palestine and Moslems all over the world, including those in the United States, to rise against the Allies, join the fifth column, commit acts of sabotage, and kill the Jews. Several members of his staff attended to radio activities. Haj Amin's broadcasts to the Middle East had noticeable effect on Arabs throughout that region during the dark hours of the War in 1941–1942. In addition, Haj Amin supplied the Middle East with propaganda papers and pamphlets in Arabic.[17]

Espionage and Sabotage

From his headquarters in Berlin and Oybin the Mufti organized a network of espionage. He had a sub-office in Geneva, Switzerland (directed by the notorious Axis agent Emir Shakhib Arslan) which served as a link between Haj Amin and his agents in Egypt and Turkey. He had another sub-office in Istanbul with branches all along the Syrian-Turkish frontier—in Mersine, Alexandretta, Antioch, Adana and Diarbekr. These received information directly from his agents in Palestine, Syria, and Iraq, and were in close contact with the members of the German Intelligence working in Turkey: Hoffman, German Consul General in Adana; Paula Koch in Alexandretta; Rudolf von Roser; Chapeaurouge in Istanbul; Von Hentig, etc.

Through this organization, valuable military information regarding British troop movements was transmitted to the Germans. News items about sabotage activities or uprisings like the Transjordan Frontier Force mutiny, although kept under strict censorship throughout the Middle East, were regularly and immediately announced on the Berlin radio.[18]

The Mufti's agents were infiltrated into the Middle East either by land through Turkey, Syria, and Iraq or by parachute. Several parachutist expeditions were discovered by the British, and their members, with their equipment (explosives, arms, ammunition, cameras, wireless transmitters, money in gold), were apprehended.

The first group to be caught were four parachutists, two Arab and two German, who dropped in Palestine in October 1944. They were rounded up near Jericho. One turned out to be a relative of the Mufti. The equipment found was impressive. It included leather suitcases, detailed maps, wireless transmission and calibration sets, Schmeisser submachine guns, Arab burnooses and kaffiyeh, khaki drill uniforms, airtight packets of food, medical stores, a number of first field dressings, a book of military instruction in Arabic, compasses, electric torches, cameras, films, and spares.

That was in October. A month later, four more parachutists were dropped forty miles west of Mosul. The incident is reported in the records of the American Legation in Baghdad which was quoted in the *New York Post* by Edgar Mowrer on June 6, 1946:

. . . . the men were sent not only to serve as intelligence agents but also to foment discontent and disorders wherever possible, and. . . . on behalf of the Mufti. . . . to exploit anti-Zionist feeling, and to prepare the way for the return of the Mufti from Germany.

The four members of this expedition had been in Iraq at the time of the Rashid Ali revolt in May 1941, and had escaped to Berlin. There they were recruited by the Mufti and trained in automatic weapons and wireless telegraphy. They left on November 26, 1944, and reached the dropping area in Iraq in moonlight. The party landed near a village some forty miles west of Mosul. They buried their equipment with the help of the local villagers and changed into civilian clothes. But the Mukhtar, headman, of the village informed the police of the incident the following morning.

British Intelligence officers frequently reported such Mufti-instigated sabotage parties. Elaborate reports made by Wing Commander Domville at Cairo (December 1, 1941), by Rex Marriot, defense security commander, Baghdad, and by Wing Commander H. K. Dawson Shepherd, defense security officer, Baghdad (December 9, 1944) gave essential details about these Axis-Arab missions.[19]

With the help of local Arabs, both parachutists and infiltrated agents on several occasions cut telephone and pipe lines in Transjordan and Palestine, and sabotaged railways and bridges in Iraq. Haj Amin boasted that because of his activities the British were forced to maintain large garrisons throughout the Middle East in order to prevent a general uprising and widespread sabotage. He claimed that only the constant vigilance of thousands of Allied troops prevented larger sabotage activities. Throughout the war every bridge and every weak point had, indeed, to be manned and guarded throughout the Middle East. In carrying out both sabotage and espionage, Haj Amin worked in close collaboration with the German *Abwehr*.[20] Major General Erwin Lahousen of the *Abwehr* wrote on June 2, 1942, in his secret diary: "The Italian national, Captain Simen, took part in discussions with the Grand Mufti concerning the utilization of the connections with the Grand Mufti for the purpose of *Abwehr* II, in order to demonstrate the solidarity of the Axis powers." A month later, on July 13, 1942, Lahousen made the further entry in his secret diary:

A meeting between the chief of the *Abwehr* [Admiral Canaris, who was also Hitler's representative in arranging for the Franco revolt against the Spanish Republican government] and the Grand Mufti of Jerusalem took place in the apartment of the chief. I [Lahousen] took part in the discussion. The Mufti made an offer to the chief that the followers of the Arabian Freedom Movement, which was led by him, as well as the followers of the former Iraq Prime Minister, Gailani, were to be used for purposes of sabotage and sedition in the Near East in accordance with the purposes of *Abwehr II*.[21]

A Parachutist and Sabotage School for Arabs was established in Athens; for special courses in wireless transmission, high explosives, and demolition, Arab students were sent to a school in The Hague.*

North African Contacts

Not least in importance were the Mufti's contacts with the pro-Axis leaders of the Moslems of North Africa. He submitted to the German military command a plan to recruit 500,000 Moroccan, Tunisian and Algerian soldiers. In Germany he opened a special North African Bureau (*Maktab el Magreb*) whose budget came from the *Büro des Grossmufti* in Berlin. During the North African campaign (which shattered his plans for a North African army) Haj Amin broadcast on numerous occasions to North Africa and urged the Moslems to help the Axis impede the Allies as much as they could.[22] He also played an important role as go-between in the secret Nazi negotiations with King Farouk of Egypt. In a confidential memorandum to the German Foreign Office on June 1, 1942, Ambassador Ettel, one of Hitler's roving envoys, reported that "the safest and most reliable way to deliver a message to King Farouk is via his father-in-law Zulficar

---

* The Mufti also worked closely with the Nazi specialists on the Middle East, including Palestine-born Templars, Christian colonists who settled in Palestine at the end of the Nineteenth century. They spoke fluent Arabic. Ever since Hitler's rise to power they had been the leading Nazi agents in the Middle East. Some managed to reach Germany after the outbreak of war, and some had gone there before.

Pasha . . . a close friend of the Mufti . . . [who] therefore can be reached most effectively via the Mufti. . . . The latter is prepared to cooperate to the best of his ability." The Mufti suggested dispatching "his trustworthy and discreet secretary, Dr. Mustafa el Wakie" with an official letter for Zulficar Pasha and was "prepared to also give a [personal] letter along to his friend Zulficar Pasha." The message was duly transmitted to King Farouk by a "confidential agent." During his stay in Egypt, the agent had two lengthy conversations with the King and was told that, "as in the past, the King was still hoping for an Axis victory"; he was also instructed by Farouk "to convey his best wishes to the Mufti of Jerusalem and to all those who work with him for the success and the victory of the Axis.[23]

In the summer of 1943, when Rommel's armies were victoriously advancing in the whole of North Africa and threatened the entire Middle East, Haj Amin sent to Hitler a jubilant message, which was found in German files under the heading "Volume 13, Letters and Telegrams from Foreign Heads of State." The message, dated July 4, 1942, read:

Allow me, Fuehrer, to express to you the sincere joy of the Arabian people and my best wishes on the occasion of the Axis victory in North Africa. These successes were crowned by the solemn declarations of the German and Italian Governments, in which the sovereignty and independence of Egypt were recognized and assured. These wise policies of the Axis powers, which guided the German-Italian armies from victory to victory, will produce a very good echo not only in Egypt but also in all the other Arab lands and in the entire Orient, for they offer the best proof of the noble aims of the Axis governments and assure the other Arab lands of their liberty and independence. The Arab people will further continue to fight on your side against the common enemy up to the ultimate victory.

During the Nazi occupation of Tunisia (November 1942–May 1943), Haj Amin is reported to have maintained, in Rome, "friendly contact" with Habib Bourguiba, then the leader of Tunisia's nationalist Neo-Destour Party (and now President of the Tunisian Republic).[24] As late as July 1944, the Mufti was still broadcasting over the German radio frantic appeals to the Moslems in French North Africa not to serve in the army of General De Gaulle, on the ground that De Gaulle is helping the Jews against the Nazis who are defenders of Moslem interests.[25]

Far East Contacts

Haj Amin was also busily cultivating his ties with the Far Eastern end of the Axis. Early in 1942 he sent a message to Emperor Hirohito, eulogizing Japan as "champion of the liberation of the Asiatic peoples from the yoke of British and Jewish capitalists and Bolsheviks." Expressing gratitude for the active solidarity which Japan had extended to the Arab nationalist cause, he assured the Emperor "in the name of the Arabs" that they were praying "for the final victory of the Japanese arms."[26]

A few days earlier, December 29, 1941, a monitored short-wave broadcast in Spanish from Radio Berlin, directed to South America, had released the following news:

The Grand Mufti of Jerusalem, now in Berlin, granted an interview yesterday to a representative of the Japanese Domei Agency. He declared that a movement for Arabic independence has ben organized and is ready to strike as soon as the British Empire shows symptoms of collapse. The Arabic movement proposes a cultural development under the guidance of Japan, Germany and Italy.

With regard to the Japanese successes in the Pacific, the

Grand Mufti said: "Japan's successes benefit the whole of Asia and all the Asiatics who are suffering under the Anglo-Saxon yoke.

Numerous broadcasts in the following years greatly aided Japan in its subversive propaganda in India and Asia, and linked Haj Amin as closely with the designs and purpose of Japan as he was with those of Italy and Germany. Nearly three years later he was still paying considerable attention to the Far East. In a Berlin broadcast on September 20, 1944, he said:

In our last holiday broadcast I told you of Germany's pledge of independence to Albania. On this occasion, I wish to announce to you Japan's pledge of independence to sixty million Moslems in Java and Sumatra. We desire victory for Germany and Japan because the interest of the Arab and the Moslem can never be fulfilled except through close cooperation with them under all circumstances. We can expect nothing from the Allies who are controlled by world Jewry.

Neither were the Moslems of India forgotten. In a monitored broadcast in Arabic from Rome Radio, on August 22, 1942, Haj Amin said:

I know well the hatred you feel for the oppressor who has destroyed your power and ruined your existence. I know you are Moslems and that your only aim is the independence of your country, for you are convinced that the British are the worst enemies of Islam and that they have always worked against Islam and the precepts of the Koran. . . .

The opportunity given you to liberate yourselves from the British yoke is a propitious one, and Moslems in all countries must not let it escape. The presence of the British in India is a slur on all peoples of Moslem countries. All Moslems must be forbidden to give military help to England.

The Arab Legion

In 1942, a few months after his arrival in Germany, Haj Amin started organizing an Axis-Arab Legion from among the Arab students in Germany, the Arab prisoners of war, and the émigrés who had followed him to Germany. They wore the German uniform and had "Free Arabia" patches on their shoulders. This *Arabisches Freiheitskorps* was a part of the German Army and protected lines of communication in Macedonia. The legionnaires had been instrumental in ferreting out American and British parachutists landed in Yugoslavia, whom the local population was seeking to hide and protect from the Nazis.[27] The Legion also served on the Russian front and suffered heavy casualties. A report carried by a London paper (*Daily Sketch*, February 12, 1944) stated:

Some time ago, through the activities of the Mufti of Jerusalem, [there was] recruited in all Axis and satellite countries an Arab Legion that was composed of Arab students in Europe and former members of the French Foreign Legion. When trained, this legion, which had been promised service in the Nazi invasion of the Middle East, was sent instead to the Russian front, and has been completely wiped out in the recent Caucasus fighting.

The numbers involved were not large. For there were not limitless groups of Arabs in Europe. And since there were comparatively few serving with the Allied Forces, the Mufti could not even count on desertions or prisoners of war to reinforce his Arab Legion.

In September 1944, the British government announced that it had acceded to the request of the Jewish Agency for Palestine to provide a specifically Jewish fighting force, and that a Jewish Brigade Group would be formed.

Some 26,000 Palestinian Jewish volunteers had already
been serving with the British forces since the beginning of
the war.* They were organised in "Palestine Battalions"
and in Palestinian units with larger formations. But here
was a specific Jewish fighting unit, commanded by a Jewish brigadier, with the status of an independent combat
unit, assigned to a section of the Italian front.

In response to this move, Haj Amin got von Ribbentrop
to consent to the formation of an Arab Brigade. He spoke
at a large protest rally in Berlin, on November 2, 1944, a
rally which was broadcast on the Arabic hour of Berlin
Radio, and at which the creation of an Arab Brigade was
announced:

> The heart of every Arab rejoiced at the declaration, on this
> same day a year ago, of the German Foreign Minister Herr
> Von Ribbentrop: "Old ties of friendship bind Germany to the
> Arab world. Today more than at any other time she is your
> natural ally. . . . The hour approaches when the Arab people
> will once again build their future in freedom."
> In contrast to this clear German pronouncement, the Allied
> lies are transparent. They are Judaizing, colonizing, exploiting,
> mandating, as they did in Morocco, Palestine and the
> Sudan. . . .
> . . . Therefore it is the duty of the Arabs to beware and to be
> ready to oppose with force and with determination this dan-
> ger, to prepare their armies, to unite, and to create both legal
> and illegal armies in order to save the land from the Jewish

* In Palestine itself, the call for Jews and Arabs to join British units
met with strikingly different reactions in the two communities: of the
about half a million Jews 85,781 men and 50,262 women between the
ages of 18 and 50 volunteered for service, and 21,851 men and 3,933
women actually served in the British Army; out of an Arab population
twice as big only 3,000 volunteered; in other words, the ratio of Jewish
to Arab volunteers was six to one. Colonel Halford L. Hoskis, known for
his pro-Arab leanings, says in his 1954 study, *The Middle East Problem
Area in World Politics:* "The Palestine Arab population, reflecting its
indifference to the issues of the war and the pro-Axis efforts of the Mufti
of Jerusalem, showed little disposition to take any active part in the
war" (p. 103).

army and its Allied supporters. The Arabs must be ready to sacrifice themselves as their forefathers did.

When Haj Amin had concluded his appeal, the announcer read the following statement:

Yesterday an Independent Arab Brigade was formed as a reply to Great Britain's decision to arm the Jews of Palestine in a Jewish Brigade. This British decision had the effect of stimulating Arab and Moslem circles in Germany and other Axis nations to ask for the creation of an Arab unit to fight the common enemy. . . . The Arabs and Moslems residing in Germany have petitioned the government of the Reich to form an independent Arab unit to fight side by side with the Axis powers. The government of the Reich has agreed to this demand. Arab anger was demonstrated by the mass of Arabs who responded to this call and who streamed from all corners of Germany and its allied countries to volunteer for the Arab Brigade.

Three weeks later, on the occasion of the Mohammedan Feast, the *Id-ul-Adha*, Haj Amin went on the air again, again over Berlin Radio, with a long appeal to Arabs and Moslems. Despite the announcement just quoted, made on November 2, recruiting was probably not spectacular. For Haj Amin's address on November 25 concluded as follows:

We have pleasure in announcing good news to the Arabs regarding the approval of the German government of the formation of an Arab unit to act against the Jewish Brigade formed in Palestine. From this the Arabs can judge the vast difference between Germany and Britain. Britain wants to frustrate all Arab hopes of their independence; Germany desires the contrary.

In fact, nothing specific was ever heard of this Arab Brigade. If it served at all, it must have been in Europe, where its service could not have been spectacular. But failure was not due to any lack of anti-British, pro-Nazi vigor on the part of the ex-Mufti. And things might conceivably have been different had this Arab force been used in the Middle East.[28]

Early in 1945, Reich Minister Dr. Goebbels received a delegation of those Mufti Arab volunteers who handed him a considerable donation for the German Red Cross as a sign of their close link with National Socialist Germany. In a short address, Goebbels expressed his gratitude and stressed his belief that the fight of the German armed forces, whose ranks included Arab volunteers, was directed against "the traditional enemies of the Arabs—Jewish world tyranny and British-American plutocratic imperialism."[29]

An intelligence report published in the January 1945 issue of *Current Foreign Relations,* issued by the State Department in Washington, spoke of "four German agents, members of the Arab Legion," who had recently been dropped by parachute into Palestine; two of them were immediately arrested. "Their mission was to work on behalf of the Mufti of Palestine by exploiting anti-British sentiments for his possible return from Germany. It is thought that these men may be the vanguard of some 45 Iraqi members of the Arab Legion to arrive later."*

Moslem *Wehrmacht* Units

The Mufti's military activities on behalf of the Axis were by no means limited to recruiting of ethnic Arabs only. He used his spiritual influence among Moslem groups in a large variety of countries. His major work of recruitment—by far the most serious from the military point of view—was with the Balkan Moslems.

---

* In order to avoid being executed, those parachutists who were caught insisted that they were "soldiers in the Mufti's Legion" and, thus, entitled to the treatment accorded to prisoners of war.

While in passage to Rome, he communicated with the Balkan Moslems under Italian occupation in Yugoslavia and Albania. In his vast correspondence with Ribbentrop and Himmler he repeatedly claimed credit for the organization of Moslem military units to fight for the Axis. In the Balkans alone he rallied tens of thousands of Moslems into the Axis *Wehrmacht*. In the spring of 1943, he visited the puppet state of Croatia and vigorously harangued the Croat Moslem *Waffen* S.S. division which fought the Yugoslav partisans and committed the worst atrocities against the Serb population; "The situation in Croatia and Palestine," he claimed, "was identical as they were fighting the same battle against the same enemies, namely the British and their Jewish allies."[30] In January 1944, Haj Amin paid a second visit to the same Moslem S.S. division, which by the end of 1943 amounted to some 20,000 men, and spent three days with these Axis troops. At the close of his visit he made a declaration of principles which was to have guided every Moslem all over the world; his speech was reproduced in full by the German Transocean agency on January 21, 1944:

This division of Bosnian Moslems, established with the help of Greater Germany, is an example for Moslems in all countries. There is no other deliverance for them from imperialist oppression than hard fighting to preserve their homes and faith. Many common interests exist between the Islamic world and Greater Germany, and those make cooperation a matter of course. The Reich is fighting against the same enemies who robbed the Moslems of their countries and suppressed their faith in Asia, Africa and Europe. Germany is the only Great Power which has never attacked any Islamic country. Further, National-Socialist Germany is fighting against world Jewry. The Koran says: "You will find that the Jews are the worst enemies of the Moslems." There are also considerable similarities between Islamic principles and those of National-Socialism, namely in the affirmation of struggle and fellowship, in stressing leadership, in the idea of order, in the high valuation of work. All this brings our ideologies close together and facilitates cooperation. I am happy to see in this Division a visible and practical expression of both ideologies.

The Mufti called on the Moslem recruits to avenge themselves against the Christian population of Yugoslavia who, he charged, were to be punished for their past anti-Moslem attitude; numerous eye-witness accounts of wide-scale atrocities against Christians, which resulted from these incitements, have been collected by the Yugoslav government.[31]

In the spring of 1944, a German broadcast, issued by the Mufti from Zittau, Saxony, and recorded in Ankara, contained a call to Moslems in Yugoslavia to hold prayer meetings for seven days for the success of Hitler's forces. Anxious to bolster his reputation among the Croat Moslems, Haj Amin lavishly distributed money provided by the Axis.[32] The *Donauzeitung* of December 31, 1942, reported that he donated 140,000 Kune to the Moslem charity organization at Sarajevo, after having already donated 100,000 Kune for the same purpose some weeks earlier. He also was in direct contact with various Balkan quislings such as Ante Pavelic, with whom he arranged the organization of the Moslem *Wehrmacht* units; with Professor von de Mende he established a school for politico-religious Moslem army preachers (*Imams*) in Germany.[33]

Moslem Units in Soviet Russia

Particularly intense was the sustained effort to establish and to consolidate pro-Axis military units from among the thirty million Moslems in the Soviet Union. The Mufti's anti-Soviet broadcasts were both numerous and fully attuned to the German line. He was in close contact with several Moslem quislings, such as Ali Khan of the Northern Caucasus; Major Dudanginski, head of the Azerbaijan Legion; Dr. Szymkewicz, Mufti at the German-occupied *Ostland* area (Poland and occupied regions of U.S.S.R.); Mohammed al Gazani, Moslem poet and one of the leaders of the anti-Soviet Moslem Union; as well as with the Turkestan National Union Committee.[34] It was largely due to Haj Amin's propaganda that on the arrival of the German armies in the northern Caucasus in 1942, five indigene tribes—the Chechens, the Ingushes, the Balkars, the Karachais, and the Kabardines—welcomed them with bread and salt. On August 30, 1942, the Mufti's representative, Said Hamil, was appointed liaison officer between the German Army and Moslem tribes in the Soviet Caucasus. A Moslem priest was sent by the Mufti to accompany five German agents in a parachute jump behind the Soviet lines southeast of Grozny for a sabotage operation known in code as "Mohammed."[35] In the wake of the German retreat in the winter of 1942–1943, large segments of the five tribes, fearing the vengeance of the returning Soviet armies, had, together with their women and children, followed the retreating German Army until they reached temporary refuge in large camps in Crimea and along the lower Dnieper.* Many of the able-bodied men among them enrolled in General Vlassov's army, while others were formed into special military units and were utilized against the Soviet partisans.[36]

Another Caucasian Moslem group of volunteers for the German Army was recruited from among the Azerbaijan prisoners of war. In November 1943, a *DNB* broadcast announced that the first Azerbaijan field battalions who

---

* Of those who remained, some 600,000 were deported to central Asia and Siberia, where hunger, disease, cold and hard labor took their heavy toll. It was not until 1957 that the survivors were permitted to return.

had been actively fighting against Bolshevism for over a year, "proved their valor, were included in German Storm Troops and decorated by the German Army," and that an Azerbaijan Conference had taken place in Berlin on November 7, under the leadership of Major Dudanginsky, of the Azerbaijan Legion.[37] A dispatch to the Secretary of State from the U.S. Legation in Bern, dated November 16, 1943, specifically mentioned that this conference was attended "by the Grand Mufti of Jerusalem" and "representatives of the peoples of Caucasus, the Ural and Turkestan."

The Moslem prisoners of war of Turkoman extraction provided a considerable number of recruits for the German forces. They wore the same uniform as all other SS units, except for a red fez marked with the German emblem and swastika. On their collars, instead of German emblems, they wore insignia depicting a scimitar held in a Moslem's fist, flanked by swastikas.[38] The first group of these volunteers took their oath of allegiance in November 1943, in the vicinity of Vilno,[39] the second, in January 1944, near Kovno.[40] In January 1943, units of theTurkestan Legion were reported on guard at the Atlantic Wall.[41]

The Reich Paid the Bill

The Third Reich invested heavily in the activities of the Mufti, Rashid el-Gailani, and other Arab dignitaries in the Axis service.

Document NG–5461, Office of Chief of Counsel for War Crimes, contains a specification of expenditure, in German marks (at that time, two and a half marks were equivalent to one dollar) for that purpose:[42]

	Monthly	Yearly
Mufti account: for rents, personal upkeep, wages, salaries (residences in Berlin; houses I, II, III, IV; Hotel Adlon; Hotel Zittau; the Jewish Institute, Klopstockstrasse)	66,850	802,200
In foreign currencies	25,000	300,000
Special expenses, "made once" (furniture, etc.)		21,100
El Ghailani account: for rents, personal upkeep, wages, salaries (residence in Berlin, Houses I, II, III, IV, and ten other houses)	86,580	1,038,960
In foreign currencies	30,000	360,000
Special expenses, "made once" (furniture, etc.)		155,800
Five months at sea resort Banzin, "made once"		82,000
Fauzi el Kaudzi* account: for rents, residence in Altenberg	600	7,200
Prince Mansour Daud† (a cousin of King Farouk): for rents, personal expenses	12,750	153,000
Kamil Mrowa account: paid "in foreign currency"§	2,500	30,000
Upkeep for miscellaneous other Arabs .	10,300	123,600
150 Arab students, Paris, "living expenses in foreign currency"	160,000	1,920,000
Total		4,993,860

* Document NG-5461 includes an explanatory note, as follows: "Fauzi el Kaudzi [German spelling] is the well known rebel leader from Palestine, who in 1941 returned from Iraq to Greece seriously wounded and was subsequently brought to Germany. Fauzi el Kaudzi held the rank of colonel in the German Army and in addition to the pension from Raschid Ali el Gailani, he received financial support from the Wehrmacht. The support from the Wehrmacht was reduced in the course of the year 1944 and finally amounted to only about 30 bottles of cognac a month."

† According to Document NG-5461, the Prince "came to Germany in 1943 with his wife and two children and attached himself to the Grand Mufti. Later [he] joined the Waffen-SS as an ordinary soldier."

§ According to Document NG-5461, Mrowa was "stationed in Sofia

The Mufti was receiving sizable funds from both the budget of Himmler's S.S. and the special budgets of the German Foreign Office. An affidavit submitted at the Nuremberg trial by former German consul, C. Rekowski, gives the specification of the monthly payments to Haj Amin from the special funds at the disposal of Von Ribbentrop's Foreign Ministry (table on page 145.)[43]

The regular total monthly expenditure thus amounted to 91,850 German marks, or 1,102,200 marks per year. Rekowski explained in his affidavit that the Mufti was not expected to account for the use of the subsidies under 1 and 1a, and "when, as was the case more than once, the amount was not sufficient, an increase was demanded and allotted."

In addition, Legationsrat Wilhelm Melchers testified on August 11, 1947, that the Mufti was being "paid also by the S.S.," receiving "important privileges, like gasoline, autos . . . also considerable amounts of money." Melchers explained that "he [the Mufti] was valuable because he went to the Moslem areas in the Balkan countries and successfully recruited for S.S. divisions."[44]

The Nazis Reciprocate

The Nazi regime, on its part, missed no opportunity of stressing the community of interests between the Third Reich and the Mufti-led Arab cause. On November 2, 1943, the twenty-sixth anniversary of the Balfour Declaration, Heinrich Himmler, in his capacity as S.S. Reichsführer and Minister of the Interior, sent to a special meeting in Berlin the following telegram, which was subsequently broadcast by the German radio:

Object	Rent	Expense for mainte- nance and repair	Food, incl. the personnel	Compen- sation and salaries for the personnel
1. Personal sustenance		50,000		
1a. Personal sustenance in foreign currency		25,000		
2. Residence in the Goethe Street, Berlin Zehlendorf	800	500	300	250
3. Office [same address]	250	100		
4. Residence Zaue, House I and II	600	300		100
5. Residence Oybin, near Zittau	1,100	900	3,000	1,200
6. Hotel Adlon, Berlin	2,000		2,000	
7. Houses II and III at Pieskow	400	300	500	200
8. Hotel in Zittau	700		300	
9. Jewish Institute in the Klopstockstrasse	600	100		50
10. Driver				300
	6,450	77,200	6,100	2,100

[capital of Bulgaria] allegedly to listen to the radio stations of the Middle East. . . . Mrowa sent his reports to Berlin daily."

To the Grand Mufti:

The National Socialist Movement of Greater Germany has, since its beginning, inscribed upon its flag the fight against world Jewry. It has therefore followed with particular sympathy the struggle of the freedom-loving Arabians, especially in Palestine, against the Jewish interlopers.

Five weeks later, on December 10, 1943, the official German News Agency Transocean reported that on the Arab-Moslem holiday of *Aid el-Kebir*, Joachim von Ribbentrop, the Reich's foreign minister, addressed a message to both the Mufti and Rashid el-Gailani: "Traditional bonds of friendship join Germany with the Arab people. Today more than ever Germany is the natural ally of the Arabs. The elimination of the so-called Jewish National Home and the liberation of all Arab countries from subjugation and exploitation by the Western Powers is an unalterable aim of the policy of the Greater German Reich. May the hour not be far off when the Arab people, in complete independence, can build up its future in unity and self-determination."

Nazi press and political literature were assiduously wooing the Mufti. The rabidly anti-Semitic periodical *Die Action* published in March 1942 an interview by N. H. Sanki under the title, "An Hour with the 'Faithful.' His Eminence the Grand Mufti of Palestine Speaks About the Arab National Aims." The following year there appeared a book by Kurt Fisher-Weth: *Amin al-Husseini, Grossmufti von Palestine* (Berlin, 1943, 95 pp.), and the Mufti was invited to write a Preface to a Nazi source book on Britain's Palestine policy, by Mamrin al Hamui, *Die Britische Palaestina-Politik, Dokumente zur Zeitgeschichte* (Berlin, 1943, 365 pp.). "Grossmufti of Jerusalem, Kurort Oybin" was mentioned in a German Propaganda Ministry document of March 1944, in a mailing list of pro-German volunteer formations receiving literature from the ministry. Haj Amin was also invited to represent "Arabia" at the abortive International Anti-Jewish Congress scheduled by Alfred Rosenberg for July 1944.[45]

The collapse of Mussolini's government in September 1943 resulted in attaching the Mufti's Arab supporters even closer to Germany. A *Nachrichten und Pressedienst* report from Antakia, dated September 10, 1943, thus described Arab reaction to this new turn of world events:

During the last ten years Fascism has, for ideological and political reasons, found many adherents and sympathizers among the Arabs of the Near East, and has awakened many hopes of powerful support for the Arabs' fight for freedom against Great Britain and France. . . . A proof that these opinions had taken root was the fact that the enemy broadcasting stations tried nearly every day to disparage and slander Italy and Fascism. . . . Since the overthrow of Mussolini, however, this attitude has undergone considerable change. . . . The news of the philo-Semitic measures taken by the Badoglio Government, which is entirely analogous to the re-establishment of Jewish influence in Algiers, has greatly contributed to this change of opinion among the Arabs.

During these last few weeks it has been observed that Italy, without the atttraction of Fascism, is no longer able to pursue an active Near Eastern policy to impress the Arab soul. All the more do Arab circles now expect an independent active German Near Eastern policy, since Germany has been freed from her former agreements with Italy.

The Mufti's Anti-Jewish Crusade

It was only natural that in the Mufti's numerous and variegated broadcasts, anti-Jewish incitement had played an outstanding and ever increasing part. It became particularly vitriolic on March 19, 1943, on the occasion of

Prophet Mohammed's birthday. In a broadcast over the Rome wireless he reiterated his old allegation, which had caused so much bloodshed in Palestine in the past, that the Jews had designs on the holy places of Islam, especially on the El Aqsa Mosque. The danger of Judaism to the Arabs, argued the Mufti, was not confined to Palestine, as the Jews, associated with the Allies, were now planning to make North Africa a shelter for Jewish refugees from Europe; this, he said, explains Dr. Weizmann's statement that North Africa will form a bridge between New York and Jerusalem. Warning the Arabs that in the case of an Allied victory "Jewish influence will be the arbiter of the world," Haj Amin urged them to sabotage the Allied war effort. He addressed himself in particular to Arab emigrants in America:

The Arabs and Moslems will not be deceived by Britain, for not only have they long known its true intentions but they have also known those of its Ally—America. I want to draw the attention of the Arab emigrants in America to this fact, reminding them of their glorious past when they supported the National Movement. I would remind them that their efforts will be wasted if, God forbid, America and her Allies are victorious in this war. For if that happened, the Arabs would never rise again. I therefore am confident that those Arab emigrants in America will refrain from helping Roosevelt or from taking part in a war which he has brought on his country.

. . . Arabs and Moslems, on this occasion of the birthday of the Prophet, who crushed Jewish ambitions in the past and completely eliminated them from Moslem countries, thereby setting us an example, on such a day Moslems and Arabs should vow before God utterly to crush Jewish ambitions and prove that faith in God is greater than imperialism and far more powerful than the devilry which surrounds international Judaism.

Eight months later, a rally to protest the publication, twenty-six years ago, of the Balfour Declaration was held

in the large *Luftwaffe* Hall in Berlin. The proceedings
were broadcast and a recording was rebroadcast the following day. Haj Amin was the principal speaker. The
broadcast opened with a color piece from the announcer:

We are in the Luftwaffe building in Berlin, where Arab
leaders are gathered to protest against the Balfour Declaration.
The Hall is festooned with Arab flags and poster portraits of
Arab patriots. Arabs and Moslems from every land pour into
the hall. Among them are Moroccans, Palestinians, Lebanese,
Yemenites, men from the Hedjaz, Indians, Iranians and Moslem representatives from all over Europe. Among the latter are
a great many Germans friendly to the Arabs, high government
officials, civilian and military, one of the S.S. chiefs, representatives of foreign embassies and at their head representatives of
the Japanese Embassy. The audience runs into hundreds, and
here now I see the Mufti of Jerusalem making his way into the
hall. He is shaking hands with a number of notables and
mounts the steps to the stage to deliver his address.

Haj Amin then took over with a vitriolic tirade against the
Jews and the British and glowing praise for the Axis:

Moslems throughout the Arab lands are united against the
enemy which faces them today in Palestine and elsewhere—
namely the British.

The Treaty of Versailles was a disaster for the Germans as
well as for the Arabs. But the Germans know how to get rid
of the Jews. That which brings us close to the Germans and
sets us in their camp is that up to today, the Germans have
never harmed any Moslem, and they are again fighting our
common enemy (applause) who persecuted Arabs and Moslems. But most of all they have definitely solved the Jewish
problem. These ties, and especially the last, make our friendship with Germany not a provisional one, dependent on conditions, but a permanent and lasting friendship based on mutual
interests.

The greatest of Britain's crimes is wanting to drag the Arabs
into a war against the Germans and Japanese, who never
committed a wrong against the Moslems.

O Araby, never fear the propaganda of your enemies. You never fought the Jews without their being the loser (applause). Time is on our side in our fight against them even though the Allies want to help them." (Stormy and prolonged applause.)

The gathering closed with the announcer's declaration: "The Arabs pledge the Mufti to fight on the side of Germany."

Continuing his anti-Jewish crusade, Haj Amin, on November 11, 1943, in a broadcast over Radio Bari, called on "my people" to fight the British and the Jews to the death; if the Arab peoples ever hoped to obtain their liberty and independence, unity and self-government, these could only be achieved through an Axis victory:[46]

Today the Axis peoples are fighting for the liberation of the Arab peoples. If England and America win the war, the Jews will dominate the world. If, on the other hand, the victory is carried off by the Axis, the Arab world will be freed. The Axis is befriending us. Fight for its victory.

A few days later, referring to events in Lebanon, the Mufti broadcast to the Arab world a stern "warning against the treacherous game and the fraud being practiced by the Allies against the Arab countries."[47]

On March 1, 1944, when the pro-Zionist Wright-Compton and Wagner-Taft resolutions were before the U. S. Congress, the Mufti issued from Berlin a call to the Arabs "to rise and to fight."[48]

No one ever thought that 140,000,000 Americans would become tools in Jewish hands. . . . How would the Americans dare to judaize Palestine while the Arabs are still alive? . . . . The wicked American intentions toward the Arabs are now clear, and there remain no doubts that they are endeavoring to establish a Jewish empire in the Arab world. More than 400,000,000 Arabs [?] oppose this criminal American movement. . . . Arabs! Rise as one and fight for your sacred rights.

Kill the Jews wherever you find them. This pleases God, history, and religion. This saves your honor. God is with you.

This call by the Mufti was used as a peg on which to hang a wider German appeal in a broadcast three hours later from the same station, Radio Berlin. The regular Arab commentator, announcing that "the revolution had started in Palestine," told the Arabs that the Americans, British and Soviets wanted to control the Near East and oppress the Arabs. The broadcast concluded:

Germany fights against the Jews, the British, the Americans and the Russians. Germany assures the Arabs of complete independence. Arabs, we are about to end this war. We are now reaching the crossroad. Distinguish between your friends and enemies. The German soldier is your protector and defender.

Destruction of the Palestine Jewish community by the Nazi war machine was a recurrent item on Haj Amin's agenda.[49]

A report, marked "Secret," by the Air Force Command Staff (No. 35526/43 g. /IIID4/, October 29, 1942) reveals that "an air attack on Tel Aviv, the citadel of Palestinian Jewry and emigration [immigration?], has been repeatedly proposed during the last half year by Arabs, especially by the Grand Mufti." The same report also discussed the suggestion of an air attack on the building of the Jewish Agency in Jerusalem on November 2, the twenty-sixth anniversary of the Balfour Declaration, when, according to the Reich Security Office, a "Zionist session" was to be held. Stressing that Jerusalem had no great military importance," the Air Force Command believed that "an attack on one of many military objectives along the Palestine coast and in the coastal region should be considered" and added: "Even the Grand Mufti, as the Reich Security Headquarters has said, would consider this sufficient." Yet Field Marshal Goering, to whom the matter had been previously submitted for decision, turned it down on July 17 because no sufficiently large task force was available.

In the spring of the next year, the Mufti renewed pressure for such an action. Another official German report, this time by Foreign Air Force West (No. 9753/448 /D4/, March 30, 1944), entitled: "In re: Grand Mufti's Urging of a Bombing Attack on Tel Aviv on April 1," pointed out that "the Grand Mufti had already repeatedly proposed bomb attacks on Tel Aviv and Jerusalem in order to injure Palestinian Jewry and for propaganda purposes in the Arab world."* Referring to Goering's previous ruling, the Air Force Command again refrained from action.

The Mufti and "The Final Solution"

It is hardly accidental that the beginning of the systematic physical destruction of European Jewry by Hitler's Third Reich roughly coincided with the Mufti's arrival in the Axis camp.

Up to mid-1941, the official German policy vis-à-vis the Jews was one of forced mass emigration from the Reich's "vital space." After the annexation of Austria in 1938, the "Jewish Emigration Office" headed by Adolf Eichmann, succeeded, within eight months, in impelling 45,000 Jews to leave the country. The Office took no interest in the ultimate destination of the expellees, and Eichmann is known to have cooperated with Zionist leaders toward the

---

* In a letter to Himmler, dated September 28, 1944, General Berger of the *Waffen S.S.* reported: "Today the Mufti came to see me for a long talk. He talked about his work and noted happily that the day is nearing when he will head an army to conquer Palestine." (Quentin Reynolds, Ephraim Katz, Zwy Aldouby. *Minister of Death: The Adolf Eichmann Story* [New York, 1960], pp. 175-176).

acceleration of such a mass exodus. The same policy was applied in Czechoslovakia when, in July 1939, Eichmann was transferred to Prague to head the branch of the "Central Office for Jewish Emigration" in the German Protectorate of Bohemia and Moravia. The announced goal was the emigration of 70,000 Jews within a year, and within the first six months some 35,000 Jews had left the Protectorate. Given exit permits, they were dumped at various European ports. Thousands were put aboard German ships with forged British certificates for Palestine or with bogus Latin-American visas. In 1938–1939 alone, a total of 80,000 Jews had left Austria and Czechoslovakia under Eichmann's "auspices"—and under duress. As it turned out, they thus escaped being gassed in Auschwitz by order of the same Adolf Eichmann.

In the second half of 1939 the emigration scheme was suddenly abandoned. Yet, for months to come, the alternative to emigration was still not slaughter but isolation in ghettos, deportation to the East, and slave labor. The program of wholesale physical extermination began only after the Mufti's arrival on the scene. The formal decision to annihilate the Jews who had survived the ghettos, forced labor, starvation, and disease, was taken at the Wannsee interdepartmental conference on January 20, 1942, two months after the Mufti's landing in Berlin.

It would be both wrong and misleading to assume that the presence of Haj Amin el-Husseini was the sole, or even the major factor in the shaping and intensification of the Nazi "final solution of the Jewish problem," which supplanted forced emigration by wholesale extermination. There is, however, abundant first-hand evidence of the part the Mufti played in making foolproof the ban on emigration.

Sealing Off the Routes of Escape

Within Germany proper, there were no loopholes to which the Mufti could object. But he felt that the puppet governments of Hungary, Rumania, and Bulgaria were not being sufficiently strict in preventing their Jewish subjects from escaping to Palestine. Throughout the war years, small groups of Jews from the Axis-dominated countries somehow succeeded in evading the ghettos and gas chambers and in making their way to Palestine, first via Greece and later, when the Greek ports were closed to Jewish refugees, overland via Bugaria and Turkey. In 1941–1942, a total of 1,090 reached Palestine; early in 1943, the first group of Youth Aliyah children arrived from Rumania and Hungary, and by the end of the year, 1,128 Jews had passed through Turkey. The total for 1941–1945 was 18,783.

However insignificant these numbers, in relation to the tragic plight of the masses of European Jewry, this trickle of escapees was a challenge to the Mufti's designs. Particularly irritating was their destination: Palestine. And Haj Amin spared no effort to seal off this sole route of salvation.

In the summer of 1944 he directly approached the satellite governments with virtually identical letters, urging them to bar any Jewish emigration to Palestine. In a letter dated June 28, 1944, addressed to the Hungarian foreign minister, he wrote:

Lately I have been informed of the uninterrupted efforts made by the British and the Jews to obtain permission for the Jews living in your country to leave for Palestine via Bulgaria and Turkey.
I have also learned that these negotiations were successful,

since some of the Jews of Hungary have had the satisfaction of emigrating to Palestine through Bulgaria and Turkey, and that a group of these Jews had arrived in Palestine towards the end of last March. The Jewish Agency, which supervises the execution of the Jewish program . . . quotes, among other things, its receipt of a sufficient number of immigration certificates for 900 Jewish children to be transported from Hungary, accompanied by 100 adults.[50]

Insisting that any Jewish emigration be stopped, the Mufti significantly added: "If there are reasons which make their [the Jews] removal necessary, it would be indispensable and infinitely preferable to send them to other countries where they would find themselves under active control, as for example Poland, thus avoiding danger and preventing damage."

When these letters to the three Axis satellites were written, Poland had already begun to function as the main center of extermination. The alternative to emigration offered by the Mufti was—deportation and subsequent annihilation. A month later, on July 24, 1944, he also approached the Reich's Foreign Office:

Berlin July 25, 1944

To His Excellency
  The Minister for Foreign Affairs
    Berlin

Your Excellency:

I have previously called the attention of your Excellency to the constant attempts of the Jews to emigrate from Europe in order to reach Palestine, and asked your Excellency to undertake the necessary steps so as to prevent the Jews from emigrating. I had also sent you a letter, under date of June 5, 1944, in regard to the plan for an exchange of Egyptians living in Germany with Palestinian Germans, in which I asked you to exclude the Jews from this plan of exchange. I have, however, learned that the Jews did depart on July 2, 1944, and I am afraid that further groups of Jews will leave for Palestine from Germany and France to be exchanged for Palestinian Germans.

This exchange on the part of the Germans would encourage the Balkan countries likewise to send their Jews to Palestine. This step would be incomprehensible to the Arabs and Moslems after your Excellency's declaration of November 2, 1943 that "the destruction of the so-called Jewish national home in Palestine is an immutable part of the policy of the greater German Reich" and it would create in them a feeling of keen disappointment.

It is for this reason that I ask your Excellency to do all that is necessary to prohibit the emigration of Jews to Palestine, and in this way your Excellency would give a new practical example of the policy of the naturally allied and friendly Germany towards the Arab Nation.[51]

Yours, . . .

A similar letter was sent two days later to Heinrich Himmler in his capacity as S.S. Reichsführer and Minister of the Interior.[52]

The Mufti was both persistent and indefatigable in his efforts to prevent the Jews from leaving, in whatever form. Legationsrat Wilhelm Melchers said in his evidence taken during the Nuremberg trial, August 6, 1947: "The Mufti was making protests everywhere—in the Office of the [Foreign] Minister, in the antechamber of the Secretary of State, and in other Departments, such as Home Office, Press, Radio, and in the S.S. headquarters. It goes without saying that the [Reich] Foreign Ministry was expecting protest demarches in matters concerning Balkan Jews, just on the part of the Mufti. They were, of course, welcome in certain places. . . . The Mufti was an accomplished foe of the Jews and did not conceal that he would love to see all of them liquidated." His main concern, however, was the liquidation of Palestine Jewry. "The

[Jewish] National Home must disappear and the Jews [there] must get out," he once told Melchers, and he "did not care where they would go: *Ils peuvent aller s'ils veulent au diable*" (They are free to go to hell).[53]

As a rule, the Mufti's demarches had an immediate effect. On May 13, 1943, he personally delivered to Von Ribbentrop a letter of protest against the plan to arrange the emigration of 4,000 Jewish children:

> It has come to my attention from reliable sources that the English and American Governments asked their representatives in the Balkans (especially in Bulgaria) to intervene with the governments and request that they be given permission to allow Jews to emigrate to Palestine. In connection with this, the British Minister of Colonies, Sir Oliver Stanley, announced in the British Parliament that the discussions for the emigration of 4,000 children escorted by 500 adults from Bulgaria have been ended successfully and he hopes that similar occurrences will be achieved in Rumania and Hungary. The Arabs see in this emigration a great danger to their lives and existence. The Arab peoples put themselves at the disposal of the Axis without any hesitation in the fight against communism and international Jewry. The Jews will take out with them from the Balkans many military secrets and will give them to Allied agents who are waiting their arrival at the port. I request your Excellency to act with all possible effort to avoid this plan of the international Jewry and Anglo-Americans without delay. This service will never be forgotten by the Arab people.[54]

Following this request, Horst Wagner of the *Abteilung* II of the German Foreign Office forthwith sent a telegram to the German ambassador in Sofia instructing him to draw the attention of the Bulgarian government to the common German-Arabian interest in preventing this rescue action.[55]

Discussing with engineer Endre Steiner at Bratislava the prospects for emigration of a group of Polish Jewish

children, S.S. Hauptsturmführer Dieter Wisliceny, Eichmann's deputy for Slovakia and Hungary, insisted that "the
destination of [their] possible emigration may under no
circumstances be Palestine." To the question as to why
such limitation had been imposed, Wisliceny laughingly
asked whether Steiner "had not heard of the Grand Mufti
whose name was Husseini . . . [and who] was in closest
contact and collaboration with Eichmann. . . . In order not
to have this action disapproved by the Mufti, Palestine
could not be accepted by any German authority as the
final destination."[56] Somewhat later, Eichmann himself
told Dr. Rudolf Kastner in Budapest: "I am a personal
friend of the Grand Mufti. We have promised him that no
European Jew would enter Palestine any more. Do you
understand now?"[57]

In every case connected with the emigration of Jews
from Germany's "vital space," there always was mention
of some promises given to, or an agreement concluded
with, the Mufti not to permit the exit of any numbers of
Jews, large or small. A document submitted at the Eichmann trial by the prosecution established that when the
German minister to Bucharest had formally objected to an
order by Marshal Antonescu, the Rumanian prime minister, to allow the emigration of 80,000 Rumanian Jews, he
did so "in accordance with our agreement with the
Mufti."[58] In answer to questions put to him at the Jerusalem trial, Eichmann said on June 27, 1961, that though
even before the Mufti's arrival there had been "objections
to emigration to Palestine because this might strengthen
the country [Palestine] and create in the field of foreign
relations a new factor which would one day join the enemies of the Reich," a consistent "policy of the Foreign
Ministry . . . began after the agreement with the Grand

Mufti"; he also spoke of an "agreement between Mufti and [head of the Gestapo] Himmler."[59]

Referring to the successful intervention by the Mufti against the planned evacuation to Palestine of 4,000 Jewish children, Robert N. W. Kempner, the American deputy chief prosecutor at the Nuremberg trials, on July 1, 1948, asked the former Reich secretary of state, Gustav Adolf von Moyland Steengracht: "How could you conclude agreements with anyone who was not a head of a [foreign] State, but your own employee whom you had been paying thousands of gold pounds?"

Steengracht's embarrassed answer was: "Yes, but it wasn't me who had made these agreements. I had just come into a situation where everything had already been completed."

Kempner bluntly formulated this state of affairs by saying: "Herr von Steengracht, first you are paying someone, and then this man, your employee, says: 'The children must not go to Palestine.' "[60]

The Mufti and Eichmann

There also is direct evidence as to the Mufti's influence in the implementation of the physical destruction of European Jewry.

In June 1944, Dieter Wisliceny told Dr. Rudolf Kastner, representative of the Budapest rescue council, that he was convinced that the Mufti had "played a role in the decision to exterminate the European Jews." "The importance of this role," he insisted, "must not be disregarded. . . . The Mufti had repeatedly suggested to the various authorities with whom he was maintaining contact, above all to Hitler, Ribbentrop and Himmler, the extermination of European Jewry. He considered this as a comfortable solution of the Palestine problem."[61]

Wisliceny was even more explicit in his conversation with Engineer Endre Steiner of Bratislava:

The Mufti was one of the initiators of the systematic extermination of European Jewry and had been a collaborator and advisor of Eichmann and Himmler in the execution of this plan. . . . He was one of Eichmann's best friends and had constantly incited him to accelerate the extermination measures. I heard him say that, accompanied by Eichmann, he had visited incognito the gas chamber of Auschwitz.[*][62]

Wisliceny elaborated on these private wartime revelations in a signed official depostion submitted on July 26, 1946, to the Nuremberg tribunal. He testified that after the Mufti's arrival in Germany he had paid a visit to Himmler and shortly afterward (late in 1941 or early in 1942) had visited Eichmann in his Berlin office at Kurfürstenstrasse 116. According to Wisliceny, Eichmann told him that he had brought the Mufti to a special room where he showed him maps illustrating the distribution of the Jewish population in various European countries and delivered a detailed report on the solution of the Jewish problem in Europe. The Mufti seemed to have been very much impressed; he told Eichmann that he had requested Himmler—and received a promise to this effect—that when, after the victory of the Axis, he would return to Palestine, he would be accompanied, as his personal ad-

---

[*] S. Wiesenthal relates in his *Grand Mufti—Agent Extraordinary of the Axis* that Haj Amin visited not only Auschwitz but also Maidanek. In both death camps he paid close attention to the efficiency of the crematoria, spoke to the leading personnel and was generous in his praise for those who were reported as particularly conscientious in their work. He was on friendly terms with such notorious practitioners of the "final solution" as Rudolf Hess, the overlord of Auschwitz; Franz Ziereis of Mauthausen; Dr. Seidl of Theresienstadt; and Kramer, the butcher of Belsen.

viser, by a trusted agent of Eichmann. The latter inquired whether Wisliceny himself would not be disposed to take such an assignment; the offer was declined. "Eichmann was strongly impressed by the personality of the Mufti," continued Wisliceny. "He told me then—and often repeated it later—that the Mufti had also made a strong impression on Himmler and exerted considerable influence in Arabic-Jewish affairs."

A photostatic copy of Wisliceny's deposition was shown to Eichmann by chief inspector Avner Less during pre-trial interrogation (the full German text of the interrogator's questions and the accused's answers was made available to this author). Eichmann recognized Wisliceny's signature under the deposition and did not question its authenticity. He insisted, however, then—and later before the Jerusalem District Court—that he had "met the Mufti only once, and never again; this was at a reception which was arranged by the S.D. [Security Service] in the Mufti's residence . . . most of the heads of departments in the Reich Security Head Office, including myself, were presented to him. . . . We—neither my subordinates nor myself—never had any further contact with the Mufti." He admitted that, once, "three Iraqi majors" (one of them, he heard, was the Mufti's nephew) had "spent . . . on a study tour . . . a day or two" in his department on the Kurfürstenstrasse. But that, he claimed, was all. When interrogator Less asked why Wisliceny would have distorted the facts, Eichmann suggested that this was done in the hope of finding favor in the eyes of the Nuremberg judges. Dr. Robert Servatius, Eichmann's defense counsel at the Jerusalem court, put to his client the question: "Did anyone propose to you, on behalf of the Mufti, that you join him as an expert on Jewish affairs?" The answer was a firm "No, no, there was never any such proposal." One of the three judges, Benjamin Halevi, then asked: "But you were undoubtedly presented to the Mufti as an expert on Jewish affairs?" To this, the answer was more hesitant:

I can't answer yes or no [at this point there was a burst of laughter in the courtroom]. I don't remember today what happened. But it is possible—I must make this reservation—that perhaps this was done by Department VI which arranged the reception.[63]

Eichmann was, however, unfailing in denying any close relation or cooperation with the Mufti. The latter, on his part, even claimed not to have ever met or known Eichmann, let alone incited or advised him on mass killings of Jews. In reply to reports to this effect, he told a press conference in Beirut on May 4, 1961:

The Nazis needed no persuasion or instigation either by me or anybody else to execute their program against the Jews. . . . I do not know Eichmann, I have never met him, and I had no, repeat, no occasion to observe his activities or for that matter to visit the Nazi extermination camps for Jews, as the Zionists so falsely claim. I also do not think that Eichmann could be the source of these fancies which can only be called the fantasies of the Machievelian imagination of the Zionists.[64]

The Mufti's sweeping assertion that he had "never met" Eichmann is easily disproved by the latter's acknowledgment of their having been introduced to each other. But the actual degree of their acquaintance and cooperation remains a moot point which was far from adequately elucidated by the Jerusalem trial.

Another question not cleared up at the trial was that raised by a piece of evidence submitted by the prosecution: a page of the Mufti's diary, dated November 9, 1944, and containing the words, in Arabic, "very rare diamond, the best savior of the Arabs," and immediately underneath, in Latin letters, "Eichmann." Called to the witness stand, Chief Inspector Avraham Hagag, Arabic and handwriting expert of the Israeli Police, testified that the sentence in Arabic was definitely in the handwriting of the Mufti. So were two other Arabic notations: "Before Tripoli is evacuated, the Jews should be cleaned out and their property confiscated," and "Bomb Tel Aviv, the Dead Sea [Works], Rutenberg and Haifa, and the military installations there." Yet, when Eichmann's defense counsel asked: "Was the word 'Eichmann' written by the Mufti?" Hagag answered: "I didn't have enough material [in Latin letters] to make a comparison and form an opinion." To the counsel's further question, "Are the other two notations in German written in the same handwriting as the 'Eichmann'?" the reply was "No."[65]

Whatever the precise degree of the Mufti's personal involvement with Eichmann's genocide activities, his broadcast from Berlin on September 21, 1944, bears witness that he was fully cognizant of the method and scope of Nazi extermination of the Jews. "Is it not in your power, O Arabs," he asked, "to repulse the Jews who number not more than eleven million?"

This reference to "eleven million" was puzzling at the time. It was common knowledge that before World War II, world Jewry numbered nearly seventeen million. The Mufti's figure was therefore disregarded as a slip of the tongue or a mere propaganda device. In 1944, nobody was as yet aware of the actual scale of Jewish extermination. But the Mufti obviously was. There was no error and no guessing in his arithmetic. As close associate, confidant, and collaborator of the top men involved in the Nazi "final solution of the Jewish problem," he knew precisely the extent of the annihilation: six million.

Abandoning the Sinking Ship

At the time of the Allied landing in Normandy, on June 6, 1944, the Mufti was attached to the staff of Admiral Dönitz. The relentless advance of the Allied armies induced him to return to Berlin. Continued air raids made life in the Nazi capital uncomfortable and, together with several other dignitaries, Haj Amin transferred his residence to the Austrian town of Linz, where he was received by August Eigruber, the *Gauleiter* of the Oberdonau province, with military honors usually bestowed only on heads of states. In a booklet published in Salzburg in 1947 with the permission of the Allied military authorities, S. Wiesenthal revealed that throughout his sojourn in the Linzer Hotel the Mufti was under constant surveillance by the Allied Intelligence: a Jewish girl, whom the booklet designates only by initials B.S., an escapee from a Nazi concentration camp at Lemberg, was provided with forged Aryan identification papers and worked at the hotel as chambermaid; assigned to Haj Amin's room because of her knowledge of French—the only European language he was able to converse in during his stay in the Third Reich—she was in a position to overhear some of the Mufti's conversations with Nazi leaders and to supply valuable information through her fiancé, who maintained contact with the Allied Intelligence Service.* Later, again in the company of prominent German and foreign dignitaries, Haj Amin settled in Bad Gastein; the hospitable Eigruber put at their disposal the best hotels of this fashionable spa.[66] There he maintained close contacts with

---

* Ironically, the Mufti was so pleased with the maid service that before leaving the hotel he left the girl a good-sized tip (S. Wiesenthal, *op. cit.*, p. 53).

the highest Nazi authorities, and as late as April 5, 1945—
a month before V-E Day, when the Third Reich was
crumbling but its rulers were still determined to continue fighting in one way or another—the following financial agreement was concluded:

AGREEMENT

between the Government of the Greater German Reich and
the Grand Mufti of Palestine, Hadji Amin el Husseini.

The Government, through its Foreign Office, concludes the
following agreement with the Mufti:

1. The Government puts at the disposal of the Mufti funds
required to fight for liberation against the common enemy.

2. An account is being opened for the Mufti with the Reich
treasurer.

The Mufti can draw against this until further notice 50,000
reichsmarks a month.

The account will be charged with expenses of the Foreign
Office and other headquarters of Reich organization incurred
for the Mufti or the movement conducted by him. These expenses—commencing April 1, 1945—shall not exceed 12,000
reichsmarks a month.

3. The Mufti agrees to pay back the credit advanced. Amor-
tization and interest payments will be later agreed on.

4. This is effective retroactively, as of April 1.

Signed, in Berlin, April 4, 1945.

For the Foreign Office
S/Steengracht*

The Grand Mufti of Palestine
Amin el Husseini[67]

A seasoned practitioner of the hazardous art of grand
style political gambling, Haj Amin always knew when the
gamble was over and lost, and never missed the opportunity of grabbing the very last chance of removing himself
from the scene of his current failure. He had had wide
experience in this field: in Palestine in October 1937, in

* Secretary of State, Gustav Adolf von Moyland Steengracht.

Lebanon in October 1939, and in Iraq and Iran in May and October 1941. This time, too, he was determined not to be caught by the advancing Allied armies. Anticipating —as we shall see, quite erroneously—the unenviable fate awaiting him should he fall into the hands of the victorious Western democracies, Haj Amin made his preparations for a last-minute escape well in advance. A German commercial airliner, reserved in advance, was ordered to stand by. Speculation was rife that the Mufti would seek to gain sanctuary in the holy Moslem city of Mecca, where he would be safe from extradition and punishment even though Saudi Arabia was officially at war with the Axis Powers. Under Koranic law, once in the Holy City he could not be refused sanctuary.

Haj Amin had, however, chosen a less distant and less holy place of refuge. When he boarded a plane on May 7, 1945, the destination given to the pilot was neighboring neutral Switzerland.

The British Game

5

A Villa Near Paris
1945–1946

Seeking Sanctuary

ON MAY 7, 1945, A PLANE LANDED AT THE AIRFIELD OF
Berne. A middle-aged man with misshapen ears and close-
cropped scanty grayish beard stepped down, followed by
two unarmed aides. To the Swiss authorities he introduced himself as Haj Amin el-Husseini, the Grand Mufti
of Jerusalem. The Swiss government, which pledged itself
not to give asylum to any Axis war criminal, firmly told
the fugitive Mufti that he could not remain in the country. He was handed over to the French frontier guards at
Lindau. After a brief internment at Lindau, Haj Amin was
transferred to Paris. However, it was not before May 19
that an official French communiqué announced that the
former Mufti of Jerusalem had been arrested by the
French political police. A villa at Rambouillet, near Paris,
was assigned to him as forced residence. It was generally
assumed that this was going to be a very brief sojourn,
preliminary to his being handed over to the British.

The British Game

Yet the British government proved to be surprisingly unenthusiastic about any action to secure the Mufti's extradition. Repeated questioning in the House of Commons evinced evasive, contradictory, and truly puzzling responses.

As early as May 30, 1945, Sir Oliver Stanley, the secretary of state for the Colonies in the Churchill government, was asked in the House of Commons by Mr. Denman whether the ex-Mufti of Jerusalem was now in the hands of the British authorities, and what it was proposed to do with him.

The answer was: "No, Sir, he is in the hands of the French authorities; as regards the second part of the question, I have no statement to make at the present."[1]

There the issue rested for a full five months.

On October 24, George Hall, Stanley's successor in Attlee's Labor government, was asked by Captain Gammans whether or not he "had any information as to the whereabouts of the ex-Mufti of Jerusalem"; Squadron-Leader Segal supplemented this inquiry by asking "whether His Majesty's Government still has any intention of bringing him [the ex-Mufti] to trial as a war criminal."

The reply of the Colonial Secretary was again: "The Mufti of Jerusalem is in the hands of the French authorities. As regards the second part of the question, I have no statement to make at present."

Captain Gammans then asked: "Would the right Hon. Gentleman say how he [the Mufti] got into the hands of the French authorities and where he came from?"

Secretary Hall: "No, Sir. Not without notice."

At this point, Miss Rathbone introduced a supplementary query: "In view of the fact that [Haj Amin's] activities were mostly carried on in Palestine, could not representations be made to the French to give up the ex-Mufti, so that he could be tried as a war criminal?"

Hall: "That is a question which should be put to my right Hon. Friend the Foreign Secretary [Ernest Bevin]."

The Foreign Secretary never answered Miss Rathbone's question.[2]

The issue was, in a different form, revived on November 28 by George Porter who asked Secretary Hall what was the reply given to the request of the Arab League for the return of the former Mufti of Jerusalem to Palestine; and whether the Secretary would inform the Arab League that this henchman of Hitler's was an enemy of the British Empire and a war criminal and that he would be treated as such.[3]

Hall: "I have received no request of this nature; the second part of the question does not therefore arise."

Porter: "Does not the right Hon. Gentleman think it is time some definite relationship was determined as between this individual and the British Government?"

Hall: "We must get the man first."

Nine days later, on December 7, Mr. McEntee again asked the Secretary of State for the Colonies where the former Grand Mufti of Jerusalem was; and whether any steps were being taken to charge him as a war criminal. Hall replied: "I have nothing to add to the answer which I gave to a question by the Hon. and Gallant Member for Hornsey [Captain Gammans] on 24th of October."

On December 12, the matter had been shifted from the Colonial to the Foreign Office. Ernest Bevin was asked by George Porter whether he was aware that the Mufti of Jerusalem was under house arrest in Paris, whether any request had been made to the French government for him to be handed over for trial; or what steps he had taken to have this man handed over to the British authorities.[4]

Bevin: "I would refer my Hon. Friend to the reply given by my right Hon. Friend the Secretary of State for the Colonies on 24th October to the Hon. and Gallant Member for Hornsey [Captain Gammans]."

Porter: "May I ask my right Hon. Friend, in view of a previous reply given to me that it was necessary to get this man, whether he will not consider this as information which will help him to 'catch his man'?"

Bevin: "We have made representations, but I am afraid I cannot add to the answer I have given at the moment."

Miss Rathbone: "Seeing that this man did the utmost harm to the Allied cause while living in Palestine, is it not really the right of the Palestinian authorities to have him handed over?"

Bevin: "I am not anxious to see him returned to Palestine."

The year 1945 passed without the British government taking any action regarding the Mufti. In the light of revelations made in January 1946 concerning the Mufti's sinister role in the extermination of European Jewry, the House of Commons got excited. On February 26, Mr. Hoy asked the Secretary of State for Foreign Affairs whether his attention had been drawn to the material recently produced at the trials of war criminals in Nuremberg about the part played by Haj Amin el-Husseini, former mufti of Jerusalem, in instigating and encouraging the Nazi plan of exterminating European Jewry; and what steps he had taken, or proposed to take, to have him tried as a war criminal.[5]

Hector McNeil, Under Secretary of State for Foreign Affairs, replied: "A special inquiry is being made to obtain accurate records of any relevant evidence that may have been given to the International Military Tribunal. This matter will be considered together with any other relevant matters. As regards the second part of the question, I have nothing to add to the reply given by the Secretary of State for the Colonies to the Hon. and Gallant Member for Hornsey [Captain Gammans] on October 24."

A similar inquiry by Mrs. Ayrton Gould on March 11 met with a new noncommittal answer by Hector McNeil.[6]

On April 5, Foreign Secretary Ernest Bevin told the Commons that the French government had "not so far agreed" to the request of the British government to hand over Haj Amin el-Husseini.[7] To this the Parisian daily *Le Monde* (successor to *Le Temps*) replied in its issue of April 7 by publishing, on the first page, the following communiqué of a semiofficial character:

THE EXTRADITION OF THE GRAND MUFTI HAS NOT BEEN REQUESTED BY GREAT BRITAIN

A mouthpiece of the Quai d'Orsay formally denied the information according to which Great Britain has demanded the extradition of the ex-Mufti of Jerusalem, Haj Amin el Husseini, from the French Government.

It will be recalled that during the debate of Wednesday in the House of Commons, Mr. Bevin declared that France had refused to accede to the British demand for extradition.

Two days later, a spokesman of the Quai d'Orsay told the Paris correspondent of the *New York Post* that the Mufti was "free to come and go as he wishes," and that Mr. Bevin had "never asked legally for the Mufti's extradition." "We have an extradition treaty with Britain, signed in 1876, and the proper procedure would be for Britain to make a formal request accompanied by a dossier on the case stating specifically the crime committed and the basis for the extradition procedure."[8]

The French statements provoked a lively discussion in

the House of Commons.[9] On April 15, the Laborite M.P., Monslow, asked the Foreign Secretary whether in view of the official announcement by the French Foreign Office that His Majesty's Government had not asked for the extradition of Amin el-Husseini, the ex-Mufti of Jerusalem, but only for his transfer from French to British custody, he would now take appropriate steps to obtain his extradition.

Hector McNeil, Under Secretary for Foreign Affairs, replied: "The offences with which the Mufti might be charged are not extraditable offences under the Anglo-French Extradition Treaty. No useful purpose would, therefore, be served by applying for his extradition."

Another Laborite M.P., Barnett Janner, then asked whether the Foreign Office was aware that the ex-Mufti had "enlisted forces against this country in Germany and were they not going to do something about it?"

Hector McNeil: "I am not asked about doing something. I am asked about extradition and I must point out that this does not fall inside the extradition agreement with France."

Laborite M.P. George Thomas then asked why, if the same government had informed the French government that the ex-Mufti did not come within the category of war criminals, he was regarded as a quisling; and if, in view of the ex-Mufti's activities on behalf of Nazis and Fascists during the war in Germany and Italy and elsewhere, and the part he had played as instigator of and collaborator in the plans for the extermination of European Jews by Hitler, the Foreign Secretary would now take appropriate steps to obtain his extradition, so that he could be tried as a war criminal.

Hector McNeil: *"The Mufti is not a war criminal in the technical sense of the term, since he is not an enemy national, not a person who served in the enemy forces. The matter in respect of which he could be accused would be that, being a person who owed allegiance to the Crown, he committed offences against his own national law."**

Barnett Janner: "Will you see whether you can obtain the ex-Mufti, by some method or another, in order that he may be tried?"

Hector McNeil: "If I am asked about some method or another, I must have notice of the question."

S. S. Silverman asked whether in fact request had been made to the French government for the transfer of the ex-Mufti from French to British custody, and would that request be repeated.

Hector McNeil: "I must have notice of that."

The British government had thus officially absolved the Mufti of the charge of being a war criminal. The Foreign Office spokesman qualified him rather as a kind of "quisling"—a charge he knew could not be sustained. A quisling to whom? He owned no allegiance to Britain. He simply gave his allegiance to Hitler. And the two charges that could be made against him were: first, his activities in Palestine, before the war, inciting the Arabs to murder and destruction; and second, precisely as a war criminal, his part in the prosecution of Hitler's war. The British government knew well that Haj Amin had actually organized Axis activities in the Middle East. For reasons best known to itself, His Majesty's Government chose to ignore the abundant evidence to this effect. It deliberately *reduced* the crushing charges against the Mufti as a war criminal to vague "quislingism."

The *Manchester Guardian* was the sole English daily to challenge openly the stand taken by the government. In an editorial published on April 29, this courageous bearer of English liberalism expressed the hope that "this [was] not the last word" of the government: "At a moment

* Author's italics.

where the Allies are seriously considering action against Franco because he supported Germany in the war, it would hardly be credible that they restore the Mufti in all his tainted glory." The newspaper recalled the Mufti's open support to Hitler, and said he gave "moral authority to the extermination of the Jews."

Events proved that refusal to demand the Mufti's extradition as a war criminal *was* the Labor government's "last word." It even went further. By April 1946, it still pretended to have asked the French government that the Mufti be transferred from French to British custody. In May, "authorized French sources" disclosed that British Foreign Secretary Bevin had merely requested the French Foreign Office "to keep the former Mufti of Jerusalem [in France] and see that he does not leave for any country in the Near East." French Foreign Minister Georges Bidault had marked Mr. Bevin's proposal "accepted."[10]

The reasons that prompted the French to welcome British leniency toward the ex-Mufti will be examined in the next chapter. But British attitude was obviously dictated by the hope of using Haj Amin as a tool in British efforts to consolididate a continuous Moslem block stretching from Africa to India and amenable to British orientation. The Mufti's close collaborators were boldly capitalizing on this speculation. Testifying before the Anglo-American Committee of Inquiry on Palestine, his first lieutenant Jamal el-Husseini said: "If you [the British] now give this country [Palestine] its rights, the Grand Mufti will be to you a second General Smuts."

This comparison was, of course, both irrelevant and impudent. Haj Amin's record had in no way paralleled that of the noble Boer. But it appealed to the British government, which apparently believed that the Mufti's influence would have a restraining effect on Arab anti-British intransigence.

The Abortive Yugoslav Move

At one stage of the game, the Yugoslav government had done what Great Britain's government had refrained from doing: in July 1945, it officially placed Haj Amin on the United Nations' list of war criminals, accusing him of organizing the S.S. Moslem Division in Bosnia and Herzegovina and of causing the murder of thousands of Serbs and Croats who had refused to become Nazi collaborators.[11] This move of the Tito regime was energetically countered by the Arab League. Azzam Bey, secretary general of the League approached the Yugoslav minister in Cairo urging him to ask his government not to demand the Mufti's extradition; a similar request was made by the Egyptian government. Azzam Bey also approached the French legation in Cairo in this matter, and the French government was reported to have entered into negotiations with Marshal Tito for the withdrawal of war criminal charges against the ex-Mufti.[12] Apparently in the wake of these démarches, Dr. Radimir Zivkovic, Yugoslav representative on the United Nations War Crimes Commission in London stated on October 4, 1945, that "he had received no instructions from the Belgrade Government to demand the extradition to Yugoslavia of Haj Amin el-Husseini"; he added that the case of the United Nations against the latter was being studied "on a political level by the governments concerned."[13] In January 1946, Dr. Gawrilowic, the Yugoslav envoy in Washington, confidentially told a Jewish representative that there was, in his opinion, "something very fishy about the whole business," and that he "had learned from non-Yugoslav sources in London that his own government had ceased to press for the trial of the ex-Mufti."[14] The Yugoslav action petered out.

The French Game

In the meantime, Haj Amin had been living comfortably under French surveillance at the villa "Les Roses" in a Paris suburb. He had a chauffeur, two bodyguards, and a personal secretary. The surveillance was a purely nominal one. As early as August 30, 1945, French authorities, confirming press reports of a "privileged treatment," explained that "custom demands such treatment for the head of a great Arab community."[15] Two months later, he was permitted to open an "office" in Paris, and was frequently seen strolling on Paris boulevards in European clothes. There were no restrictions on visits by Arab nationalist leaders; among such visitors was Yunis el-Bahri, the Arab "Lord Haw-Haw" of Nazi broadcasts in Berlin, who had been, since 1941, under a death sentence from the Iraqi government for his participation in the Mufti-sponsored pro-Axis revolt of Rashid Ali el-Gailani. *Middle East Opinion* of Cairo reported that the Mufti's trusted collaborator Mussa el-Alami came from London to Paris "in accordance with a pre-arranged plan":

During their first meeting, which lasted several hours, they reviewed the situation in Palestine. On the day following, a further meeting, which lasted two days, took place between the Mufti, Alami and a number of official Arab personalities of London and Paris.[16]

A spokesman of the Quai d'Orsay told a *New York Post* correspondent in April 1946 that the Mufti "was not under any confinement or house arrest of any kind." Admitting that Haj Amin was kept surrounded by a cordon of police, the Foreign Ministry official insisted that this was for his protection only.[17]

The French position was that they had nothing against

the Mufti and that the British had not asked for him. London, in turn, contended that, after all, the fugitive Mufti was in the hands of Paris. The two governments thus "passed the buck" to each other when asked what they intended to do with Haj Amin. This left him virtually unaccountable to anybody and able to enjoy complete liberty.

An all-time peak of dissimulation was reached by the French government on April 17, 1946, when, in a broadcast in English to North America, it attacked the Mufti as a war criminal, and on the very same day broadcast to the Levant in Arabic a note from the secretary general of the Arab League thanking France for the "privileged position" and protection accorded to "His Eminence the Mufti." Contemporary American Intelligence sources reported that Haj Amin was maintaining regular correspondence with friends in both Syria and Lebanon through the use of French deplomatic channels and that he had been insistently advising Moslem leaders to show greater leniency toward the French and to strive for an understanding with them. Some French politicians believed that continued tension in Palestine would adversely affect Great Britain's and the United States' position with the Arabs, and thus pave the way for a rapprochment between France and the Moslems of the Middle East and North Africa. Others felt that recent anti-Jewish policies of the Nazi-sponsored Vichy government had remained in Arab memory as a valuable asset, likely to strengthen the French position in the new turn of events. A grateful Mufti would then be of considerable usefulness. French politicians, like the British, had been speculating on Haj Amin's popularity as a means of rallying the Moslems in support of French interests in the Middle East. According to a Reuters dispatch, a spokesman of the Quai d'Orsay averred that the French government was ready to release the Mufti to any Arab state willing to receive him.

A noted Israeli correspondent in New York, Dr. Jacob Rubin, who was living in Paris in 1946, told this author that in mid-May of that year a group of demobilized soldiers of the Jewish Brigade and of sympathizers with the Irgun Zvai Leumi (underground Jewish military organization in Palestine) had conceived the plan of kidnaping the Mufti in his suburban villa and later disposing of him. When they came to consult Dr. Rubin, he strongly objected to the plot, arguing that such an action would inevitably provoke Arab retaliatory attempts to kidnap and kill Jewish leaders—be it Dr. Chaim Weizmann, David Ben-Gurion, or Menachem Begin. Before any final decision could be taken, the Mufti left France for Egypt.

An earlier story of a similar kind was related to this author by Mr. Shmuel Katz, now a publisher in Tel Aviv. In the autumn of 1937, when, after his flight from Jerusalem, the Mufti lived in Lebanon, continuing freely his subversive activities, Mr. Katz was told by a veteran foreign correspondent that an Arab friend of his, ostensibly a Mufti follower, offered to have the Mufti assassinated for the sum of two hundred pounds ($800 at that time); the payment was to be made only after the deed was accomplished. The offer was forwarded to Vladimir Jabotinsky, whom Mr. Katz considered his political and spiritual leader. The answer was in the negative: "Would you like to see the Arabs bumping Weizmann or Shertok? . . ."*

* In August 1946, when Haj Amin was already safely entrenched in Cairo, a "Senior Arab League authority" told the United Press that he had received from a Hungarian Jew residing in Palestine a letter warning him that "your blood will be spilled wherever you go" (*New York Post*, August 19, 1946).

The American Game

The attitude of the United States was evasive and discouraging. Early in September 1945, Congressman Emanuel Celler approached the then U.S. secretary of state, James F. Byrnes, with the request that Haj Amin el-Husseini be taken from his comfortable French villa, imprisoned with the major war criminals at Nuremberg, and tried as promptly as possible. Urging the Secretary to demand that the United Nations War Crimes Commission ask for Haj Amin's extradition from France, Celler charged that "outrageous diplomatic maneuvering" may result in the Mufti's going off scot-free; failure to punish the Mufti would be regarded in the whole Orient as a sign of British and American weakness. The Secretary of State did not act upon this suggestion.

On June 11, 1946—after Haj Amin's "escape" from Paris —Bartley C. Crum, member of the Anglo-American Inquiry Committee on Palestine, addressed a telegram to Secretary of State Byrnes urging the United States government, acting in cooperation with the British government, to take all necessary measures for the immediate apprehension of the Mufti and for his extradition and trial: "May I respectfully suggest that the State Department obtain from the official records available to counsel in charge of the prosecution of war criminals in Nuremberg and Vienna, and from our own intelligence department, copies of the written agreements between the Mufti and the Nazi Government." The Secretary's answer was that he knew of no plans for the United States to ask France how the Mufti had left Paris: "The State Department has no information on the matter, and would not go into the question of whether the Mufti was a war criminal."[8]

The United Zionists Revisionists of America published a statement which bluntly put before the administration the question as to why the United States government "permits itself to be a party to the infamous conspiracy aimed at covering up the acts of this arch war criminal and protecting him from deserved punishment."

Do President Truman and his administration intend to allow the Mufti to perpetrate his bloody deeds and to continue his murderous campaign against the Jews of Palestine and the Middle East?

The American people have a right to know why the Mufti was not placed by the American Government on the list of international war criminals.

Did not Roosevelt and Churchill promise "severe and strict punishment" for all those guilty of complicity in the Nazi atrocities? How can Secretary Byrnes now state that America "has no interest in bringing the Mufti to trial?"

We call upon the Congress of the United States to draw aside the curtain of backdoor diplomacy and to bring out into the open the insidious intrigues and secret commitments involved in the power politics of the Middle East.

We call upon the Senate of the United States to investigate why the American Government refuses to bring this notorious Nazi collaborator before the bar of justice.

The ex-Mufti is a living legacy of Nazism and Fascism, the bearer of Mussolini's and Hitler's spirit, the perpetrator of the Axis' "unfinished work." He must be brought to trial.[19]

No United States action followed.

This aloof attitude of the United States constituted a major obstacle to bringing the Mufti to trial as a war criminal before the Nuremberg Tribunal. In reply to a telegram from Edgar Mowrer, the *New York Post* columnist who had submitted documentary proof that the Mufti was party to the murder of millions of European

Jews, Supreme Court Justice Jackson, chief prosecutor of the war crimes trials, stated on June 18:

Would be much interested to examine your documentary evidence. If it even remotely incriminates any of the defendants at Nuremberg, or the Hitler regime in general, it may be helpful in the present case. If it incriminates only the Mufti, it could not be used in this trial because of the executive order appointing me to proceed and the London Agreement which gave the tribunal jurisdiction to try criminals of only European Axis countries.

Only change of policy to include Asiatics in subsequent proceedings would have to be made in Washington and it requires the concurrence of all interested powers.[20]

No "change of policy" took place. Neither Great Britain, nor France, nor the United States were prepared, individually or collectively, to take determined action to bring the Mufti to trial.

On August 28, 1946, Dean Acheson, then Under Secretary and Acting Secretary of State, announced that the State Department was preparing a white paper on the Mufti's wartime activities, based on documents seized in Germany by the Allied armies. The white paper was not published. Mr. Acheson stepped out of the State Department, and those who succeeded him refrained from honoring his promise.

In 1949, Dean Acheson returned to the State Department, this time as secretary of state—a position in which he was free to act. But he apparently did not feel obliged to redeem his pledge.[21]

Arab Adoration Unabated

Both the British and the French were undoubtedly correct in assuming that Haj Amin el-Husseini continued to be the idol of the Palestinian Arabs, in whose eyes he was, like Hitler to the Germans, still the greatest national hero. His flight and his association with the Axis had enhanced rather than shattered his halo. The predominant feeling was that he, like Prophet Mohammed, had left his people "to struggle for the people's liberation." In January 1945, L. O. Pinkerton, the American consul general in Jerusalem, in a report to the State Department, the contents of which became known in Palestine, estimated that the Palestine Arab Party, founded in 1935, and headed by Tewfiq Saleh el-Husseini, was still "by far the strongest party [among the Palestine Arabs] partly by reason of loyalty to the Mufti and partly because of adherence to the Husseini family. They claim to be as strong potentially as all other parties, and I believe their claim may be justified by facts." Pro-Mufti manifestations of this feeling were numerous and widespread. Internment in France only activated the zeal of the Mufti's admirers throughout the Middle East. They widely circulated the story that on May 9, and 10, 1945, a group of Palestine Arab soldiers serving with the British Middle East Army and stationed in Lebanon, staged a noisy pro-Mufti demonstration at Beirut. Riding in a British military vehicle, they displayed British, Egyptian, Saudi, and Iraqi flags, carried a large picture of the Mufti, and shouted: Haj Amin, *sayf al-Din!*" (Haj Amin, sword of the faith!). In the latter part of the same month, inhabitants of the Husani Arab quarter of Jerusalem were awakened about midnight by the singing of a crowd extolling Haj Amin and shouting that "by his sword they would break down the wall." On June 1, at a meeting of the Palestine Arab Party attended by some 7,000 people, a large picture of the Mufti displayed on the stage received a hearty ovation, and a resolution was unanimously adopted demanding his return to Palestine. The party addressed an appeal to King George, Prime

Minister Churchill, Foreign Secretary Eden, the Arch-
bishop of Canterbury, and members of the House of
Lords to set their leader free and enable him to return to
Palestine.

The pro-Mufti action was not conducted by Palestine
Arabs alone. It was energetically supported by Moslem
and Arab leaders in other countries as well. Mohammed
Ali Jinnah, head of India's powerful Moslem League,
cabled to London for Haj Amin's release.[22] Sidi Mohammed, Sultan of Morocco, asked the French government
for the Mufti's transfer to Morocco, where he would be
safe under the Sultan's protection, and reportedly told the
French that, according to information received from Arab
League headquarters in Cairo, the British government
would welcome such a solution because trial of the Mufti,
under present conditions, might spoil relations between
the Arab world and Great Britain.[23] In Egypt, the student
body of Al-Azhar University adopted a resolution demanding Haj Amin's release.[24] The speaker of the Egyptian Senate announced that the Egyptian government had
pleaded with London to allow him to come to Egypt,
guaranteeing that he would not escape to Palestine. Similar efforts were made by Azzam Bey, the secretary general of the Arab League, who, during his stay in London,
sent a special envoy to Paris with a full report on the activities of the League and assurances that he was doing
his utmost to enable the Mufti's return to Palestine.[25]

The Palestine Arabs were psychologically fully prepared for Haj Amin's resumption of leadership, thanks to
both his disciples' untiring devotion and the mandatory
government's failure to even attempt to bring him into
disgrace.

When the Allied armies scored a decisive success in
North Africa, no efforts were made to discredit the Mufti

by showing that his collaboration with the Axis was, in the final analysis, contrary to the interests of the Palestine Arabs. Instead, immediately after the inauguration of the North African campaign the British administration began progressively to restore political liberties to Palestine Arab nationalists. Most of the Mufti's henchmen, who had been arrested or deported between 1936 and 1939, or who had fled in order to escape arrest had been gradually freed and were returning to Palestine. Seven leading members of the Mufti's family who had taken an active part in his intrigues in Baghdad and Teheran and were subsequently surrendered to the British by Iranian authorities, had been allowed, early in 1942, to return to Palestine. It was stated in the House of Commons on February 2 that this group included "leading members of the Mufti's family clan,"[26] as well as Musa el-Alami, who had acted as legal adviser and chief of the anti-British propaganda service in Baghdad. Said Ziyed, who was from 1936 to 1939 the main organizer of weapons and ammunition contraband for Arab armed bands, and who fled to Istanbul in 1939, later quietly returned to Palestine and lived there undisturbed. Mahammed Arjawal, another leading dealer in arms contraband, also escaped, but had returned by the spring of 1944. When asked on December 11, 1943, whether assurances could be given that Jamal el-Husseini and Amin al-Tamimi, "two of the leading assistants of the ex-Mufti of Jerusalem . . . will not be permitted to return to Palestine from Rhodesia" (where they had been interned since 1937), Colonial Secretary Oliver Stanley told the Commons that "there was no intention of releasing them."[27] Nevertheless, in October 1945, Jamal and several other members of the former Arab Higher Committee had been freed and were, in February 1946, permitted to return to Palestine. Finally, under a VE Day amnesty, 138 Arab political prisoners who had been imprisoned during the period of the Arab revolt, (some of them had been serving life sentences), were released. The vast majority of these prisoners had been fervent followers of Haj Amin; upon release from concentration camps they sang their praises of the Mufti, and the agitation for his return to Palestine, which was going on for a long time, became more insistent.

Under the Labor Party regime, most of the exiled Husseinis and their fellow travelers received unconditional amnesties, and the Arab nationalists could not understand why the mandatory, in granting these pardons, should have stopped short of the Mufti, particularly since no formal charges had been proferred against him.

Moreover, throughout the war, the British government continued to consider Haj Amin el-Husseini as the mufti of Jerusalem. In reply to a question of Samuel Hammersley, a conservative member of the House of Commons, "why no appointment has yet been made to fill the posts of Mufti of Jerusalem and President of the Moslem Supreme Council," Colonial Secretary Oliver Stanley explained on December 1, 1943, that "the post of Mufti of Jerusalem is a purely religious office with no powers and administrative functions," and that Haj Amin was "technically still Mufti" [of Jerusalem] because "no legal machinery in fact exists for the formal deposition of the holder of that office," nor is there "any known precedent for such deposition." The Colonial Secretary added that though Haj Amin remained the mufti of Jerusalem, the importance of this point was academic since the government did not plan to allow this Moslem cleric, "who had openly joined the enemy, to return to Palestine in any circumstances." The government also did not "propose . . . to intervene" regarding the presidency of the Supreme Moslem Council, "a matter which is giving rise to no trouble, and which is not impeding the adequate transaction of business in those affairs for which the Council is responsible."[28] Seventeen months later, on May 8, 1945, the official British Broadcasting Company (BBC), announcing Haj Amin's capture by the French, still referred to him as "His Grace the Grand Mufti of Palestine." In a letter to the London *Times*, L. B. Namier, professor of modern history in the University of Manchester, reminded the British public that "the personage in question never was either Grace nor Grand, and that his spiriutal province was Jerusalem, not Palestine." "Why this sudden aggrandissement from British quarters?" asked Professor Namier.

In fact, it was only after his installation in Hitler's Third Reich that Haj Amin started styling himself *"His Eminence the Grossmufti"* or Grand Mufti (*al-Mufti al-Akbar*), dropping altogether the territorial qualification "of Jerusalem" (which he had used since the 1920's), thus extending his ambitions beyond Palestine's borders. Spiritual leaders of Islam indignantly denied the very existence of such a title. The sheikh-president of Cairo's Al-Azhar University indignantly told Pierre van Paasen:

His Eminence? In Islam, there are no "eminences" and no "grand" muftis. Before Allah all men are equal. And it ill behooves a religious teacher to assume such redundant titles. . . . A mufti is a teacher in Islam. And even to that title Haj Amin should have no claim, for he has not finished a single course of studies here at the University. He owes his appointment to political influence and family connections. He is a politician.

One More "Escape"

Rumors to the effect that plans were being formed to organize Haj Amin's "escape" from his "protective custody" in Paris and his triumphal return to the Middle East started circulating as early as February 1946. Neither the French nor the British authorities paid any attention to these rumors.

On Tuesday, May 28, 1946, the Mufti went, as he had frequently done before, to Paris. He was seen returning to his villa "Les Roses" the same afternoon. It later transpired, however, that the man in the green turban who was supposed to be Haj Amin, was one of his aides.[30] The Mufti himself spent the night in Paris, and the next day, May 29, a clean-shaven man in European clothes boarded at the Orly Airport an American Skymaster plane of the Trans World Airlines.* He carried a Syrian passport in the name of his former political secretary in Berlin, Beirut lawyer Marouf al-Dawalabi (who later became Syrian prime minister), issued on November 28, 1945. It took the French police some ten days to discover the Mufti's disappearance. On June 8, embarrased Quai d'Orsay briefly announced that he had left France.[31]

Public opinion was nearly unanimous in the belief that he could not have done so without some amount of connivance on the part of the French authorities. Solomon Grumbach, president of the French Assembly's Foreign Affairs Commission, called on the government for an investigation and a full report on how the Mufti had been held in France and the method by which he had escaped. Grumbach bluntly accused his country of having treated the Arab master of Middle Eastern intrigue "most agreeably," despite his "pro-German, anti-British background"; he simultaneously arraigned the British, asking: "Why did England, which logically could and should have put his name on the war criminals list, not do so?" Years later,

* According to the United Press, "diplomatic circles in Paris" believed that the Mufti had obtained an American air priority with French help (*New York Times,* June 10, 1946).

Clare Hollingworth (special correspondent to the London *News Chronicle* and the *Economist* who had traveled extensively in the Middle East) went much farther in her book *The Arabs and the West:* "There is little doubt that anti-British French officials, smarting then as now under the loss of their Levant States, ascribed, as time went by, entirely to British intrigue, connived at this 'escape.' "[32]

At the time of Haj Amin's smooth departure, Gaston Deferre, French Under Secretary for Information, told reporters that the Mufti had been kept "under house arrest." But both the semiofficial French news agency Havas and the authoritative *Le Monde* admitted on June 12 that he had been merely under "discreet surveillance" and was free to move about at will since "he had given his word not to change his residence without informing the French authorities." The French officials accepted this assurance at its face value, and were obviously greatly embarrassed when, on June 8, Isaac Darvich, the Mufti's nephew and secretary, delivered at the Quai d'Orsay Haj Amin's handwritten letter thanking the French government for the hospitality extended to him. Réné Desvaux, chief of the Paris Judicial police, was suspended for his credulousness, but no other measures were taken.[33] *Le Matin*, the Paris moderate daily, charged on June 13 that Desvaux was used by the government as a scapegoat and that as early as October 1945 the Quai d'Orsay had ordered the police to give Haj Amin complete liberty of movement.

There also was some speculation that at least in certain London circles Haj Amin's cavalier departure from France was seen without grief. Ussef el Issa, editor of the Damascus Arab newspapers *Alef Baa*, told Edgar Mowrer of the *New York Post* on June 18: "Of course the British had a hand in it [the Mufti's 'escape']. It suits their policy admirably to have him turn up in the Middle East just now. The Mufti means trouble and the British Empire thrives on trouble. Trouble in Palestine will demonstrate how necessary it is for the British to stay and maintain order."*

Fifteen years later, the popular French daily, *Paris-Press-l'Intransigeant* (January 5, 1962) published a sensational article, "There Is No Longer a Mufti Mystery." The article reminds us that, in the late spring of 1946, Léon Blum was in the United States negotiating Franco-American financial arrangements designed to spearhead French economic rehabilitation. He discreetly informed his government that American Zionist circles who reportedly exercised considerable influence in the financial world, had insisted that the Mufti be delivered to the Allied tribunal, and that he committed himself to this demand. This had greatly embarrassed the French Government. The Quai d'Orsay, headed at that time by Georges Bidault, decided that the only possible solution was to let the Mufti "escape." French police received orders to "close their eyes." The Franco-American financial accord was signed on May 29, 1946; the Mufti "escaped" the same day. "This was no mere coincidence," the paper insists; it also offered

---

* The Cairo Paper *Al Mussawar* wrote on July 12, 1946, that prior to the flight of the Mufti from France, a representative of the British government had attempted to negotiate with him the conditions on which he would be allowed to return to Palestine. The Mufti, however, refused all negotiations, insisting that his repatriation must be permitted unconditionally. This attempt having failed, the British emissaries claimed that they had contacted the Mufti on their own accord without the knowledge of their government.

A Foreign Office spokesman officially absolved the French government of blame for the Mufti's "escape": while the British government had asked the French to keep a close eye on the Mufti, he was not under arrest and there were no legal grounds for holding him. As an afterthought the spokesman added that should the Mufti return to the Middle East, "Britain would have to decide whether to ask for his arrest." (*New York Times*, June 10, 1946.)

an explanation for the "intriguing" fact that in the years to come the Mufti had played no active role in politics connected with French North Africa: he gave his word of honor never to act against France—and "he kept his promise."

Former president of the Zionist Federation in France André Blumel, who at that time had served as Léon Blum's *chéf de cabinet,* denied the veracity of this version when interviewed by one of this author's informants in Paris; other knowledgeable French political leaders, however, confirmed it.

6

Back in the Middle East
1946–Present

The Whereabouts of the Mufti

THE MUFTI'S COMPLICES IN EGYPT HAD APPARENTLY BEEN
informed of his impending arrival, for when, on May 29,
the TWA plane landed at the Cairo airfield, "Marouf al-
Dawalabi" was warmly greeted by four members of the
Arab Higher Committee: Dr. Hussein Khalidi, Ahmed
Hilmi Pasha, Emil Ghouri, and the Mufti's right-hand
man, Jamal al-Husseini.[1]

For more than three weeks Haj Amin remained in hiding. For a time, his whereabouts were the object of speculation, deliberately fed by Arab leadership. On June 10,
the United Press reported from Jerusalem that Arab supporters of the Mufti had purposely "thrown a veil of
mystery over his whereabouts." A dispatch from Damascus, dated June 9, asserted that Haj Amin had arrived
there aboard a British plane and "received a wild ovation."* Another U.P. dispatch said that "automobile pro-

---

* A spokesman for the British Embassy in Paris indignantly denied
that "the Mufti had left France in a British plane," but added with

cessions were leaving all principal towns in Palestine for
Damascus," to greet the great guest. The next day, June
11, "Arab League circles" in Cairo told a Reuters correspondent that they had "good reasons to believe" the
Mufti flew first in a French plane to Syria and then continued by air to Saudi Arabia to seek sanctuary at King
Ibn Saud's court. On June 13, a "super-secret session" of
the Arab League in Bludan, Syria, reportedly discussed
when and how to display the Mufti to the Arabs. In the
meantime, Haj Amin was reported to be living in seclusion
in the village of Hosh el-Mitban, which had banned sight-
seers; yet, Syrian President Shukri el-Kuwatly was said to
have invited all Palestine Arab leaders to his home near
Damascus to meet the Mufti. The Syrian government,
however, was officially denying the very fact of the
Mufti's presence in the country.[2]

The confusion was facilitated by the British authorities
in Palestine who enforced a total news blackout on any
item connected with the Mufti. A newspaper which dared
to mention him was suppressed for two weeks. Yet the
BBC did broadcast about the Mufti's "escape," and many
Arabs in remote villages tuned their radios in to hear the
news. They were not perturbed by lack of information on
the destination he had reached. "Damascus, Mecca or
Medina are as much Haj Amin's home as Jerusalem," said
Auni Bey Abdul Hadi, spokesman for the Arab Higher
Committee, "though we are confident that he will come to
bless us here in Al Kudr [Arab name for Jerusalem]. . . .
This is one of the happiest moments in the Arab Middle
East." The Associated Press reported from Jerusalem that,
reflecting this festive mood, most of the narrow streets in

---

grudging sportsmanlike admiration: "I've got to hand it to the fellow—
that's the fourth time that he's eluded us." (*New York Times*, June 10,
1946.)

the Old City and many streets in the Arab quarter of the New City were decorated with flags, flowers, and olive branches; the Mufti's pictures appeared everywhere.[3]

As late as June 19, the British government pretended not to be aware of Haj Amin's whereabouts. "It can be assumed," Minister of State Philip Noel-Baker told the House of Commons, that "when the Mufti had left Paris he was hoping to reach an Arab country; we are considering what steps would be taken if this assumption proves to be correct." In any event, he assured the House, the British government would not permit the Mufti to return to Palestine.[4]

The King's Guest

Uncertainty (genuine or assumed) as to, and camouflage of, Haj Amin's actual residence ended on June 20 when an official Egyptian communiqué announced that "at eight o'clock tonight, Haj Amin el-Husseini, Mufti of Jerusalem, called at the Abadin Palace, signed the royal visitors' book and asked for an audience from King Farouk. The audience was granted, and the Mufti told the King: 'I have taken refuge in your palace.' His Eminence decided to stay as the King's guest." King Farouk advised the British government of his decision to grant sanctuary to the fugitive Mufti. In the early hours of the following morning it was officially reported from Cairo that the guest "left King Farouk's Palace and is staying at the King's Inchass estate," an hour's drive from Cairo.[5] The same day, Labor Prime Minister Clement Attlee reported that His Majesty's ambassador in Cairo was "in consultation with the Egyptian Prime Minister as to what measures should be taken."[6] The following day, the Egyptian foreign minister stated at the close of a cabinet meeting: "Britain has made no request to Egypt to hand over the Mufti, and even if one had been received, it would be rejected." On June 24, press correspondents who had interviewed both Sir Ronald Campbell, the British ambassador, and Egyptian Premier Sidki Pasha, reported: "A broad agreement regarding the position of the Mufti seems to have been reached between Britain and Egypt." Sidki Pasha explained that the Mufti was a political refugee and not a war criminal; as such, he had sought "rule of the desert" sanctuary, and was a guest of King Farouk.[8]

For a time Haj Amin's freedom of movement and political action was restricted. "The Mufti is greatly inconvenienced," wrote the pro-Government weekly *Ithinin* on July 1, 1946, "as he is unable to appear in public; he does not, however, complain about this since he appreciates the delicacy of the position caused by his presence . . . [which] has not only had a bad effect on Anglo-Egyptian negotiations, but has also caused certain tension between the British Ambassador and the Egyptain Government." The paper even felt that "a great mistake had been made in allowing the Mufti to come to Egypt." Another Cario weekly, *Ahar Saat*, felt differently:

> While in France, the Mufti enjoyed great freedom. He was permitted to receive visitors and to move about as he pleased. When he became tired of staying there he took refuge in a country which he could legitimately regard as his own. Egypt has received him, by the grace of her King, with open arms. However, the Egyptian Government has seen fit to intervene, on constitutional grounds, so that the Mufti has to remain hidden as if he were imprisoned, unable to move about or receive people. . . . Was France not after all a much pleasanter and more comfortable place? Why does the Egyptian Government regard it as necessary to restrict his freedom? Does it wish to protect him from any untoward happening? This

should not require restrictions on his freedom. In any case, no one would dare to lay a hand on him. Anyone with such a design would realise what misfortune would be in store for those responsible for any hostile act against this person. If the reason for the restrictions on his freedom is purely political, then what is its legal, constitutional or international justification? There is no international law which may compel an independent country to restrict its hospitality. . . . The matter is far too important not to deserve all our attention. We shall raise this question again at every opportunity.*

There was no need for protracted pressure. Two weeks later, on July 16, Premier Sidki Pasha announced that restrictions would no longer be imposed on Haj Amin's movements. Four days later he was officially received by King Farouk and visited by Jamil Mardam, Syrian minister to Egypt.[9]

The British government's attitude toward the Mufti's openly anti-British political activities, centered in Egypt, was anything but consistent. On April 1, 1947, a spokesman for the British Information Service in Washington disavowed any knowledge of a report from Jaffa that Haj Amin was preparing to leave Cairo for Jerusalem and firmly announced that the ex-Mufti was "not wanted and would not be welcome in Jerusalem, and, if detected, would be arrested." Nine days later, the London Foreign Office denied a report from Cairo that the British government had protested to Egypt against Haj Amin's political activities. However, admitting the possibility that the British ambassador to Cairo Sir Ronald T. Campbell, might have "made representations on his own initiative,

---

* Similarly the opposition *Kotla* (Wafdist bloc) Party, denounced "any restriction on his [the Mufti's] freedom, which contradicts humanity and weakens Egypt's position in the Arab world." The Party demanded that he be given complete freedom of action in order to be able to "do his national duty toward Palestine," the Associated Press reported in the *New York Post*, June 22, 1946.

and had not yet informed London," the Foreign Office spokesman added that "as far as he knew no such step was contemplated at present."[10] Reversing this stand, Hector McNeil, Minister of State for Foreign Affairs, told the House of Commons on May 5 that His Majesty's Government had made "frequent representations to Egypt protesting the continued political activities of the ex-Mufti of Jerusalem"; he, however, refused to go on record as saying that the British government would bar the former Mufti from Palestine under all circumstances.[11]

Back in the Saddle

After his return to the Middle East, Haj Amin once more took his place as the central figure in the higher Arab councils, eclipsing and silencing many of the rulers and political leaders who had directed Arab affairs during his absence in the service of the Third Reich. The immediate effect of his reappearance was to unnerve most of those leaders. The old memories of the Mufti's effective methods of persuading—or destroying—those who disagreed with him were dramatically revived. The more moderate Arab leaders, fearing isolation and worse, chose to join in adulation of the Mufti.[12] "Haj Amin's reputation among the Palestine Arabs was now greater than at any time since his presidency of the first Arab Higher Committee in 1936–1937; he once again became the symbol of the Palestine Arab national aspirations," remarked J. C. Hurewitz.[13]

The Arabs proved to be the only people in the whole world for whom close collaboration with Hitler and Mussolini was not a crime, not even a blemish on the record of a national leader. There was no need to prompt the

French, Norwegians, Belgians, and Yugoslavs to condemn their Axis collaborationists, to bring them to trial and punishment. For the French, Marshal Pétain had been for more that two decades the hero of Verdun, the great old soldier and patriot. And still the French nation did not hesitate to brand him a traitor, to sentence him to death, and only after that to commute the death sentence into life imprisonment. And Pétain headed a long list of French collaborationists brought to trial and punished by special purge courts. Up to November 1, 1945, 52,439 cases were heard and a total of 2,366 death sentences were pronounced.[14] The example of France was followed by other countries: Quisling, Degrelle, Joice, Bardossi had been, without the slightest hesitation, branded by their own nationals for the inexpiable sin of collaborating with Hitler and Mussolini, seeking favors from them, trying to exploit the dominating position of the Axis for what they thought to be in the interests of their respective peoples. By far not all of them did it for their own selfish purposes. Some sincerely believed that they were rendering a patriotic service to their country. But next to none of the Axis collaborators all over the world escaped blame, judgment, and condemnation by the very same nation whose interests they had proferred to serve.

Haj Amin el-Husseini was the sole and glaring exception to this pattern. Arab leadership, both in Palestine and in the Arab League countries, might have been somewhat embarrassed by his record of active collaboration with Nazi Germany and Fascist Italy and by his vituperation of the victorious Allies. The Palestine daily *Haboker* on February 4, 1946, reported that the Arab League emissaries in London and Washington were making the utmost effort to prevent the publication of documents produced at the Nuremberg trial which exposed the Arab quislings.

(The paper had to resort to the generic term "quislings" because British censorship in the country was still forbidding specific mention of the Mufti's name in the press.) The committee of editors of the Hebrew Press submitted to the chief secretary of the Palestine government a strongly worded protest against the censorship's ban on the republication locally of Edgar Mowrer's revelations printed in the *New York Post:* it was the clandestine "Voice of Israel" that had on the afternoon of February 3 broadcast a full account, in Hebrew and English, of Mowrer's dispatches.[15]

Embarrassed or not, Arab leadership presented a bold and united pro-Mufti front. The wealthy and aristocratic Nashashibi party, considerably depleted by Mufti-ordered assassinations, still hated him bitterly, but did not dare to refuse allegiance at the risk of being called traitors to the Arab cause. On the opposite side of the socio-political spectrum, the League for National Liberation, founded in 1943–1944 by a group of Arab communist intellectuals (Emil Tuma and Emil Habibi) regarded the Mufti as a national hero who had not hesitated to oppose "British imperialism." Though eliminated from the Arab Higher Committee, the League kept in close contact with the Mufti and his first lieutenant, Jamal el-Husseini; its representatives repeatedly visited the "National Leaders" in Cairo and Beirut.[16]

The only Arab leader who felt unhappy about Haj Amin's return to the Middle East was his old adversary, Abdallah ibn ul Hussein, the ruler of Transjordan. In his *Memoirs,* published in English translation in 1954, he speaks derisively of "a certain individual who arrived in Egypt and began to work to the detriment of the Arabs and Palestine; this person was al-Haj Amin al-Husaini, known as the Mufti." Abdallah specifically mentions that this "certain individual" had received from Shukri el-Kuwatly, President of Syria, "a large sum of money amounting to 250,000 Syrian pounds [about $92,500 at the 1953 rate of exchange], which was only a small part of what he received from other sources."[17] But even Abdallah deemed it at that time necessary to withhold adverse public comment.

"The First Arab Leader, the Mufti"

Unconditional allegiance to the Mufti was resolutely voiced by Arab witnesses who, in March 1946, appeared before the Anglo-American Committee of Inquiry.[18]

Speaking on behalf of the Palestine Arab Higher Committee, Jamal al-Husseini said in his introductory remarks that he "regretted the absence of their leader the Mufti, whose place could not be filled." Asked by Bartley C. Crum, an American Committee member, whether the Arabs had applied specifically for the reurn of the Mufti to Palestine in order to appear before the Committee, the witness replied: "Yes, only a fortnight ago." Then Richard Crossman, one of the British members of the Committee, began firing a series of questions referring to the Mufti's activities in Germany during the war:

Crossman: Has your attitude towards the Mufti been strengthened or weakened as a result of his activities during the past five years?

Jamal Husseini: His [the Mufti's] position has remained the same; he acted in the interests of his people. The Arabs are not the enemies of the Germans, like the Jews, and they had to seek the best means for safeguarding their cause in the event of Germany winning the war.

Crossman then asked the witness whether the term "first leader" meant that Jamal and the Arab Higher Com-

mittee considered the Grand Mufti their leader in democratic philosophy.

Jamal: Yes.
Crossman: You feel that during the last five years, his [the
Mufti's] whole policy and activity has been a struggle for
democracy?

The reply was that the mandatory government had pursued the Mufti from one place to another, until he had no
other place but Germany to go; there he worked for the
good of his nation.

Crossman: You feel that what he did during the war was not
collaboration in any sense with the Germans?
Jamal: The Grand Mufti in Germany was working for the
interests of the Arabs, who had no direct interest in the war.
Here in Palestine we stood with you [the British]. The Mufti in
Germany told them: "If you win, you must give us our rights."
Crossman: You felt a spiritual neutrality in this struggle?
Jamal: Generally, yes, but actually we helped [the British].

When the witness contended that the British were in
fact acting similarly by helping "totalitarian Russia,"
Crossman retorted: "But Mr. Churchill was fighting the
Germans." To this Jamal replied: "And he [the Mufti] was
fighting the English."

To the question why the Mufti had gone to Germany
rather than to neutral Switzerland, the answer was: "To
save his neck."

Crossman: You mean the Germans brought him to the country? In view of his record during the war, does the Arab
Higher Committee think the Mufti still enjoys the full confidence of the Palestinian Arabs?
Jamal: Yes.

Not less definite was the stand taken by the second
Arab witness, Auni Bey Abdul Hadi, secretary general of
the Higher Arab Committee.

"Would you regard the organizing of a *Waffen* S.S. Regiment as a hostile act [toward the Allies]?" asked Crossman. "Yes," Auni replied. Whereupon Crossman produced a photograph taken in January 1944, published in the Nazi paper *Wiener Illustrierte,* showing the Mufti giving the Hitler salute, and inspecting a regiment of *Waffen* S.S. consisting of Moslem recruits. Auni glanced at the photograph and said: "We regard the Mufti as a great Arab patriot."

Crossman then asked: "Why did the Iraqis condemn Rashid Ali as a traitor, and you regard the Mufti as a great Arab patriot?" The answer was that the Iraqis had condemned Rashid Ali because what he did was contrary to the Iraqis' interests.

In reply to Bartley Crum, Auni fully associated himself with Jamal Husseini's statement that there was no substitute for the Mufti, who was still the greatest Palestinian Arab leader.

Emil Ghouri, secretary of the Palestine Arab Party, also urged the return of "the first Arab leader, the Mufti."

Renascence of the Arab Higher Committee

By the time he reappeared on the Middle East political scene, the Mufti's Husseini clan was once more on the ascendance in the Palestine Arab community. The ground was prepared well in advance.

In November 1945, Syrian Prime Minister Jamil Mardam went to Palestine on behalf of the Arab League to reconcile the feuding Arab factions. He succeeded in reconstituting the Arab Higher Committee with the participation of all the six existing Arab political groups: the Mufti's own Palestine Arab Party, representing the interests of the Husseini clan; the National Defense Party, organized in 1934 by Ragheb Bey Nashashibi, former mayor of Jerusalem, to represent the interests of the large and wealthy Nashashibi family, the sworn enemies of the Husseinis; the Reform Party, founded in 1937 and headed by western-educated Dr. Hussein Khalidi, who advocated progressive reforms of the feudal Arab society but was actually toeing the Mufti's line; the National Bloc Party, a regional organization centering in the Sychem-Jenin area and comprising a number of mayors of the northern Arab towns and their entourages; the Arab Youth Congress, a Christian Arab organization; and the extreme pan-Arab *Istaqlal* Party headed by Auni Bey Abdul Hadi.

The presidency of the resurrected Arab Higher Committee was left open for the absent Haj Amin, who at that time lived under liberal French surveillance in a Paris suburb; to the post of acting chairman was appointed his plenipotentiary, Jamal el-Husseini, who had returned from wartime exile. Yet this six-party formation lasted less than half a year. Jamal behaved and acted in an openly dictatorial manner, suppressing or disregarding any opposition on the part of his five partners. On May 29, 1946, the leaders of these five groups seceded and announced the establishment of a rival Arab Higher Front.

This outright rebellion against the Mufti camp could have become the point of departure for a completely new reorientation of political forces within the Palestine Arab community. This possibility was, however, frustrated by (1) the failure of the British government to give immediate support and encouragement to the anti-Mufti front, (2) the spectacular arrival of the Mufti in Cairo just ten days later, and (3) quick action on the part of the Arab League.

The League Council convened on June 13, 1946, in

Bloudan, Syria. The Mufti, then still biding his time, was not present, but he had every reason to be satisfied with the outcome of the meeting. The League ordered the dissolution of both the Arab Higher Committee and the Arab Higher Front. They were replaced by the newly established Higher Palestine Executive, with the Mufti as chairman, Jamal el-Husseini as deputy-chairman, Dr. Hussein Khalidi as secretary, and Hilmi Pasha and Emil Ghouri as members. The Bloudan "Dictat" was a complete victory for the Mufti. His party received three seats (the Mufti, Jamal el-Husseini, and Hilmi Pasha) on the new committee—an absolute majority. The Defense Party of the Nashashibis, the National Bloc, and the Istaqlal Party were denied any representation whatsoever on the new supreme body. Representatives of the Arab workers, organized in the Federation of Palestine Workers and in the Federation of Arab Trade Unions, were also excluded.[19] John Marlowe is convinced that "from this time onward not only was Husseini supremacy fully restored in Palestine, but the influence of Haj Amin on the Arab League tended more and more to eclipse the moderate counsels of Azzam Pasha, the Secretary General, and to encourage the Arab League to aim, not at persuading Great Britain to adhere to the White Paper policy, but at compelling Great Britain to evacuate Palestine."[20]

Jamal el-Husseini served as acting chairman in formal dealings with the Palestine government. But the major policy of the Higher Executive was directed by the Mufti from Egypt. On April 10, 1947, the Arab newspaper *Al Difa'a* (Self-Defense) reported that the central offices of the Palestine Arab Higher Committee would be transferred to Cairo in a move designed to strengthen the Mufti's direct influence in Arab politics.

Armed Backing

In addition to political backing provided by the Arab Higher Committee, the Mufti was able to count on substantial organized armed support in Palestine. Andrew Roth published in the November 16, 1946, issue of *Nation* a revealing correspondence on "The Mufti's New Army," consisting of two para-military youth organizations: the *Nejada* (Rescuers) and the *Futuwa* (Power). Their combined strength was estimated at about 10,000 young men. Though pretending to be nothing more than "older Boy Scouts," neither body made any secret of the fact that they possessed arms and were practicing their use; members were given their khaki uniforms free and wore them openly. While *Nejada* owed allegiance to the Moslem Brotherhood, *Futuwa*'s political sponsor was Mufti's cousin, Jamal el-Husseini. At the end of September 1946 the two groups merged and their leaders were reported holding secret meetings in a walled villa in Alexandria under the tutelage of the Mufti.[21] The British authorities in Palestine who relentlessly suppressed any form of Jewish para-military formations, good-naturedly tolerated the activities of both *Nejada* and *Futuwa*. When Jamal el-Husseini reviewed at Jaffa several hundred khaki-clad *Nejada* members, who took an oath of allegiance to Arab nationalism, and then made an aggressive appeal to their Arab patriotism, the British-controlled radio station fully broadcast the whole proceedings.[22]

By the end of 1946, the actual combined strength of the two united armed groups was reported to have reached 20,000, including camel corps, trained infantry, and mobile units capable of moving wherever ordered at a moment's notice. Gene Currivan cabled to the *New York*

Times from Jerusalem that "the decision for unification was reached . . . during recent consultations in Cairo with the Mufti" and that the force thus created was "operating under the inspiration, if not direct control of the Mufti:"

It is understood that Palestine will be divided into six administrative districts, with commanders recommended by the Mufti in control of each district, and a high council directing the over-all administration. All members of the army will pledge allegiance to the Mufti who will virtually be commander in chief although his actual participation will be through deputies.[23]

Villa Aida

Summing up the towering position acquired by the Mufti in the Arab world, Clifton Daniel wrote from Cairo to the *New York Times* in August 1946 that "despite such activities, which have been sufficient cause for hanging in other countries," Haj Amin "not only kept his head but has enhanced his prestige among his own people, who have all but sanctified him by this time."[24]

There is now a pilgrimage that every Arab and Moslem notable and patriot must make in Alexandria. The new shrine of political Islam is the Mufti's house, Villa Aida, near Roushdy Pasha Station of the street-car line that runs out from Alexandria to the suburb of Ramleh. The two-story villa stands directly beside the tramline. There is an Egyptian soldier about every eight or ten yards around the garden, and the Mufti has personal body-guards inside.

Everyone approaching the house is stopped and asked if he has an appointment. If so, he is taken to the Mufti's secretary, who passes upon his admissibility. If not, he is turned away. All these precautions are taken for the Mufti's protection and not his detention, says the Egyptian Government, which is sensitive to allegations that he is held prisoner. Visitors say that the Mufti is uneasy about his personal safety, and understandably so for a man who has been so often on the brink of disaster.

Clifton Daniel pointedly stressed that to call at Villa Aida was for Arabs "not only a matter of courtesy: it is also becoming customary again to consult him on the affairs of Palestine in particular, and problems of the Arab world in general; it is safe to say that no recent Arab decisions on Palestine policy have been taken without his opinion being rendered, at least indirectly."

One More Round-Table Conference

The report of the Anglo-American Committee of Inquiry, released at the end of April 1946—in particular its recommendation for the immediate admission of 100,000 Jewish immigrants—was unconditionally condemned by the Arabs and was not endorsed by the British government. Further Anglo-American consultations on a ministerial level had, in July 1946, produced the so-called Morrison-Grady cantonization scheme, which was rejected by both Arabs and Jews. In the meantime, on June 29, four members of the Jewish Agency for Palestine were arrested by the British in Jerusalem in retaliation for the continuation of Jewish armed resistance to the mandatory's policy.

Faced with a stalemate, the British government again resorted to the expedient of a round-table conference, which had been tried out—and which had failed—in 1939. Invitations were extended to the seven member-states of the Arab League, the Mufti's Arab Higher Committee, and the Jewish Agency.

The Jewish Agency, while inclined to accept the invitation, insisted on the right to choose its representatives for participation in the London talks, which was in effect a demand for the release of the interned Agency members. The Arab states were ready to participate. Azzam Pasha, secretary general of the Arab League, said, on August 12, 1946, in Alexandria, that he had received assurances from the British that the talks would not be based exclusively on any "fixed policy," such as the British-United States Cabinet Committee's provincial plan for Palestine, but would be free and open to any proposition the Arabs wished to make. He added, however, that "there had never been any question of the Arabs' sitting at a round table with Jewish representatives." Asked whether the Mufti's Palestine Arab Higher Committee would be consulted in framing a policy on Palestine, Azzam Pasha replied "certainly": consultations would take place with Jamal el-Husseini, vice-chairman of the Committee, who is in constant contact with Haj Amin el-Husseini, exiled mufti of Jerusalem and chairman of the Committee. Asked whether the Mufti would be consulted, Azzam Pasha said: "Why not? He is an Arab and has a right to express his opinion on Palestine."[25]

The problem of the Mufti proved to be the stumbling block in regard to his Higher Committee's participation in the London Conference. The member-states of the Arab League had on August 22, in a joint note, asked the British government to recognize him as the leader of Arab Palestine.[26] Three days later, the Higher Committee decided in Jerusalem not to accept Britain's invitation to the Conference unless its chairman, Haj Amin, were invited to head the delegation. The British government had, on the other hand, made it clear far in advance that the Mufti would not be acceptable as a delegate.[27]

On August 26, Jamal el-Husseini, vice-chairman of the Higher Committee, submitted to the High Commissioner for Palestine, Lieut. Gen. Alan G. Cunningham, a formal request that the Mufti be included in the Palestine Arab delegation to London. The High Commissioner "pointed out the difficulties in meeting this request," said an official British communiqué. He also raised the question of including in the Palestinian Arab delegation persons not affiliated with the Arab Higher Committee, such as "suitable representatives of municipalities, commercial life and labor." The Higher Committee spokesman rejected this proposal.[28]

For a time, the British government seemed to have had second thoughts as to the nonadmissibility as delegates of both the Mufti and the detained Jewish Agency members. A spokesman for Prime Minister Clement Attlee made it clear that the British would rather not have them at the Conference, but went on to say that "we would not let the Conference break down on this issue."[29] However, when the Conference opened on September 9, Jewish Agency members were still under detention (they were not freed before November 6) and the Agency was not represented; nor was the Arab Higher Committee. When, on August 29, it was announced in Jerusalem that the Mufti would not be admitted to the Conference, Dr. Hussein Khalidi declared that Palestine Arabs "will flatly refuse to go to London and will insist that other Arab nations also refuse to attend the Conference."[30] Member-states of the Arab League did not heed this demand, however, and sent delegations to the Conference. Making virtue out of necessity, the Mufti said in a cable to these delegations: "Although representatives of Palestine Arabs are not participating in the London conversations for reasons they were not responsible for, they nevertheless firmly believe that the delegations of the Arab Governments will fight for the case of Palestine which is the case of all Arabs."[31]

No progress toward an agreed solution was made during the first stage of the Conference. It was interrupted, with the proviso that it was going to be resumed early in 1947. It was expected that by that time both the Jewish Agency and the Arab Higher Committee would reconsider their non-participation. The expectations did not materialize in regard to the Agency: the twenty-second Zionist Congress, held at Basel in December 1946, resolved that "in the existing circumstances the Zionist movement cannot take part in the [London] conference."[32] The Arab Higher Committee, on the contrary, decided this time to accept what the Mufti described as an "open and unrestricted invitation." Asked whether he himself would be a delegate, he replied: "I shall not go to London but I have approved of the delegates who will represent Palestinian Arabs." Just as in 1939, Haj Amin, though personally proscribed by the British, was able to nominate the Palestine Arab delegation and to determine its stand by remote control. All delegates were summoned to Cairo for consultation with the Mufti before proceeding to London.[33]

The second stage of the London Conference (January-February 1947) proved to be as inconclusive as the first. On February 4, the Mufti declared at a press conference in Cairo that neither partition nor the British "federalization plan" was acceptable to the Palestine Arabs; he favored placing the Palestine problem before the United Nations where he hoped the decision would be in favor of the Arab cause.[34] The delegation of the Arab Higher Committee was, accordingly, determined not to accept even the most pro-Arab proposals advanced by the British foreign secretary Ernest Bevin, and the delegations of the Arab States fell into line.

The Mufti Delegation Before the United Nations

Winding up the abortive London conference on February 14, 1947, British Foreign Secretary Ernest Bevin announced that Great Britain would take the entire Palestine problem to the United Nations. A special session of the U.N. General Assembly convened on April 28.

One of the first and most controversial issues on its agenda was the granting of a hearing to the Jews and Arabs. The principal contender on the Jewish side was the Jewish Agency for Palestine. The General Assembly decided by a vote of 44 to 7, with 3 abstentions, to recognize the Jewish Agency's right to be heard. The British delegation constituted itself as the main protagonist for recognizing the Mufti-led Arab Higher Committee as the sole spokesman for the Palestine Arab community. In response to a question by Warren R. Austin, United States delegate, as to whether the mandatory recommended that the Arab Higher Committee be heard by the United Nations as representative of the views of the Arab population of Palestine, British delegate Sir Alexander Cadogan, replied unhesitatingly that it did so recommend. Accordingly, the subsequent draft resolution submitted by the United States referred to the Arab Higher Committee as "representative of the views of the Arab population of Palestine." On May 6, 1947, the chairman of the First (Political and Security) Committee of the U.N. General Assembly officially informed the secretary of the Palestine Arab delegation that the Committee was granted a hearing on the same basis as the Jewish Agency for Palestine.[35]

This decision was the more surprising since just at that time all fifty-five United Nations delegations had received from The Nation Associates an amply documented memorandum establishing that the Arab Higher Committee was controlled by the ex-Mufti of Jerusalem and that three members of the delegation had been active agents of the Germans and Japanese during the war, ranking with the "worst of the Axis war criminals." The Arab Higher Committee was described as the "creature" of the Arab League. Its chief, the exiled Mufti, was a "full partner" of Germany and Japan before and during World War II and was now an escaped prisoner who had found asylum in the palace of the King of Egypt in Cairo. Emil Ghouri was once exiled from Palestine for extremist activities and sent to Egypt and Iraq. The memorandum quoted the British General Service Intelligence in listing him as one of a group "who are responsible for propaganda, intrigue and subversive activities inside and outside Iraq." He was accused of having been partly responsible for "internal terror against Arab opponents of the Mufti and Arabs who sell land to the Jews." Wasef Kamal, it was charged, had to leave Iraq after the 1941 rebellion against the British, and from there escaped to Turkey, where he served as agent of the "German secret service, from which he received a salary." Ghouri and Kamal arrived in New York on April 28. The third delegate, Rasem Khalidi, was, according to the memorandum, denied a visa by the State Department because of "his activities in Nazi Germany": he was one of the closest collaborators of the Mufti and a former announcer on an Axis-Arabic radio station.[36]

Most members of the Arab Higher Committee, reported the *New York Times* (May 12, 1947), refused to comment officially on the charges; there was "a general feeling among Arab delegates that the Axis issue should be forgotten." Emil Ghouri himself told a correspondent of the United Press, after he had seen the memorandum, that "the more the Zionists try this sort of propaganda, the tighter the Arabs will stick to the Mufti." The Mufti, he said, "is our leader, and it is only democratic to let us be led by the man we want. It's not up to an outsider to tell us our leader is bad."[37]

The Nation Associates memorandum specifically indicated that its reproduced documents and thirty-five photographs showing the Mufti and other Arab leaders in the company of Adolf Hitler, Heinrich Himmler, and Dino Alfieri, Mussolini's ambassador to Berlin, were copies of originals "now in the possession of our [United States] State Department."

This evidence was withheld from the United Nations and the American public by the State Department. On June 6, Senator Robert F. Wagner, Democrat of New York, addressed a letter to Secretary of State George C. Marshall, urging its publication:[38]

It is my understanding that the Department of State has in its possession a number of documents pertaining to the wartime activities of Nazi and Fascist leaders and collaborators, particularly pertaining to the former Mufti of Jerusalem, who now serves as chairman of the Arab Higher Committee, and his collaboration with the Axis powers during the war. Because this material is of such unquestioned interest to the [U.S.] Congress and to the American people, and because the United Nations is now investigating the Palestine question, I deem it most urgent that the Department of State should publish all the material it has in its possession regarding this important matter.

I am particularly anxious that the extent of the ex-Mufti's role in the Iraqi revolt of 1941 be disclosed, as well as his activities as an agent of the Axis since 1941, and his role in the extermination of the Jews, as revealed in documents discussed by Bartley C. Crum in his recent book, *Behind the Silken Curtain*. A very revealing article was published in the May 17 issue of *The Nation* in connection with the ex-Mufti's activities. It is entitled "The Grand Mufti in World War II."

Since the facts presented by the publication of this material will, I feel sure, help the United States and other members of the United Nations to reach a decision on Palestine at the United Nations Assembly, and will help to determine our course of action in the Middle East, I am counting on your help and co-operation.

Wagner's appeal remained unheeded.

Whitewashing the Mufti

The attempt to disqualify the Arab Higher Committee, on the grounds that the Mufti actively collaborated with Nazi Germany, failed. By that time—only two years after the collapse of the Third Reich—the stigma of having been Hitler's militant associate apparently no longer loomed so large in the United Nations. Jorge Garcia-Granados, the outspoken delegate of Guatemala, delivered, it is true, a powerful indictment of the Mufti's record. But Jamal el-Husseini, the chairman of the Palestine Arab delegation, felt free to accept the challenge and on October 18, 1947, devoted a great part of his address to the vindication of his cousin and leader:

The honorable delegate of Guatemala has accused the Mufti of having been one of the initiators of, and one of the most active collaborators in, the plan for the systematic extinction of the Jews during the war. We emphatically deny this accusation. It is surprising that the honorable delegate should base himself upon so-called testimony at Nuremberg, given at a trial in which the Grand Mufti was not involved and to which he had no opportunity to reply.

Moreover, the British Government had declared in the House of Commons that the Grand Mufti could not be considered a war criminal. The French Government also had extended to him, it will be recalled, their kind hospitality.

On the other hand, the Germans did not need any foreign

person to lay their policy, and in fact they had embarked upon the program of the persecution of the Jews since 1933. One can discern in all these accusations against the Grand Mufti the efforts of the Jewish Agency, which aims at besmirching a political and a nationalist leader, who has stood firm against Zionist ambitions and designs.[39]

Emboldened by the opportunity to defend the Mufti before the United Nations forum, his representatives eagerly grasped every pretext to improve his reputation.

Speaking on behalf of the Jewish Agency for Palestine at the fifty-fourth meeting of the First [Political and Security] Committee of the United Nations, Moshe Shertok, on May 12, 1948, mentioned that "at the head of the Arab Higher Committee of Palestine stands a man who, apart from other well-known aspects of his activity, was directly involved during the war in the Nazi policy of the extermination of the European Jews." No name was specifically mentioned in this rather casual remark. But at the very next meeting, the same afternoon, Emil Ghouri, secretary of the Palestine Arab delegation, hastened to pin it down to "His Eminence, the Grand Mufti," and presented a spirited defense of the Mufti's political record. Said Mr. Ghouri:

I can understand that the acts of anyone who seemed to cast his lot with the Axis during the war must seem to be wicked and detestable. . . . But I am also convinced that if the reasons that drove him to take the course he took were fully known, fair-minded men would at least see that there was another side to this matter; that in fact, it was the policy that was adopted in Palestine that finally forced this course of action on the Mufti. . . .

I beseech you to put yourself in the place of the Arabs of Palestine in the period between the two wars. . . . For twenty years Britain, as it seemed to them, had been pursuing a monstrous policy aimed at taking their country away from them and giving it to another people. . . . The attitude of the Mufti represented a natural stand taken in self-defense, a stand which any threatened nation would have taken in order to protect itself. . . .

The Jews are questioning the record of an Arab spiritual leader. Does it properly come from the mouth of a people who have crucified the founder of Christianity?[40]

The last part of Mr. Ghouri's statement referring to the Mufti was stormy; he was interrupted by the chair five times. Yet the chair also rebuked Mr. Shertok by warning against making "controversial statements which provoke even more controversial replies," and added: "It [Shertok's remark] possibly might be considered by some as an unfortunate statement which provoked what I am sure would be considered by others as at least an equally unfortunate reply."[41]

The Mufti-Ordered Boycott

In the discussion on the terms of reference of the U.N. Special Committee on Palestine (UNSCOP), Arab representatives insisted that the Committee should be limited to the investigation of the situation in Palestine and not concern itself with the plight of the Jews in Europe, which, they insisted, had no connection with the solution to the Palestine problem. By a majority of 36 to 8, with 4 abstentions, the U.N. General Assembly voted that UNSCOP was free to inquire into areas other than Palestine, i.e., to study the Jewish situation in Europe.

Following the Mufti's instructions, conveyed from Cairo, the Arab Higher Committee had decided to boycott the proceedings of UNSCOP. In a statement to his Jerusalem mouthpiece, *Al-Wahda*, Haj Amin declared that the United Nations was dominated by "imperialistic interests" and that "despite all difficulties and thorny obstacles placed in our way by imperialists and Zionists, we shall continue defending our just cause and shoulder the burden of the struggle until our right is restored to us— we shall protect our homeland that is now surrounded by menacing dangers."[42]

The opposition press reacted at first unfavorably to this Mufti strategy. But when UNSCOP arrived in Palestine, all Arab groups, including the Communists, obeyed the injunction. Where persuasion did not work, coercion was applied.[43] "The very real fear of violent reprisals if they defied the Mufti's command was powerful deterrent, and the Arab community was solid in its attitude of negation."[44] Moreover, from mid-June on, Mufti followers in Palestine, with one eye on UNSCOP, became increasingly belligerent. Jewish liaison officers and journalists accompanying UNSCOP were not allowed to visit certain Arab establishments or municipalities. Mass demonstrations were staged in Haifa, Jaffa, and Jerusalem. Popular wrath was aroused not only against the Zionists, the British, and the Americans, but also against the Arab "traitors" who continued to violate the anti-Jewish land and economic boycotts. "Zionists must not have an inch of this country," declared a message from the Mufti. "It is your duty to gain back every inch of your land."[45]

A Surprising Move

The majority report of UNSCOP, signed in Geneva on August 31, 1947, advocated the partition of Palestine into two states, one Jewish and one Arab, linked by an economic union. Backed by both the United States and the Soviet Union, the partition scheme was endorsed on November 29, against determined Arab opposition, by the

U.N. General Assembly by the required two-thirds majority vote: 33 to 13, with 10 abstentions.

The Mufti's Arab Higher Committee repeatedly went
on record as uncompromisingly and violently opposing
any form of partition and any peaceful settlement of the
Arab-Jewish controversy on Palestine. It came therefore
as something of a sensational disclosure when two years
and eight months later in the July 27, 1950, issue of the
Jaffa Arab daily *Al Yom,* an article by Sharif el-Shanti
appeared revealing that on November 27, 1947, just two
days before the partition resolution of the United Nations
General Assembly, the Mufti approached the Jewish
Agency for Palestine with an offer of direct negotiations
for solution of the Palestine problem. His emissary in
Haifa, Ahmed el-Iman, received the following message:
"The Mufti requests you to contact immediately Dr.
Mordecai Eliash [a noted leader of the Zionist religious
party Misrachi, who after the establishment of the State
of Israel became first Israel Minister to England] and ask
him to propose secret talks between the Jewish Agency
and the Mufti prior to the final decision of the United
Nations General Assembly. These talks are to be conducted without the mediation of any of the Arab countries." According to *Al Yom,* the Mufti also promised a
compromising attitude with a view to bringing his proposed negotiations to a successful conclusion. The negotiations were to be conducted at the Mufti's residence in
Lebanon. A reply from the Jewish Agency was requested
within twenty-four hours.

Dr. Eliash submitted the Mufti's proposal to a meeting
of the Jewish Agency Executive in Jerusalem. The meeting unanimously rejected the idea of entering into any
talks with the Mufti but emphasized readiness to negotiate with any Arab leader except the Mufti, who had not

only provoked bloodshed against Jews in Palestine but also aided Hitler in his mass annihilation of Jews. It was Sharif el-Shanti, writer of the *Al Yom* article, who had transmitted the Agency's refusal to the Mufti.

Both the Mufti and the Jewish Agency refrained from either refuting or confirming el-Shanti's revelation.

Unannounced Visit

On October 8, 1947, Haj Amin landed at Beirut airport in a surprise visit—his first trip out of Egypt since June 1946, when he fled Paris and set up his headquarters at Cairo.[46] He arrived in the Lebanese capital's airport at 7:30 A.M., without a visa, and without the knowledge of the Lebanese government. Riyad el-Solh, prime minister of Lebanon,

was getting out of bed when a flustered aide interrupted him with: "Excellency, Haj Amin el Husseini has just landed in Beirut." "Nonsense," snorted the Prime Minister, "the Mufti is in Cairo." But a phone call confirmed the fact that an unidentified DC-3 had landed at the airport, bearing a stocky man in flowing Arab robes, with a bodyguard of six young men.

Riyad dressed hurriedly, and minutes later, his official limousine whisked into the airport enclosure.

The surprise guest was made welcome, and by 8:00 A.M. he was already conferring with Riyad and President Bechara el-Kouri at the president's summer home in Aley, a small resort town high on Mount Lebanon, overlooking Beirut and the Mediterranean Sea. After ninety minutes with them, he was taken to the Prime Minister's home, to rest in seclusion, and later to a former hotel in Aley, just across from the Tanios Hotel, where the Arab League was meeting. A government communiqué, announcing the

Mufti's arrival, said that he was received "with enthusiasm" and that he was a guest of the state. Lebanese police were patrolling the street outside the hotel he was staying in, while "distinguished guests" were reported coming and going, some in Arab garb but most in Western clothes and fez.[47]

The official reason for Haj Amin's arrival was chairing the meeting of the Arab Higher Committee, and he was not expected to attend the Arab League session, on the agenda of which Palestine figured as first and main item. It was, however, commonly accepted that he came to Beirut because he thought the time was ripe to apply direct, personal pressure on Arab leadership for decisive action on Palestine.

From his new headquarters Haj Amin was, according to a firsthand report circulated by the Overseas News Agency, "manipulating the world's biggest unofficial bureaucracy behind a heavy curtain of mystery." His "hotel" was

crammed with a clientele consisting of legal and military experts, religious and political advisers, lieutenants, secretaries and a horde of bodyguards; this is the hard core of a political machine so tight-knit and widespread that it can roll a blanket of propaganda across the Middle East with an alacrity and ease of a man unrolling a 9 by 12 carpet.[48]

The Onslaught

The U.N. partition decision served as a signal for an all-out Arab onslaught. In his final statement presented on November 24, 1947, before the United Nations Ad Hoc Committee on Palestine, Jamal el-Husseini, vice-chairman of the Mufti's Arab Higher Committee, warned: "By imposing partition on Palestine you will precipitate the country into a virtual blood bath. . . . The boundary line proposed, if ever decided upon, shall be nothing but a line of fire and blood." No effort was spared to make good this warning. For the Mufti the stakes were too high to permit merely token resistance. It was through his claim to be "Mr. Palestine" that he became a kingpin in the Arab world, a force to be reckoned with in the councils of the Arab League. Having lost this claim he would become a king without a throne and a land. Armed intervention in Palestine would also give him the golden opportunity of settling—as he did in 1936–1939—quite a few accounts with the Arab leaders who had been opposing him, thus eliminating prospective rivals in his drive for power.

Directed by the Mufti, who was then in Damascus, the Arab Higher Committee proclaimed a three-day general strike, from December 2 to 4, 1947, to be followed by mass demonstrations after the midday prayers on Friday the 5th.[49] But even prior to that there was launched a campaign of indiscriminate violence against the Jewish community. Within the first twenty-four hours—on November 30, 1947—eight Jews had already been killed near Nathanya. Ambushes, arson, bombings became the order of the day.*

All this was, however, but a prelude to organized armed intervention from outside the country. In its initial stage it was fully dominated by the Mufti's Arab Higher Committee. Glubb Pasha, commander of the Transjordan Arab Legion, testified that at first, neither the Mufti himself nor the Egyptian and Syrian governments had believed that it would be necessary to use regular armies; they were per-

---

* The opposition favored postponement of open hostilities until after the end of the citrus season and to allow time for the help promised by neighboring Arab states to materialize. (Netanel Lorch, *The Edge of the Sword* [New York, London, 1961], p. 37.)

suaded that a force of irregulars would be sufficient. In December 1947, recruitment of irregulars was started in Syria and a motley force was collected under the title "Arab Liberation Army." The recruitment was financed by the Mufti's Higher Committee, which was well supplied with funds.* Noted American journalist Joseph Alsop wrote in December 1947 in his syndicated column that Haj Amin's political activities were "lavishly financed" by Saudi Arabia's Ibn Saud and Egypt's King Farouk.[50] "But," he added,

the Mufti is not dependent on the generosity of these monarchs. With astute foresight, the Mufti managed to get a large proportion of his Nazi financial backing out of Germany even while the war was still on. He now is known to have a large cache of gold in Iraq, and a considerable fortune in Switzerland, largely in the form of easily negotiable Swiss watches.

With this money, and with a well organized, highly paid and fanatical gang of triggermen, the Mufti's influence is increasingly paramount in Arab politics.

A report for the year ending June 1948, published by the Higher Committee in the Damascus press, showed an income of £2,376,000 of which £2,080,000 were spent "for the war in Palestine."

Early in January 1948, the first detachments of the Liberation Army began to infiltrate into Palestine from Syria and Transjordan. On February 11th, the British delegate to the United Nations Palestine Commission admitted that infiltrated Arab bands were "increasingly ex-

---

* Prior to the U.N. partition decision, the Haifa Orphans Committee was conducting among Arabs resident in the United States a drive for the Committee's philanthropic purposes. Al-Bayan, Arabic biweekly published in Washington, on December 13, 1947, printed a cable of thanks to the Arabs of Chicago from the Mufti. In the same issue of the paper there appeared, however, an announcement that all collections for the Haifa Orphans Committee had been suspended to enable Jamal el-Husseini to tour Arab communities in the United States to raise funds for the struggle in Palestine.

ercising considerable administrative control over the whole area" of Samaria, and on March 3 the British colonial secretary told the House of Commons that 5,000 Arabs had invaded Palestine since November 29. On March 16 he added that Fawzi Kaukji, military leader of the Arab revolt of 1936–1939, had "slipped through the border guards" and arrived in Palestine.[51] (In fact, Kaukji had already arrived by February 12.)

There was constant rivalry and friction between the motley ingredients of the Arab military force. Lt. Col. Netanel Lorch relates in his competent study, *Israel's War of Independence, 1947–1949:*

The Mufti of Jerusalem was content to let the Arab League undertake the financing of the war effort and the mobilization of manpower in neighboring Arab countries, but he wished to maintain in his own hands effective control over all forces in Palestine and their activities. The Arab League was by no means inclined to recognize the Mufti as "the sole authority." As soon as the Mufti realized that, he began to act independently, appointing his own men as commanders in various areas of the country, who competed with commanders appointed by the Arab League. The Mufti's following among Palestinian Arabs was by no means negligible; yet, as long as the Arab League controlled the distribution of arms now being more and more urgently requested by delegations that arrived at the Damascus headquarters from most of the Arab cities of the country, the League could call the tune, and impose its own command.

Thereupon the Mufti went to Egypt and prevailed upon the King and government, who viewed with apprehension the possibility of Iraqi or Syrian domination of Palestine, to entrust him with most of the rifles in the Egyptian quota for the Liberation Army, over a thousand and their ammunition. The Mufti distributed them as he saw fit. Arms which had been handed by the military committee of the Arab League in Damascus to the Mufti's messengers for transfer to Haifa never reached their destination. The Arabs of Haifa had been notoriously lax in expression of loyalty to the Mufti. . . . There was no lack of rivalry among commanders at lower levels.

At one point, relates Lorch, the Mufti proposed a compromise solution; that two commanders should be appointed for each area, one by himself, the other by the Arab League. Ismael Safwat, an Iraqi general appointed by the League as inspector general of the Liberation Army, insisted on unity of command as a basic principle of war. It was finally decided that the southern part of Palestine and the mountains of Judea were the Mufti's domain. In addition, the force of Moslem Brothers from Egypt was stationed in the Gaza area under the command of Tariq el Afriki, a Sudanese close to the Mufti though not directly responsible to him. Yet, even after this compromise was agreed upon, says Lorch, Safwat "complained that the Mufti's men acted independently, put pressure on the villagers to join their units, and ignored the instructions of the Arab League, according to which all forces in Palestine were under the command of the Inspector General."

At that stage, Haj Amin seemed to be at the peak of his political career—an undisputed leader of the Arab national rebellion and future ruler of a Palestine Arab state. Even King Abdallah of Transjordan, an old-time enemy of the Husseinis, did not at that time dare to challenge Haj Amin's influence. Asked what prevented him from collaborating with the Mufti, he piously replied: "I do not doubt the good intentions of the Mufti, and we would welcome his visit to Amman. There can be no animosity among Arabs at present. May Allah bless the Mufti and give him peace."

The Mufti's "Charter"

On March 19, 1948, the United States abruptly reversed its positive stand in regard to partition. The American U.N. delegation asked the Security Council to suspend the activities of the U.N. Palestine Commission aimed at the implementation of the partition decision and advocated the establishment of a "temporary trusteeship regime" for Palestine.[53]

This turnabout of U.S. policy was widely interpreted as capitulation before Arab violence and an attempt to appease Arab opposition. Yet, on March 25, Haj Amin, speaking as chairman of the Arab Higher Committee and "for the Palestine Arabs in general," firmly rejected any form of trusteeship over Palestine. At a press conference of the Arab League in Cairo, a spokesman for the Mufti and the Committee declared that trusteeship was considered "another type of mandate" and that the Arabs would fight it just as they had fought against Zionism and the British mandate.[54]

The determined anti-trusteeship stand taken by the Mufti was generally considered as precluding the consent of the Arab League to the United States' new proposal. Gene Currivan cabled the *New York Times* from Cairo that

On matters pertaining to Palestine all League decisions must be unanimous so that trusteeship would be doomed as long as the Arab Higher Committee opposed it. Recent statements attributed to Abdul Rahman Azzam Pasha, League secretary-general, supporting the principle of trusteeship, were denied by the League spokesman. . . . The only solution was the establishment of an independent Arab state with a governmental system agreed upon by the inhabitants of Palestine.

If an Arab state were formed, the spokesman said, Jews would receive every right that any minority receives under democracy.

Five days later the Mufti ended his lengthy boycott of the United Nations. On March 30, Isa Nakley, New York representative of the Arab Higher Committee, handed to United Nations correspondents an "Arab Charter for Palestine," signed by Haj Amin el-Husseini in his capacity as chairman of the Higher Committee and circulated to all U.N. delegations; Faris el-Khouri, delegate of Syria, was asked to transmit it formally to the U.N. Security Council.[55]

In the "Charter," the Mufti outlined Arab aims as "the establishment of a sovereign state with a constitution based on democratic principles," combined with determination to prevent the establishment of Jewish sovereignty over "one inch of Palestine soil." Omitting any specific reference to partition, trusteeship, or any other particular solution of the Holy Land problem, the Mufti said the Arabs of Palestine "hereby solemnly affirm that they do not recognize the right of any foreign power or powers to deprive them of their natural right to independence or that their country should be subject to interference from or encroachment by foreigners."

In this first direct communication to the United Nations the Mufti expressed confidence that public opinion would "look with sympathy" upon Arab aims "when the true facts are revealed and the confusion created by the perfidious campaign of Zionists propaganda to discredit our noble national movement, is exposed." The Palestine Arabs, the Mufti insisted, aim "to obtain our independence and the freedom and liberty of our country, the establishment of a sovereign state with a constitution based on democratic principles which would include adequate safeguards for minorities, the safety of the holy places as well as all civil rights and freedoms." Such a state would "treat all citizens and peaceful residents of all creeds with justice as befits a truly democratic country."

The statement laid particular stress on the peaceful character and intentions of the Palestine Arabs, who are "God-fearing people" and "by nature a democratic people"; they "wish to declare that they are not opposed to Jews as Jews." Strife in Palestine, the Mufti explained, was not based upon religious sentiments or grounds but "is the result of the invasion of Palestine during the past twenty-seven years by hordes of immigrants from foreign lands, instigated and directed by the international Zionist cabal." The Arabs therefore "consider it their sacred duty to defend their country against this invasion and are determined to see to it that these invading hordes will never succeed in establishing their sovereignty on one inch of Palestine soil."

The Arabs, concluded the Mufti's statement, were anxious to "put an end to this tragedy in Palestine and to establish peace and order in the Holy Land. Peace, however, cannot reign in that country as long as justice is denied to its rightful inhabitants," it said.

Declining Fortunes

The Mufti's "Arab Charter for Palestine" was published at a time when his fortunes in the armed showdown with the nascent State of Israel appeared promising. But very soon, the military situation deteriorated. The relations between Haj Amin and Fawzi Kaukji, who headed the Liberation Army, were anything but cordial. Aware of the Mufti's antagonism Kaukji had, immediately after his arrival, contacted local anti-Mufti elements, did his best to win their friendship and to push Haj Amin's trusted aides out of important command posts. Not until the Arab League—the sponsors of the Liberation Army—had intervened, did he agree to have two of the Mufti's men take command in the Jerusalem and Jaffa sectors: Abdal-Qadir Husseini, who was later killed in the battle for Castel, and

Hassan Salameh, who was to meet his death in the bombing of his headquarters in Ramla.

"Of course we sought to turn these relations between the Mufti and Kaukji to our advantage," recalls Yehoshua Palmon, who spent years with the Middle East Department of the Jewish Agency and later with the Foreign Ministry of Israel: "We did our best to convince Kaukji that we [the Jews] were not sworn enemies of the Arabs . . . and that we were being pushed into war by the same Mufti elements that were making trouble for him."

The meeting between Palmon and Kaukji took place at the end of March 1948, at the latter's headquarters near Nablus. Surrounded by his staff of officers, Kaukji began by saying:

This man [Palmon] speaks our language, understands our ways and risked his life to come to us in the cause of peace. I personally do not see why we should not be able to arrive at an understanding with the Jews in the Middle East. We have inherited the sword from our fathers, and the Jews the book and a knowledge of commerce. We are cousins who can live together and complement each other.

In reply, Palmon insisted that the Jews, too, saw no reason why they should not be able to arrive at a settlement and an understanding with the Arabs on a basis of good will:

I explained that we had been driven to the present situation not because we did not want peace but because the man who now stood at the head of Palestine's Arabs, the Mufti of Jerusalem, had proved to be an individual on whom no one could depend, a treacherous hypocrite, an intriguer, and a layer of snares. Here I reminded Kaukji of the Mufti's intrigues against him, and how he had violated promises he had given during the disorders of 1921, 1936 and 1939. In view of this, it was only natural that in order to defend our lives and our honor we had had to take up arms and to fight.

According to Palmon's recollection, Kaukji appeared particularly impressed by the reference to the Mufti. He angrily dwelt on Haj Amin's intrigues against him in the field and described Abd al-Qadir and Hassan Salameh as "corrupt commanders and bandits who were not worthy of being called soldiers." Responding to Palmon's plea, Kaukji agreed to preserve the status quo on the central front and hinted that if the Haganah forces should attack Abd al-Qadir, the Liberation Army would not come to his aid. Palmon gathered from the conversation that Kaukji was interested in reducing the influence of the pro-Mufti circles.[55]

It very soon became obvious that both rival Arab armed forces were no match for the vigorous Jewish counter-offensive. Two major attacks on Jewish colonies (February 15 and April 4) ended in a fiasco. "As their moral enthusiasm waned, the Liberation Army became more interested in looting—often from the Arabs of Palestine," contemptuously recalled old soldier Glubb Pasha.[56] On April 9, Fawzi's forces were decisively routed. Mufti's irregulars, recruited mostly from among local Palestine Arabs, showed little fighting spirit and their military potential had proved to be much lower than anticipated: they were easily disheartened by any setback and had created no fighting force of their own to speak of. By mid-May 1948, Abdallah's Arab Legion and regular armed forces of Egypt, Syria, Lebanon, and Iraq took full charge of the war against Israel.

The Mufti as the head of the Higher Arab Committee had virtually disappeared from the military political scene. When the first (June 11, 1948) and then the second (July 18) cease-fire came, the area assigned by the United Nations to the prospective Arab State was in the hands of Jews, Egyptians, or Abdallah's Arab Legion; one-third of its inhabitants had fled, and the rest were exhausted, apathetic, or despairing; the Mufti's bands were beaten and dispersed.

This state of affairs suited Abdallah perfectly. Other heads of the Arab League states, in particular Egypt, were, however, opposed to his aggrandizement and supported the Mufti as counterweight to Transjordan's ambitions. In the last week of June, Abdallah paid a visit to King Farouk in Cairo and had an interview with the Mufti whom he had not seen since the latter's flight from Jerusalem in 1937; but no agreement was reached. When the United Nations mediator, Count Bernadotte, presented on July 28 a "peace plan" providing for the unification with Transjordan of the entire area allotted to the Arab State by the U.N. partition resolution, plus the entire Negev and the Jerusalem area, a thoroughly alarmed Egyptian government allowed the Mufti's Arab Higher Committee to entrench themselves in the Egyptian-occupied Gaza strip.

The relations between the Mufti's followers and the Transjordan Arab Legion were extremely strained. The Legion's British Commander, John Bagot Glubb, recalls that "some Arabs of the Mufti party" had said in Haifa to one of the Legion's officers: "We reckon the Arab Legion to be a greater danger to us than are the Jews." Though realizing that "the Mufti personally had doubtless hoped one day to be himself the ruler of Palestine and that the entry of Emir Abdallah into the field perhaps weakened his chances," Glubb nevertheless considered "such pettiness almost incredible . . . he [the Mufti] surely should have preferred any Arab to control Palestine rather than his alleged sworn enemies the Jews."[56] A similar item can be found in Sidney Nettleton Fisher's authoritative *The Middle East: A History,* which relates that during the war of 1948 "agents of the Arab League refused arms to other Arabs in Palestine if they were supporters of Arab families known to be inimical to Haj Amin el-Husseini, the ex-Mufti who looked upon himself as the future ruler of Arab Palestine."[57]

Ups and Downs

It is difficult to ascertain to what extent the Mufti's aspirations were well founded.

His early attempts to persuade the Arab League to establish a provisional Palestine Arab government-in-exile along the lines of his Arab Higher Committee were unsuccessful. Member-states of the League were apprehensive lest the formation of a full-fledged Palestine government might affect the precarious balance of power within the League; some apparently were not disposed to grant the Mufti undisputed control of the Arab war effort in Palestine, for which they were providing funds, military equipment, and manpower. Disregarding the opposition, the Mufti's cousin Jamal el-Husseini in January 1948 personally canvassed the Arab capitals for support. His mission proved to be a failure. Moreover, the conference of the Military Committee of the Arab League, held at Damascus, had officially shelved the proposal for a government-in-exile. It also decided to limit the Mufti's military authority to the naming of the military commander of the Jerusalem area. Despite Haj Amin's objections, Syrian President Kuwatly, who presided over the conference, prevailed with his proposal that military and political direction of the Palestine campaign be separated. The Mufti was also advised that in political affairs as well he would not be the sole arbiter in Arab Palestine.[58]

His plans and ambitions seemed to have been irretrievably frustrated. But he was patiently biding his time, waiting for some new opportunity. In mid-April 1948, the Cairo correspondent of the *New York Times* reported that "plans for a provisional government" were again under discussion and were "awaiting approval of Iraq and Saudi Arabia." The dispatch added: "It is understood that under the plans the exiled Mufti of Jerusalem, Haj Amin el-Husseini, would lead the provisional government until elections could be held and a legislative assembly formed." Arab League leaders, however, had apparently decided that at that early stage a "government-in-exile" would constitute too ambitious a proposition. On May 12, two days before the armies of the five Arab states had invaded Palestine, it was announced that after the end of the British mandate an "Arab civil administration" be set up in Palestine "under the Arab League, to function in cooperation with the occupying Arab forces."[59] In this scheme, no place for the Mufti was foreseen. It was later reported that soon after the end of the mandate the secretary of the Arab League, Abdul Rahman Azzam Pasha of Egypt, when asked about the Mufti's position, said flatly that the Mufti was finished with politics. His religious position was recognized, Azzam Pasha said, and he would be accepted as the spiritual authority but would never again play a political role.[60]

In July 1948, the League's Political Committee had officially approved the establishment of a "Provisional Palestine Administration," which was intended to deal not with political questions but with essential local services; it was hoped that this move would open a new era in which Palestinians would "direct their own affairs and assume the obligations of their independence." Haj Amin, who had long advocated the formation of a full-fledged Arab government for Palestine, was not included in this ten-member body. Yet Ahmed Hilmi Pasha, formerly treasurer of the Mufti's Arab Higher Committee and military governor of the Old City of Jerusalem, was nominated for chairman. At least four more trusted Mufti men held key positions: Jamal el-Husseini was in charge of internal public security; Dr. Hussein Khalidi headed health services; Raji Husseini, economic affairs; and Abdul Hadi Bey Auni, social affairs. On July 26, Egypt's premier, Mahmoud Nokrashi Pasha, declared that the Administrative Council for Palestine was "quite definitely to be regarded as a prelude to an Arab Government for Palestine."[61] A week later, Arab Higher Committee officials at Lake Success disclosed that plans were progressing rapidly for setting up an Arab government over Palestine; Jamal el-Husseini, vice-chairman of the Committee, was scheduled to fly to Damascus on August 14 "to confer with leaders of the Arab Higher Committee and the seven-nation Arab League . . . on plans for the long expected establishment of a single Arab government for the Holy Land." This time, the plans were again connected with the person of the Mufti. Summarizing the new situation, in retrospect, Sam Pope Brewer, cabled to the *New York Times* (October 10) from Paris: "Haj-Amin el-Husseini, the Mufti of Jerusalem, after being politically pigeonholed—supposedly for keeps—has popped up again as a figure to be reckoned with."

In Cairo, the "Supreme Guide" of the powerful Moslem Brotherhood, Sheikh Hassan el-Banna, threw his support behind the establishment of a Palestine Arab government based on the Mufti's Arab Higher Committee.[62] On September 17, at a meeting under the Mufti's chairmanship, the Higher Committee decided to send Ahmed Hilmi Pasha and Dr. Hussein Khalidi to Amman to confer with

King Abdallah of Transjordan on the projected formation of an Arab Palestinian government, on its seat and functions, as well as on the choice of men who would be added to the existing Arab League Administrative Council for Palestine to form a cabinet.[63]

However, Abdallah firmly refused to go along with the scheme, and promptly served notice that he would not permit formation of the proposed government "within the security zone of the Transjordan Government, which extends from the Egyptian Kingdom's frontiers to the frontiers of Syria and Lebanon." He argued that the establishment of a separate Arab government amounted to recognition of partition of Palestine. In a message to the Arab League, Abdallah insisted that "formation of such a government, in our opinion, would turn back Palestine to the disturbed situation prevailing before May 15":[64]

As the Arab Legion is now fighting alone in Jerusalem, where hostilities are still in force in spite of the truce, and as this central front, including Ramallah, is under authority of the Arab Legion and the situation is still confused, we cannot allow any other hands to interfere in the responsibility of our military government, especially those who are anxious to rule Palestine.

The last part of this long sentence clearly reveals that Abdallah's catagoric rejection of the entire scheme was largely motivated by his long-standing apprehension that through it the Mufti intended to carve out for himself a base of power in Palestine. As early as January 24, 1948, Abdallah bluntly told the Cairo daily *Akhbar al-Yom:* "I have no desire to be sandwiched between Shukri al-Kuwatli in Syria and Haj Amin el-Husseini in Palestine."

All-Palestine Government

Disregarding Transjordan's opposition, the Mufti's Arab Higher Committee announced on September 22 the formation of a "Palestine Government," with the seat at Gaza, headed by Ahmed Hilmi Pasha. Three days later, Hilmi, signing himself "Premier and Minister of Foreign Affairs pro-Interim" addressed the following telegram to the secretary general of the Arab League and to the foreign ministers of all Arab countries:

I have the honor to inform you that the inhabitants of Palestine, in the exercise of their right to determine their own fate and in accordance with the decisions of the Arab League Political Committee, have decided to declare all Palestine within the frontiers such as were established at the moment when the British mandate ended, an independent state ruled by a government known as the "Government of All Palestine," based on democratic principles. I take this occasion to express to Your Excellency the positive desire of my Government to strengthen the bonds of friendship and mutual assistance between our countries.[65]

All this was but a prelude to the triumphal installment of the Mufti, who arrived in Gaza on September 28, entering Palestine for the first time in eleven years. Accompanied by Hilmi Pasha and preceded by motorcycles and armored cars, he was driven ceremoniously, through crowded streets beflagged with Arab colors, to a hall in the Falah Peasants' School. Two days later, a self-constituted Palestine National Assembly unanimously elected him as its president and proclaimed the creation of a "free, democratic Arab State in the whole of Palestine." The Mufti was to act, in effect, as "President of the Republic."[66] Egypt, Syria, and Lebanon announced recognition of the Gaza regime on October 12; the Iraqi government followed suit five days later.*[67] "The first impression that news of the new Arab Government made on observers following Middle Eastern Politics was that the Mufti was 'in' again," reported Sam Pope Brewer in the *New York Times* of October 10, 1948.

Abdallah Steps In

What was lacking, however, was recognition by Transjordan, whose Arab Legion was in full control of the entire remaining area of the Arab part of Palestine, with the exception of the Egyptian-held Gaza strip. Abdallah reacted quickly and vigorously. On October 1, a Palestine Refugee Conference in Amman denounced the newly-formed Arab Palestine government and asked King Abdallah to negotiate for them and to put Palestine under his patronage. Five thousand delegates representing both Palestine refugees and native Transjordanians passed a resolution asking the Arab League and the Egyptian government not to support the Gaza government on the ground that such support would mean recognition of partition.[67] The Transjordan authorities were aware that the Mufti was staging a comeback. Glubb Pasha, the commander of the Arab Legion, complained that the emergence of the "Arab Government of All Palestine" had

* The United States withheld recognition. Acting Secretary of State Robert A. Lovett, on October 13, 1948, told a news conference in Washington that the United States had already recognized *de facto* the State of Israel which included territory claimed by the Gaza government. The Gaza regime, he added, also had "not conformed to the normal attributes of government": it had not held elections and it did not control the area over which it claimed sovereignty. (*New York Times*, October 14, 1948.) Great Britain, bound by a treaty with Abdallah, had also refused recognition.

"revived the courage of the Mufti's armed retainers in Jerusalem. This organization had dubbed itself *Al Jihad al Muqqaddas*, or the Holy War. . . . The greater part of it had collected in the country north of Jerusalem, where it had taken little or no part in the fighting, but was menacingly positioned across the Arab Legion communications." On October 3, Glubb made this entry in his diary:

. . . behind our front line, the Mufti's emissaries are raising armed forces, which are drilling and training, but not taking part in holding the line. Now that the Arab League has declared a number of the Mufti's henchmen to be the sole legal government of All Palestine, his retainers in Jerusalem have become distinctly hostile to us.

On the same day, the Transjordan Ministry of Defense ordered that "all bodies of armed men in the area held by the Arab Legion must either be under the orders of the Legion or must be disbanded and disarmed forthwith." "Orders were issued to surround and disarm them; the operation was carried out and no opposition was encountered," related Glubb Pasha dryly.[69]

Two months later, on December 1, an assembly representing the national leaders of Arab Palestine under Transjordan occupation met in Jericho; it urged the immediate unification of the east and west bank of the Jordan under the crown of Abdallah. The Transjordan Parliament unanimously approved the Jericho resolutions on December 13, and a week later, December 20, Abdallah did what the British government had failed to do since 1937: Haj Amin was replaced as mufti of Jerusalem by Sheikh Husam ad Din Jarallah, former president of the Palestine Moslem Court of Appeal.[70] Early in 1949 there followed the Sheikh's appointment as president of the Moslem Supreme Council. Haj Amin was officially stripped of his two key positions and titles. Finally, on

August 14, 1949, Ragheb Bey Nashashibi, former mayor
of the city of Jerusalem and an arch-foe of the ex-Mufti,
was appointed Minister of Refugees and Deputy Governor of Arab Palestine, with the title of Pasha.[71]

Disintegrating Gaza Regime

Abdallah was obviously gaining in his showdown with
the Mufti, whose Gaza regime had begun to disintegrate.
Already on December 20, 1948, Auni Bey Abdul Hadi,
leader of the *Istiqlal* (Independence) Party and minister
of social affairs, joined Minister of Education Akram
Fu'aitir in announcing their resignation; both offered their
services to Abdallah.[72]* The rump "government" soon
left Gaza—its last foothold on Palestine soil—and established headquarters at Heliopolis near Cairo, where it led
the shadowy existence of a tolerated government-in-
exile.† Haj Amin's position was also jeopardized by his
close association with Hassan el-Banna, the leader of the
fanatical Moslem Brotherhood. During World War II,
both were deeply involved in espionage and sabotage directed against the Allied forces. The Brotherhood was
from the beginning particularly vociferous on the Palestine
issue and—with the Fascist *Misr al-Fatat* Party—was
among the first Egyptian bodies actually to recruit volunteers for the *Jihad* (Holy War) in Palestine. Charging

---

* "This was a heyday for turncoats, and plenty of the Mufti's old followers were edging on King Abdallah's reclame." (Ann Dearden,
Jordan [London, 1958], p. 77.)

† By the time [February 1949] that they [the Egyptians] signed an
armistice with Israel, their protégé, the Gaza government of Haj Amin
Husseini was more or less discredited. Removed to a modest villa in a
Cairo suburb, it survived only as a focus for anti-Abdallah propaganda
and conspiracies. (Dearden, *op. cit.*, p. 76.)

the Moslem Brotherhood with responsibility for a week-long riot in Cairo in July 1948, which had left 250 dead, Premier Nokrashi Pasha outlawed this organization. Two weeks later he was assassinated; other terrorist acts followed. Haj Amin's ties with the Brotherhood had become utterly compromising. In January 1949, Ibrahim Abdul Hadi, the then Egyptian Premier, urged him either to declare his "Gaza Government" dissolved or leave Egypt. The Mufti then sent to Beirut Ahmad Shūkeiri, a member of his "Administration," with the request to be allowed to move his government to Lebanon "until circumstances change in Egypt." The Lebanese government's evasive reply was that no decision could be made until after the next session of the parliament. When the U.N. Palestine Conciliation Commission called a conference of seven Arab States, on March 21, 1949, to consider the Arab refugee problem, it extended to the ex-Mufti an invitation to appear before it on March 24—the day set aside for the representatives of nongovernmental groups. The Transjordan government protested to the P.C.C. against the granting of even this second-grade status, arguing that the ex-Mufti did in no way represent the Palestine Arabs. Haj Amin had on his part telegraphed to the Commission claiming to be the only representative of the Palestine Arabs, demanding to be heard on equal footing with the delegations of the Arab States, and voicing dissatisfaction with being invited as an unofficial, nongovernmental representative. Speaking for the Commission, Mark Erthridge, its American chairman, replied that he saw no reason for changing the Commission's original decision. Haj Amin nevertheless came to Beirut in the hope of somehow gaining equal treatment with the delegations of the Arab states. When this attempt failed, he announced that he would boycott the Commission's hearings. But this intran-

sigent policy, which had often served him so well during
the days of the British administration in Palestine, did not
impress the Conciliation Commission; it simply did not
take notice of the boycott declaration. All that Haj Amin
could do was to send a strongly worded protest to Trygve
Lie, the U.N. secretary general, who, in turn, ignored it.
No Arab government supported the protest.

For a time the Mufti's Gaza regime was also excluded
from the Arab League councils. The Near East Arabic
Radio reported that it was not invited to the October 1949
session of the League in Cairo; Haj Amin's protest telegram remained unanswered. Similarly, no representative
of the Gaza regime was invited to join the League's Palestine Committee composed of representatives from each
member-state, which, for the first time in the history of
the Arab League, received full authority to deal exclusively with the Palestine problem, to take final decisions
and arrange for their implementation.

Rescued From Oblivion

This period of decline was, however, short-lived. Abdallah's obvious determination to annex parts of Western
Palestine held by his Arab Legion, and persistent rumors
of his peace negotiations with Israel had created a new
situation which rescued Haj Amin from oblivion and once
again brought him to the fore of Arab political life.

Abdallah's Arab rivals took vigorous action against his
ambitions. Apart from Yemen, all members of the Arab
League came out with strong statements condemning the
annexation move. Egypt instigated "indignant protests by
the 250,000 Arab refugees" in the Gaza area. It was but
natural that Haj Amin had eagerly joined in the anti-

Abdallah crusade. Following an all-night session of the "Gaza Government's" cabinet in Cairo, he declared that the unification scheme was not binding on the Palestine Arabs and was "nothing but an evil plot"; the "real Arabs of Palestine," who were "true nationalists," would continue the Holy War. The Beirut correspondent of the London *News Chronicle* reported that the Mufti was about to start indiscriminate terrorist activities against supporters of King Abdallah. Members of the Transjordan Cabinet had received letters threatening them with death if they continued to work against the separate existence of the Mufti-led Arab Palestine, and Transjordan authorities in the Arab areas of Palestine made large-scale arrests of Haj Amin's partisans charging them with "subversive propaganda."

This violent opposition to Abdallah's expansionist plans secured for Haj Amin and for his Gaza regime the support of most Arab and Moslem countries. Nokrashi Pasha, the Egyptian prime minister, solemnly declared that "Egypt has not and never will change its attitude toward the Provisional Arab Government in Gaza, the only body authorized to represent the Arabs of Palestine." As far away as Pakistan, Chaudhry Khaliquazzaman, president of the powerful Moslem League, announced that Pakistan would continue to support the policies of Haj Amin. He has become a valuable asset to the Arab League in its struggle against Abdallah's plans and ambitions. It was in the interests of the League's major partners, in particular Egypt's and Saudi Arabia's, to enhance the status of the Mufti's Gaza regime.

Transjordan political circles strongly resented the stand taken by these two Arab sister countries. The Amman paper *An Nahda* accused them of supporting "the former Nazi spy, the ex-Mufti of Jerusalem, who sacrificed his people in order to fill his own pockets, and who is now ready once more to plunge the country into hatred and internal war in order to achieve his ambitions." Transjordan authorities ordered the disbandment of a big refugee camp near Nablus whose inmates—mostly refugees from Jaffa and Ramleh—had been charged with carrying pro-Mufti propaganda under the guidance of Haj Amin's agents. Several suspects were arrested. *An Nahda* urged that further stringent measures be taken against the infiltration of pro-Mufti elements from Egyptian-occupied territory to the Hebron area. In December 1949, higher Transjordan and Israel Army officers met to discuss combined means to fight attacks by well-armed and uniformed gangs, officered by Mufti supporters and financed by Arab countries which backed him against Abdallah.

Transjordan's bitter opposition had, however, merely strengthened Egypt's support for the Mufti. As early as November 1, 1948, Bahad el Din Tukan, Transjordan's Minister to Egypt, reluctantly acknowledged, following the second meeting of the Arab League Council in Cairo, that the Mufti's All-Palestine (Gaza) government "has the right to vote in the Council because it was recognized by a majority of the Arab States."[73] This *de facto* status was formally legalized at the spring 1950 session of the Council. On March 25, Egyptian Premier Mustafa Nahas Pasha proposed that a representative of "our sister state Palestine" be admitted to the meetings in accordance with a special provision of the League Charter. Two days later, the Council, disregarding Transjordan's protests, invited the "All-Palestine Government" to attend the sessions.[74] To the Mufti this was a most welcome vindication of his claim to be considered the sole representative of Arab Palestine. He fared less satisfactorily in the Transjordanian parliamentary elections, held in April, 1950, which were conducted on both sides of the Jordan River. Among the few elected pro-Mufti candidates were Kamel Areikat, former deputy commander on the Jerusalem front and commander of the *Futuwa* organization; Dr. Mustapha Bushniak, who was once exiled from Palestine and was an active member of the Husseini Party; and Anwar Nusseibieh, who fought in Jerusalem under the Mufti's direction. On the other hand, in Christian Bethlehem, the only Moslem candidate to win was Sheikh Abdul Fatah el-Darwish, the well-known leader of Malha village, who was terrorized by Husseini gangs because of his good relations with the Jews of Jerusalem.[75]

Undeterred by threats of expulsion from the Arab League, Abdallah proceeded with the final annexation of the parts of Western Palestine conquered by the Arab Legion. Faced with the *fait accompli*, Lebanon, Syria, and Iraq at the last moment refused to vote for Jordan's expulsion, and only Saudi Arabia supported the Egyptian expulsion proposal. On April 13, 1950, the Council of the Arab League adopted a face-saving resolution "to treat the Arab part of Palestine annexed by Jordan as a trust in its hands until the Palestine case is fully solved in the interests of its inhabitants."[76]

Having lost its undeclared war on Abdallah, Egypt also lost much of its interest in the Mufti, whose main sponser it had been. Yet Haj Amin was not prepared to resign himself to political oblivion. He vigorously continued on his own the crusade against both Israel and his adversaries in the Arab camp.

In May 1950, the Israeli government disclosed that a "military organization for the liberation of Palestine" had recently been formed by agents of the Mufti in Syria and Lebanon, seeking to mobilize and train Arab refugees for irregular military operations against Israel. A pamphlet distributed in various Arab countries called on all Palestine Arabs, especially youth of military age, "to join our ranks and be ready to join the holy war after the completion of our preparations for returning to the motherland.[77] This appeal apparently found response. Glubb Pasha relates that Jordan authorities believed that the Mufti was organizing refugee raids in Israel from Jordan, in cooperation with "certain extremist organizations in Egypt and Syria." When, in March 1950, Glubb Pasha saw an Israeli complaint that two Jews were found murdered, he asked: "Could this be the Mufti's work, in the hope of embroiling Jordan with Israel?"[78] In a "Report and an Appeal to the Arab Emigrants in America," published in Arabic newspapers in the United States, Haj Amin urged the Arabs not to despair but to continue to support his Higher Committee, which had a two-point program by which it expected to retrieve what the Arabs had lost. The first: to keep the Palestinian Arab refugees alive by assuring them of food and shelter; and the second: to organize and prepare the Arabs residing in Palestine, and those who were refugees in the other Arab countries, for the reconquest of their land so that they might take their part in the future battle to retrieve their lost country.[79]

Assassination of King Abdallah

On July 20, 1951, King Abdallah of Jordan, the Mufti's arch-enemy in the Arab camp, who had successfully blocked Haj Amin's political ambitions in the crucial period 1948–1950, was shot to death at point-blank range as he was entering the Dome of the Rock in the Old City of Jerusalem for the Friday services. The assassin, a twenty-one-year-old tailor's apprentice by the name of Mustafa Shukry Ashu, was killed on the spot by Abdallah's bodyguard. He was reported to have been a supporter of a pro-Mufti fanatical terrorist group known as the "Holy War Organization." It was largely believed that the Mufti and his Arab Higher Committee had a hand in the King's assassination. Sir Alec S. Kirkbride, who was for many years Abdallah's adviser and friend, asserts that "the tragedy was not unexpected; the followers of the ex-Mufti . . . had determined to kill the King years before on the grounds that he was a traitor to the Arab cause."[80] Both the Mufti and the Committee heatedly denied any responsibility. Yet among the six men sentenced to death by a Jordan military court for complicity in the assassination plot, one, Dr. Mousa Abdullah el-Husseini, was a cousin of the Mufti; two brothers, Tewfiq Saleh el-Husseini and Dr. Daoud el-Husseini, were acquitted for the lack of evidence.[81]

The Mufti in turn asserted that the assassins of King Abdallah were "completely under the control" of Glubb Pasha, the British commander of the Arab Legion; he charged "the Arab Legion and the Jordan police, in other words Glubb Pasha," with "killing, robbing and persecuting Palestine Arabs in Jordan, and attacking refugee camps." Referring to the British "hints" that he was connected with the "lamentable assassination" of King Abdallah, he insisted that they were proferred to serve British "imperialist interests" in the Arab world by the creation of feuds among the Arab leaders. As a result, he said, the Jordan government had persecuted his relatives and friends and had asked Cairo to limit his activities. "Individual acts of terrorism or political assassinations never did and never will enter the program of the Palestine Arab Higher Committee or its leader," the Mufti told a press conference in Cairo.[82] Prior to that, he had sent on behalf of the Arab Higher Committee a telegram to the heads of the Arab states and to the secretary general of the Arab League, Azzam Pasha, accusing the Jordanian government of a "brutal campaign of terror" and of massacring and jailing "defenseless Palestine Arabs all over the land." Arab kings and presidents were asked to intervene urgently to check the "slaughter of innocents" and force the Jordan authorities to confine their acts to an "honest, legal investigation into the lamentable assassination."[83]

"This telegram will have a familiar ring to those who followed the ex-Mufti's pre-war and wartime activities in Palestine," dryly commented the Cairo correspondent of the London *Times*.[84] On August 2, the government of Jordan protested to Egypt against the renewed political activities of Haj Amin, and especially against his allegations that acts of "terror" had been carried out by the Jordanian army and police against the Arabs of Palestine. Jordan expressed astonishment that the Egyptian government should allow such activities to be conducted on Egyptian soil, and warned of the danger of further deterioration in Egyptian-Jordanian relations. Later, Jordan notified the Arab League that it would accept no League interference in the country's internal affairs.[85]

It is a moot point whether, and to what extent, the Mufti was directly involved in the assassination of King Abdallah. There is no evidence that he was.* But disappearance of his formidable adversary and the troubled situation it had created, undoubtedly offered him a welcome opportunity for political maneuvering. The London *Evening Standard* reported on July 31 that the Mufti was

* John Marlowe insists that Haj Amin was "morally if not legally responsible for the murder of Abdallah." (*Arab Nationalism and British Imperialism: A Study in Power Politics* [New York, 1961], p. 92.)

transferring his Cairo headquarters to the advance headquarters at Gaza, on Palestinian soil. It was expected that
his strategy would be twofold—to create a quarrel between Abdallah's sons and heirs, Talal and Naif, and to try
to subvert the Jordanian Arab Legion. Israeli sources also
related that Haj Amin was busier than ever building up
his para-military organizations, increasing recruitment
among the Arab refugees, enlisting numerous former Nazi
officers and privates, and intensifying traffic in small
arms for groups known to be linked with him.[86] Both the
U.S. State Department and the Pentagon were reportedly
"worried about what's happening in Jordan." Piecing together available information, Intelligence sources spoke
of "the Mufti's sinister plan":

A stream of agents are filtering into Jordan for the purpose
of stirring up turmoil and violence among the 460,000 Arab
refugees. The Mufti's deliberate intent is to compel the Jordan
government to resort to force to suppress these secretly-insti-
gated uprisings. The government's instrument for doing that
would be its famed British-trained, supported and led Legion.

This action, in turn, would provide the Mufti with grounds
for raising a hue and cry for help for the refugees by other
Arab countries—specifically his co-plotters, Egypt and Syria,
which would be waiting to march into Jordan and divide it
among themselves, if they could get away with such a grab.

Inevitable outcome of this plot would be fierce war throughout the Near East. . . . Russia, always fishing in troubled
waters, would be sure to stick in its insatiable paw.

After that, the fat would be in the fire—which is exactly
what the Mufti wants. He thrives on violence and chaos.

It is now pretty definitely established that secret ties exist
between him and Moscow, and that they are playing one another's game against the West in the explosive Near East cock-
pit.[87]

Less catagoric in his assessment of the Mufti-Communist
link, C. L. Sulzberger nevertheless admitted in the *New*

York Times that "the only great power to benefit by King Abdallah's murder will be the Soviet Union, whose interest in the Near East as a whole has shown visible signs of increasing":

Whether Haj Amin actually has a secret understanding with the Communists is difficult to say. It is noteworthy that his nephew, Dr. Khalil Budayri, is recognized as one of the leading Communists in the Near East and an important member of the [communist-inspired] Arab League of National Liberation.

For more than a year it has been known that the Mufti's group and the Communists have been working along parallel lines. Communism in both Israel, where the Stalinist faction is rather small, and in Jordan has been seeking the establishment of an independent state of Arab Palestine.

Such a country would become a Soviet satellite in the heart of the Near East. Presumably the Mufti has played ball to a degree on that project as a means to his end—control over all Palestine.[88]

In the spring of 1953, tentative attempts were made to heal the rift between the Mufti and the Jordan government. The Old City Arab daily *Falastin* reported in March that as a result of "a series of telephone conversations" between Cairo and Amman, the Jordan capital may expect the visit of "an unofficial Arab personality of the utmost importance,"—a commonly accepted way of referring to Haj Amin in Jordan where his name is proscribed. Two months later, the Mufti's cousin, Jamal el-Husseini, was permitted to visit the Old City of Jerusalem, and Radio Damascus' Hebrew transmission said on May 18 that the Mufti himself would be allowed to pray in the Old City's holy places during the high Moslem holiday of Ramadan. Official Amman sources, however, refused to confirm the report. The Mufti's proscription remained in force.[89]

The Pan-Islam Card

It was during the period of his decline in the Arab Middle East that Haj Amin made a determined attempt to recoup his political fortunes on a wider front of pan-Islamism, which had always been one of the basic components of his political concept and plan of action. As mentioned in Chapter One, he had in 1931 convened in Jerusalem an all-Moslem conference and was elected its president. In his campaign for an Arab Palestine he frequently made appeals to world-wide Moslem solidarity and support, both political and financial. But during the years 1920–1950 this aspect of Haj Amin's strategy had, on the whole, played a minor and subordinated role in his over-all effort, and was overshadowed by the more immediate struggle for (a) Arab independence in Palestine and (b) concerted action of the neighboring Arab nations aimed primarily at the achievement of this goal. Priority belonged to the local (Palestine) and ethnic (pan-Arab) outlook. It was only when both had become dimmed that Haj Amin decided to play the Pan-Islamic card that he had neglected for so long.

This move coincided with the general revival, in a somewhat "modernized" form, of the old slogan of the "unity of the Moslem world," stretching from Morocco across the Middle East to the Indian sub-continent and inhabited by an estimated 400 million souls.

The sponsor of this scheme in the Western world for more than half a century was Great Britain, who had pinned her hopes on securing her imperial position in Asia and Africa on the formation of a consolidated pan-Islamic movement. She had accordingly encouraged Abdul Hamid's effort in this direction. On the collapse of the

Ottoman Empire after World War I and the establishment of a pronounced secular regime in Turkey, the British policy makers switched over their main support to the idea of a pan-Arabic Union, based on ethnic—as distinct from religious—principles. They had, however, never fully abandoned the original concept of securing British influence throughout the Moslem world through rallying all Moslems round a pan-Islamic body.

By the end of the fifth decade of this century, the British-sponsored Arab League, created in 1945, had in more than one respect turned out to be a great disappointment. Its military weakness, which was so dramatically exposed in the defeat of the combined Arab armies by Israel, was only the first and most spectacular manifestation of the League's intrinsic shortcomings. Even more alarming loomed the apparently insurmountable clashes of dynastic aspirations; the appalling rise of violence and political assassinations; the corruptness of the quickly alternating political regimes. The peak of disappointment was reached when it was realized in the Anglo-American world that what they had hoped to be a bedrock of firm resistance to Soviet penetration was degenerating into a treacherous quicksand of shifting loyalties.

The masterminds of British policy had thus begun to look for another, and in their opinion more reliable, alignment of forces in the East.

The revived pan-Islamic scheme centered around Pakistan.

As early as July 1949, it was reported from London that the idea was being advanced to call upon Pakistan to take over the leadership of the Middle Eastern countries and play the same role there as India was playing in South-East Asia. As "the only modern Moslem country with an English liberal tradition," Pakistan, it was believed, could influence the development of other Moslem countries, economically and politically. The *Hindustan Times* of New Delhi said ironically that Pakistan was "being cast for the role Prussia had played in the unification of Germany."

Pakistan's political leaders eagerly responded to this suggestion. They had from the very beginning conceived of their own statehood as a Moslem theocracy and officially defined Pakistan as an "Islamic State." Deeply distrustful of neighboring India with her teeming population of 340 million, Pakistan hoped to bolster her position by being able to rely on—in addition to that of her own 80 million souls—the sympathy and support of the 400 millions of the "Moslem world" in her acute and explosive conflict with India over the Kashmir issue.

Those in control of the Arab League had for a time been eager to follow the Pakistan lead as a vehicle for the establishment of a pan-Islamic "third force" capable of influencing the course of international politics. The one most anxious to join Pakistan in the creation of such a force was Egypt, the seat and backbone of the Arab League. Dr. Bey, the Egyptian ambassador in Karachi, solemnly declared that "Kashmir is now Egypt's problem." In return, Pakistan gratefully announced that the Suez Canal was her problem, and Fazlur Rahman, Pakistan's minister of education, told Cairo newsmen that "Pakistan was ready to withdraw from the [British] Commonwealth if that can help to solve the many problems of Moslem countries, including Egypt's effort for the evacuation of British troops from the Suez Canal and the unity of the Nile Valley."

A ready-made name for such a prospective bloc of states had been offered by Chaudhry Khaliquazzaman, the Pakistan Moslem League leader, who in 1949 undertook a missionary tour of the Middle East with a grandiose scheme of uniting all the Moslem countries from Karachi to Cairo, into an Islamic Federation. "If," he said, "the Jews can be proud of calling their state 'Israel,' why should we feel shy of calling our state 'Islamistan'?"

The Champion of Pakistan

The stage was thus set for Haj Amin's appearance in a new and apparently promising hypostasis: that of an all-Moslem supreme spiritual-political leader, and specifically of a champion of Moslem Pakistan's cause, harnessed to his own cause in Palestine.

In the fall of 1950, the leading Karachi daily, *Dawn*, reported that

the Grand Mufti of Jerusalem, this great Arab leader, has firmly reiterated his faith in the return of the Holy Land to the children of the soil, and has reminded 400 million Moslems in the world over that Palestine is and should be their special concern. . . . No power in the world can underestimate this mighty bloc, nor can it be prevented from occupying its rightful place.[90]

It was in this spirit that Haj Amin had accepted the invitation to attend—and to preside over—the annual session of the World Moslem Conference to be held early in 1951 for the second consecutive year in Karachi. Enthusiastically greeting the Conference, *Dawn* wrote: "Karachi, and indeed all Pakistan, is proud to be able to welcome so distinguished and widely representative an assemblage of Moslem notables. There is special cause for gratification that the legendary figure of the Grand Mufti is not only among them but will grace the presidential chair."[91]

Haj Amin's visit was converted by Pakistan's leadership

into an event of great national significance. The *Tribune* of Ambala (India) complained that it "was deliberately exploited . . . to keep up the morale of the Moslem masses on the Kashmir issue. His tour was heralded with pre-arranged demonstrations and impression was sought to be given to the masses that the ex-Mufti was the saviour of Islam. He himself played the game well and tried to win cheap applause by making wholly irresponsible speeches on Kashmir." The "Kashmir Liberation Movement" bestowed on him the "freedom of Kashmir."[*][92]

The Indian press, which deeply resented the Mufti's association with Pakistan, was blunt in describing his waning influence in Egypt, where he had been residing since June 1946, and in the Arab League councils. The *Sunday Standard* of Bombay, in the early spring of 1951 wrote:

. . . All has not been well with the ex-Mufti. In spite of frequent photographs of his, supposedly having important talks over cups of coffee with Arab dignitaries, it is rapidly becoming apparent that this perennial trouble-causer is speedily losing whatever influence or prestige he once enjoyed.

Bazaar gossip in Egypt has it that the Mufti's vanity was sorely wounded when he was not even consulted during the recent Arab League discussion in Cairo. The Islamic World Conference will perhaps succeed in restoring his deflated ego.

New Delhi's *Hindustan Times* also registered the fact that "there is no account or other evidence of the ex-Mufti receiving or being received by any of the Arab Premiers or other high personages who were in Cairo for the

[*] Later, at a press conference in Damascus, Haj Amin denied rumors that he had accepted Pakistani nationality. "It is a misunderstanding," he said. "I was honored by being presented with the title of honorary citizen of Karachi, Lahore, and other cities I visited. That had been misrepresented as meaning that I assumed Pakistani nationality. Untrue also are reports that I have been appointed to a post in Pakistan." (*Civil and Military Gazette*, Lahore, quoted in *India and Israel*, July 1951.)

[Arab] League meeting; hence," concluded the paper, "the very special interest attaching to the 'warmest of welcomes' accorded to him and to the 'uninterrupted flow of visitors' that had 'rendered him homage' at his [Karachi] hotel." Another Bombay daily, the *Times of India*, acknowledging that Haj Amin was still "continuing to pull strings and exercise his religious influence for political ends," stressed that "Pan-Islam provides him with the means of staging a come-back, and he knows it."[93]

The Aftermath of the All-Islam Conferences

The much heralded World Moslem Conference—*Motamar-i-Islami*—convened in Karachi in February 1951, with Haj Amin in the chair. Attended by delegates from twenty-eight Moslem countries, it was dominated by two main issues dear to the hearts of its organizers: Kashmir and Palestine. Its mood was most eloquently expressed by a delegate from Syria who, in a histrionic performance, promised his co-religionists that he would be with them "sword in hand" on the battlefields of either Kashmir or Palestine. In his presidential address Haj Amin told the delegates that it was "the bounden duty of the entire Moslem world to liberate Palestine." The Moslems, he said, should not despair but should try to regain Palestine. If the "enemies of Islam" remained rulers of Palestine there would come a time when they would try to conquer other Moslem countries one by one. At the closing session, the Conference adopted a resolution urging support for the stand taken by the Moslems of Palestine for "safeguarding their rights and launching a full struggle to meet the aggressor." Other resolutions suggested that an act of aggression against one Moslem country should be regarded as an act of aggression against all and that the Moslem peoples and governments should unite to defend their tents, peoples, holy places, and lands. Haj Amin called for the formation of an Islamic bloc, saying that "the world should not be apprehensive about such a bloc, since Islam is a religion of peace."[94]

The Pakistani press was highly gratified by the Conference and the Mufti's stand. *Dawn* quoted him as saying that "the birth of Pakistan meant the establishment of a true *Dar ul Islam*" (homeland of Islam). He and other delegates to the *Motamar* "regarded Pakistan's stability as the strength of the whole Moslem world."[95] India's press was understandably critical. Wrote *The Searchlight* of Patna:

Haj Amin el-Husseini, former Mufti of Palestine, was obviously playing to the Pakistani gallery when he remarked at Karachi the other day that by all canons of justice Kashmir should belong to Pakistan. . . . It is doubtful, however, if leaders of the type of Haj Amin el-Husseini really represent the views and feelings of their own people. A priest without a parish and a political leader without following and support, so reminiscent of our [Indian] Rajas and Nawabs without an inch of land, the Mufti cannot presume to speak for the great Arab nation. Much of the misfortune that came the Arab way in Palestine was wrought by el-Husseini's blundering leadership of the now virtually defunct Arab League. The ex-Mufti gave a religious coloring to what was essentially a nationalistic cause.

Bombay's *Free Press Journal* said accusingly: "The *Motamar-i-Islami* used to be a deeply respected cultural organization, meeting in Mecca in annual session for the exchange of views and Islamic knowledge; today it is being utilized by a few disgruntled Arab elements to set the Moslem world aflame." The *Hindustan Times* (New Delhi) added: "Throughout history Islam has suffered from the ambitions of military and political adventurers. Those who cast people steeped in ignorance and poverty for ambitious world roles are merely playing to the gallery, or are grinding their own axe." The *Indian News Chronicle* (New Delhi) confidently said: "Whatever the ex-Mufti of Jerusalem has touched thus far has turned to dust, and we hope his advocacy of Kashmir for Pakistan will meet with a similar fate."[96]

No less critical was the reaction in other countries.

In Iraq, which still vividly remembered the role the Mufti had played in the May 1941 rebellion, the press warned Pakistan against "misguided admiration" for Haj Amin and criticized his nomination as president of the World Islamic Conference. The Baghdad morning daily *Al Sijil* described him as "enemy and useless idol that should be smashed." The weekly *Garandal*, asking "What is the ex-Mufti of Palestine doing in Pakistan?" recalled that he was "responsible for fomenting disputes among the Arabs," and advised Pakistan "to stop harming herself" by getting involved in his activities.

Outspokenly hostile were non-Arab Moslem countries. Afghanistan, which had an acute conflict of long standing with Pakistan over the so-called Pushtunistan, a hotly disputed area on the Afghan-Pakistan frontier, was, as expected, strongly inimical toward a Pakistan-engineered Islamistan. Indonesia followed the leadership of New Delhi rather than of Karachi. The most deliberate opposition came, however, from Turkey with her 20 million Moslems. She insisted on being regarded as a European, not an eastern nation. Ankara's ambition—then as now—was to belong to the Atlantic Treaty Organization and it had little understanding and sympathy for a purely religious vision of Islamistan. The leading Turkish daily *Ulus* said bluntly: "It is vain to nourish a project of pan-Islamic union. Cooperation between Turkey and the Arab States cannot be established upon a religious basis." The Istanbul evening newspaper *Aksam* said: "We consider that the union of the Islamic nations based exclusively on religion is not only useless, but also harmful."

The leading New York Arabic daily *Al-Hoda* published on April 8 a vigorous condemnation of the Islamistan scheme from the Lebanese point of view, written by its political correspondent in Beirut, Salah Lebky. The article insisted that "Lebanon should never go to 'Karachi'—or will lose her identity if she does."

Unwanted in Cairo?

Undaunted by adverse reaction, Haj Amin continued playing the pan-Islamic card, with Pakistan as the center of gravity.

Early in 1952 it was announced that a World *Ulama* (a body of Moslem doctors of the law who interpret the Koran) Conference would be held in Karachi; of the hundred invitations sent to Moslem countries, fifty-four had been accepted. This was a forum the Mufti was eager to attend, in particular as his position in Egypt was obviously becoming uncertain and delicate. Describing him as "a man of mystery," Michael James, the *New York Times* correspondent in Karachi, reported on February 29 that the Mufti had appeared in Pakistan's capital one day the previous month:

No one seems to know just how he got here. Heavily guarded, the pink-cheeked and neatly bearded Mufti spent a few days in Karachi's largest hotel. He then disappeared. He was somewhere in Karachi but no one knew exactly where.

He appeared at a number of minor conferences held by Moslem religious leaders here during the month and even made a few public appearances. The conferences, ostensibly, resulted in the adoption of platitudinous resolutions supporting Islamic unity.

It is impossible to know exactly where the Mufti obtains his money here. Several embassies guess that he suggests that wealthy Moslems make donations, although there are reports that the Mufti, whose external political affiliations are regarded as flexible, may benefit from financial aid from interested nations.[97]

The fact that the world conference of Moslem religious leaders would be held in Karachi rather than in Cairo, where previously it had been scheduled to take place, made competent observers of the local scene conclude that this change was effected in compliance with the wishes of the Egyptian government of Aly Maher Pasha, which was determined to cut down on the effectiveness of the fanatical Moslem Brotherhood, known to be closely connected with, and influenced by, the Mufti not only on points of religion but also in matters of political nature.

There was even a persistent rumor that after Haj Amin's arrival in Karachi he had been advised by the Cairo government that he would not be permitted to return to Egypt, and that he was compelled to ask Pakistan for asylum. Karachi authorities "refused to make any comment" as to the accuracy of this report, though it "became generally known" among members of the diplomatic corps. The Pakistan Foreign Office merely said that its deliberation on the subject was "top secret." It was recalled that the late Prime Minister Liaquat Ali Khan of Pakistan once offered Pakistani citizenship to the Mufti, probably as a move to win support among the Arab countries. At that time, Haj Amin had turned down the offer. According to a United Press dispatch of February 29 from Cairo, the Egyptian Ministry of Foreign Affairs also refused to comment on reports from Karachi that the Mufti, who had been residing in Egypt, would not be permitted to return and had therefore asked to be permitted to stay in Pakistan. A similar attitude was adopted by associates of the Mufti in Cairo: they would neither verify nor deny the report.[98]

But the next day, March 1, the United Press reported from Karachi that the Mufti himself categorically denied that he had been barred from Egypt and said there was "absolutely no truth nor any foundation" to the reports, published in New York, that he was seeking asylum in Pakistan. He came to Karachi, he stated, specifically to attend a conference of religious leaders from Moslem countries; his plans were indefinite as to the length of his stay, but he did not plan to settle in Pakistan for any reason. Using a deliberately cautious and vague formula, Haj Amin assured that he was "ultimately" returning to Egypt, though he might well visit other Moslem countries en route.* After that, spokesmen for the Pakistani Ministry of Interior and the Egyptian embassy in Karachi confirmed that the Mufti had not asked asylum.[99]

The full truth about this particular episode in the life of the "man of mystery" will probably never be established. Both the Egyptain and Pakistani governments undoubtedly were greatly embarrassed by current reports that the former was barring the Mufti from returning to Cairo,

---

* Commenting on a news cable from Cairo relating that the new Egyptian government of Aly Maher had barred the Mufti from returning to Egypt, and a report from Beirut that Haj Amin had asked the Lebanese government for asylum as a political refugee, Al Hoda, the leading Arabic daily in the United States, wrote on March 25, 1952: "We warn the Lebanese Government not to play with fire, and we ask with all sincerity that it should not succumb to the evil influence of Haj Amin and not let him endanger the security of the country. The government should refuse Haj Amin entry into Lebanon!" Another Arabic paper in the U.S., Al-Islaah, on April 2, 1952, published a report of its Lebanese correspondent confirming that the Mufti had "asked for Lebanese citizenship. . . . He was refused."

and that the latter was faced with the dilemma of granting or refusing asylum to him. In his dispatch to the *New York Times* Michael James described the problem before Prime Minister Khwaja Nazimuddin as "a difficult one":

The Mufti has a lot of influence among the more devout Moslems and rejecting his request for asylum would present a political difficulty. At the same time the government here has never actively supported the extreme steps taken by the Iranians and Egyptians toward foreign interests and has been happy to accept the recent political stabilization in Egypt.[100]

Apparently aware of the delicate situation, the Mufti at the "Congress of the Divines of Islam" (*Ihtifal Ulama al-Islam*), held February 16–18 at Karachi, wisely abstained from his usual militant political utterances. As reported in the April 1952 issue of *The Islamic Revue,* he pleaded in his presidential address for the "unity of Islamic states into a compact *bloc*":

Blocs are being formed today in the world on the basis of belief and thought. On the one hand there is the Anglo-American *bloc*. On the other hand, the nations believing in communism are forming themselves into a *bloc*. Each nation and each country is joining one *bloc* or another.

Only the Moslems in the face of so many difficulties and problems have so far failed to form themselves into a permanent *bloc*, though they are badly in need of a powerful *bloc* today.

Moslem unity is demanded of Moslems by their religion. Islam has ordered the Moslems to form themselves into one *Ummat* [nation].

Therefore, it was our duty to respond to the call of the *Ulama* of Pakistan for considering ways and means of uniting the Moslems, establishing close cooperation between the *Ulama* of the world, popularizing Islamic culture, jurisprudence and way of life, and replacing the modern laws in Moslem countries with Islamic laws.

Notwithstanding the clearly political overtones of this address, it called mainly for a religious-cultural program. There was no mention of Palestine or Israel in the deliberations of the "Divines of Islam."

An outspokenly political character was evident, however, in a three-day conference of nongovermental representatives from ten Moslem countries, which opened in Karachi on May 10, 1952. Its purpose was to establish a Moslem Peoples' Organization having as its aim the creation of a "strong constitutional bloc of Moslem States." Among the nations represented was a delegation of "Arab Palestine," headed by the Mufti, and at the closing session of the conference a resolution was passed condemning the creation of the State of Israel, which "has thrust a nail into the heart of the Moslem world."[101]

While still in Karachi and later upon his return to Cairo, Haj Amin started putting particular stress on the part which, he claimed, Great Britain and the United States had played in the establishment of the State of Israel and which, he argued, precluded any cooperation with them by the Arab and Moslem world. To *Life* correspondent James Bell, who interviewed him in October 1952 in Cairo, he said:

On the solution of Palestine depends the whole future relationship between the Moslem world on one side and Britain and America on the other. It is clear to all Moslems that those responsible for inserting the dagger of Israel in the body of the Arab world are not Jews alone, but also the British who worked many years to establish Israel; and unfortunately, in later years, the Americans shared the responsibility of this serious step.*

---

* Widely accepted is the Jewish counterclaim that the British mandatory power was systematically sabotaging the development of the Jewish National Home and was openly opposed to the establishment of the State of Israel. America's support was more than questionable under President Roosevelt in the crucial years of World War II; it was invaluable, though often erratic, under President Truman.

You musn't believe there is any possibility of real, sincere, hearty cooperation between the peoples of the Moslem world on the one hand and Britain and America on the other without a just solution in Palestine. There might be some [Arab] governments and some officials who, out of courtesy or private reasons, say we want to cooperate and would like to cooperate. But the people themselves will never be sincere in cooperation so long as Britain and the U.S. stick to their present policy toward Israel.

We don't ask Britain or America to undo what they have done or repair what they have spoiled. We ask only the simple and just thing. Britain and America should from now on take a neutral attitude in the conflict between Arabs and Moslems on the one hand and the Jewish world on the other. This neutrality should be military, economic and political. By this I mean Britain and America should not help us, and should not help the Jews. If Britain and the U.S. will adopt this attitude of neutrality, the Arabs and Moslems will be their friends. We are ready to forget what both have done and begin a wholehearted cooperation. Can you think of any more simple, just demand for friendship and real sincere cooperation?

Then his voice hardened. "If the British and Americans do not at least take a neutral attitude," he said, "we Arabs and Moslems shall take a neutral attitude in the conflict between East and West. If Britain gave a promise to the Jews, she has long ago fulfilled it. Similarly America has given Israel an important hand. Why doesn't she now be satisfied with that much and adopt neutrality? If the British and Americans will not adopt this simple demand for neutrality, the Arab people will have every reason to believe that they support the Jewish ambition to uproot Arabs from the Middle East.[102]

Even more sweeping and menacing was the stand Haj Amin had taken during his stay in Karachi in March of 1952. Addressing a news conference, he declared that unless the Western Powers, including the United States, "withdraw completely" from the Middle East, a third world war was "imminent." Withdrawl means, he explained, both "foreign troops and economic aid."[103]

The Bandung Conference

The two all-Moslem conferences in Karachi were the last major events in which Haj Amin was able to play a leading role. The initial impact of a pan-Islamic movement, with Pakistan as its standard bearer, petered out very soon, and he was realistic enough not to persist in flogging a dead horse. In addition to that, his own ties with this movement had become a liability rather than an asset. The spiritual father of the concerted effort toward all Moslem unity had been the Moslem Brotherhood (*el-Ikhwan el-Islami*) created in Egypt in 1934 by the Mufti's backer, Hassan el-Banna. The Brotherhood's relations with the quickly changing Egyptian governments were of a shifting nature, varying between open opposition and silent cooperation. In its early stage, the military coup of July 1952 had not directly affected the Brotherhood's position. But later, latent antagonism between the new regime, bent on modernization of Egypt's life, and the Brotherhood striving to preserve a definitely religiously colored way of life, inspired in every domain by the tenets of Islam, came into the open. The Moslem Brotherhood was outlawed. In the struggle for power between Naguib and Nasser, its leaders were inclined to support the former.[104] An attempt on the life of the winner, Nasser (October 26, 1954), was laid at the door of the Brotherhood, and by November 27 about 1,000 of its members were imprisoned. Under these circumstances, it became for the Mufti, still residing in Cairo, unwise to maintain any open association with the pan-Islamic movement. His recent involvement with Pakistan, which had joined in the Baghdad pact with Great Britain, Turkey, Iran, and Iraq —a pact strongly opposed by Nasser—constituted an additional liability. It would have been sheer folly for Haj Amin to continue the role assumed in Karachi in 1951 and 1952.

It was not before the spring of 1955 that one more chance presented itself to take part in a gathering of international significance: the Afro-Asian Conference at Bandung, Indonesia. Israel, though geographically an Asian country, was barred from participation, and the conference, attended by twenty-eight Afro-Asian delegations, unanimously adopted a resolution on Palestine, submitted by Afghanistan, which was very much to the Mufti's liking:

In view of the existing tension in the Middle East caused by the situation in Palestine and of the danger of that tension to world peace, the Asian-African conference declares its support of the rights of the Arab people of Palestine and calls for the implementation of the United Nations resolutions on Palestine and of the peaceful settlement of the Palestine question.[105]

The main actual promoter of the resolution was, however, not so much Haj Amin, who played a minor part in the Bandung deliberations, as Premier Nasser of Egypt, actively supported by the premier of Communist China, Chou En-lai. The Mufti was first admitted as a mere unofficial "observer" and was only at the last moment made a member of the Yemen delegation.[106]

Staging a Comeback

For years to come, the Arab stormy petrel was commonly considered a hopeless "has-been." The forefront of the tumultuous "Palestine question" was occupied by governments of the established Arab states, each playing a game of its own, without regard to, and need of, the ex-

Mufti, who had behind him no armed forces or territory and whose appeal to Arab public opinion was but a personal and emotional one. For a time, Egypt's progressively flagging support had been maintaining the fiction of Haj Amin's Higher Committee. But in August 1959, Nasser's complete disregard for the Mufti's prestige prompted the transfer of the Committee's headquarters to Beirut.*

It was from half-Christian Lebanon, where he felt himself to have regained liberty of action, that Haj Amin staged a comeback, forcefully advancing an uncompromising, more aggressive Arab policy on the "Palestine question." During the last decade, the official line pursued by Arab governments in the United Nations was insistence on the strict implementation of the original U.N. resolutions of November 29, 1947 (assigning to Israel a much smaller territory) and of December 11, 1948 (favoring the "repatriation, resettlement and social rehabilitation of refugees and payment of compensation"). Paying lip service to U.N. authority, these demands indirectly implied recognition of Palestine's partition and of Israel's existence.

In November 1959, the Arab Higher Committee, under the signature of its chairman, openly challenged such an approach. On its behalf, the Mufti submitted to all Arab governments a confidential memorandum, which was in essence an outright rejection of the United Nations de-

* A somewhat different, more drastic, version of this change of domicile was given by John Marlowe in his recent (1961) study *Arab Nationalism and British Imperialism* (p. 192):

"In August 1959 diplomatic relations were restored between UAR and Jordan. At about the same time Haj Amin el-Husseini, the ex-Mufti of Jerusalem and an inveterate opponent of the Hashemite regime in Jordan, who had, since the Palestine war, enjoyed asylum in Egypt, and who still cherished ideas of becoming the head of an Egyptian-sponsored Palestine government-in-exile, was expelled from Egypt and pursued to his new home in Lebanon with precisely the same accusations as had been levelled at him by the Hashemites for the previous twenty years."

cisions on Palestine in their totality and in all their implications.[107] Reproachfully noting that "certain Arab states
are demanding implementation of the UN resolutions,"
the memorandum insisted that "continuation of the policy
of leniency and placability will inflict more and graver
losses upon the Arabs. . . . Therefore the Arabs of Palestine request the Arab states to handle the Palestine question with a view of realizing one single aspiration . . .
stamping out Jewish aggression against Palestine and
purging it of Zionism and imperialism. In this way . . .
Palestine will be brought back in the Arab fold [as a inde-
pendent] Palestine Arab Republic. . . . A Palestine Army
must be created, trained and armed to be the vanguard of
the Arab forces which will march to regain Palestine."[108]

Those who at that time were inclined to consider this
belligerent program merely as one more outburst of the
Mufti's "verbal extremism," bereft of all practical political
significance, failed to reckon with (1) Haj Amin's truly
remarkable resourcefulness and (2) the new alignment
of forces in the Arab camp, i.e., the deepening conflict
between Egypt's Nasser on the one side and Iraq's
Kassem, King Saud of Saudi Arabia, and Jordan's Hussein,
on the other.

A past master of political intrigue, Haj Amin was for
a time able to make the most of this rivalry.

The first to jump on the bandwagon of his belligerency
was Kassem. In a speech on Iraq's Army Day, he accused
other Arab governments of deliberately ignoring and suppressing the Higher Committee's memorandum, which
had sought aid in the creation of an independent Arab
state in the whole of Palestine. "I will publish this memorandum," Kassem pledged (the full text of the document,
published on his instructions in Baghdad in January 1960,
appears in Appendix 5 of this book). He insisted, in line

with the Mufti's position, that it was high time—before it became too late and the very notion of Palestine was obliterated—to restore the "Palestine personality" and start creating the Palestinian Republic: "Time is not in our favor, brothers, it is not in favor of the Arab nation." The Iraqi premier bemoaned the actual disappearance in the public mind of the name "Palestine," so dear to the Mufti's heart:

No one can at present find a map or an area bearing the name Palestine. I have enquired of the Minister of Education, I have looked at several maps. Is there at present a map which has on it the name of Palestine? Undoubtedly, you will reply that there is not such a map. But a map exists in our hearts, and we will bring it into being.[109]

While stressing that it was for the Palestinian Arabs themselves to bear the burden of rebuilding their homeland, Kassem pledged Iraq's help: "We will help them with money, equipment, weapons and everything. . . . We are talking in the name of the Palestinians, we are their mouthpiece. . . . We must work shoulder to shoulder in order to help our brethren, the Palestinian people." Echoing the Mufti's old grudge, Kassem stressed that Palestinian Arabs had been "subjected to aggression by enemies and thieves": "by the big aggressor and thief, Israel, which stole the heart of Palestine; and by our cousins who stole and divided the outer parts of Palestine." Speaking of "our cousins who stole and divided" parts of the "Palestine Entity" (*Al-Kiyan Al-Falastin*), Kassem had obviously Abdallah's Jordan, in mind which had in 1949 annexed 2,125 square miles of Western Palestine against the Mufti's violent protests, and Nasser's Egypt, which had been since 1949 occupying the twenty-nine mile-long Gaza Strip. The Mufti, backed by Cairo, had never protested against this latter occupation and was undoubtedly em-

barrassed by this part of Kassem's barbed utterance. But
he undoubtedly enjoyed the frontal attack against Jordan,
which was branded by Kassem as "an imperialist puppet":
with the parts of Palestine territory handed over to it by
the Iraqi Army in 1948, he charged, it had incorporated
one slice within its own borders and given the rest to the
Zionists. In this manner, "the Jordanian Kingdom was established. This is the glorious deed which they have
carried out. . . . [Arab] peoples will bring them to account for what they have done against them."[110] The
Mufti himself could not have delivered a more stinging
tirade against the main target of his inter-Arab enmity,
the Hashemite Kingdom of Jordan.

Four months later, in an interview with the Sudanese
paper *Al-Ayyam* (April 5, 1960), Kassem became even
more specific. Stating that the Palestine issue had
"reached a stage that requires violent action," he stressed
that it was not only that part of former Palestine which is
now Israel where such action was required. There should
be a Palestinian Republic, he said, and "this republic
should include all the soil of Palestine. . . . We believe
that Palestine in its various parts is an Arab country. We
want the Palestine people to recover their soil in Jordan
and in the Gaza Strip."*

To lend force to his charge that all the other Arab states
were prepared to do for Palestine was call conferences
and utter empty words, Kassem ordered Interior Minister
Yahya to authorize the establishment of the *Jami'at Rab-
itat Abna' Filisteen* (League of the Sons of Palestine). All
Palestinians living in Iraq were invited to join the League,
whose stated aim was to create a kind of "Palestinian
Force" to be trained by the Iraqi Army. Officials con-

* A similar proposal was made a few months earlier by Lebanon.
(John Marlowe, *Arab Nationalism and British Imperialism*, p. 194.)

cerned with the project were saying quite openly that this force would be used to "reconquer" Palestine, whether it was in the possession of Israel, Jordan, or Egypt. On April 14, 1960, Kassem issued a muster call to the 5,000 Palestinian refugees in Iraq for the formation of a "Palestine Liberation Army."[111]

Walking the Tightrope

The reaction of the Jordan government to the Mufti's initiative, endorsed by Kassem, was both stern and contemptuous. Prime Minister Hazza Majali told the Chamber of Deputies:

> There is no longer any Arab Higher Committee or any other committee which can claim to represent and speak on behalf of the Palestinian Arabs. . . . The only legitimate representative of the Palestinians in Jordan, who are the vast majority of the Palestinian Arabs, is the Government of his Hashemite Majesty. . . . Mobilization and preparation to recover the rights of Palestine are the main features of our policy which are exactly what we are acutally practising in this faithful country.

Jordan's anger was predictable and probably reckoned with in advance. But Kassem's resolute espousal of the Mufti's cause in its totality and his call for action in the Egyptian-held Gaza area was bound to affect whatever was left of Haj Amin's position with the Nasser regime in Egypt, of which he had been a pensioner until he went to live in Beirut in August 1959. Soon after Kassem had delivered his speech, Cairo's *Arab News Agency* (A.N.A.) put him on the spot by asking what he thought of the Iraqi premier's recommendations for the immediate creation, as a preliminary step, of a Palestinian Republic in the Gaza Strip and on the west bank of the Jordan. To gain time, Haj Amin asked for the question to be submitted in writing, and the Agency obliged. In his cautiously worded answer, the Mufti—as the *Jewish Observer and Middle East Review* put it—"tried to walk the tightrope, a practice at which he had been adept over the years, except when he made his decision to plump for the Germans during World War II."[112] At that stage of the game, the Mufti was apparently still not prepared to become fully identified with Kassem and openly to challenge Nasser. The basic objective of the Higher Committee's memorandum, he told the A.N.A., was "to ask *all* the Arab states to join together and cooperate" reestablishing the "Palestine Entity": it was "not in the interest of the Arabs to discuss such problems [the establishment of an Arab government for Palestine] at this stage because we must avoid everything that may increase Arab differences."[113]

Nasser was hardly appeased, let alone satisfied, by this elusive answer. But, not to be outbid by his Iraqi antagonist, he bestirred himself to make gestures of his own along the lines of the Mufti's belligerent memorandum. On April 5, 1960, *Al Ahram* reported that a volunteer Palestine army was in formation in the U.A.R. and the Gaza Strip. On July 23, a battalion of Palestine refugees, trained in Gaza, marched briskly past the reviewing stand at a military parade in Cairo: it was hailed as the "vanguard of the Palestine Army." And two months later, in his maiden speech before the U.N. General Assembly (September 28) Nasser fiercely denounced the 1947 partition resolution, insisting that

justification based on the *fait accompli* is sinful and harmful to principles. . . . The only solution to Palestine is that mattters would be restored to normalcy and should return to the conditions prevailing before the error was committed.[114]

Kassem's and Nasser's bellicose gestures hardly amounted to anything of actual military significance. (Iraq did not even have a common frontier with Israel.) But—though they both, as a rule, omitted any mention of the Mufti's authorship—this new line of theirs closely followed his memorandum of November 1959. A special correspondent of the *Jewish Observer and Middle East Review* in Beirut, the Mufti's new residence, reported that this obvious "meeting of minds"

raises once again the position of the ex-Mufti of Jerusalem who has been actively campaigning here for a more hostile Arab policy toward Israel and himself circulated a plan which Kassem later presented as his own brainchild.[115]*

Undismayed by Haj Amin's elusive position, Kassem continued sponsoring the Mufti's cause. In an interview with Munis Altai, the publisher of *Thawrah*, a leading Baghdad newspaper, he said in August 1960: "We have allocated £250,000 a year as a preliminary contribution to the [Mufti-led] Arab Higher Committee. . . . We have also created Arab organizations which have begun operating throughout the Arab world, even in the land occupied by the Zionist gangs." Members of the prospective "Pales-

---

* The same correspondent related, however, that Haj Amin apparently "has been getting fouled up in someone's lines of communication, and an attempt has been made on his life in Beirut," where he had been staying for four months. Lebanese Intelligence officers arrested four men involved in the plot. But the Lebanese caretaker government avoided embarrassing publicity around this matter, and the Mufti was "only too happy to cooperate; it would not serve his purposes if it were to get around that he was so unpopular that a gang of assassins had hunted him down."

It is difficult to ascertain the source of the assassination plot. Both Amman and Cairo are known to have been protesting in Beirut against Haj Amin's subversive activities. When, early in 1960, there appeared leaflets signed by his Arab Higher Committee and calling on the Arab refugees to "reconquer Palestine from Israel and Jordan," the Jordanian government had asked Lebanon to expel him. Two months later, his expulsion was urged by the United Arab Republic in a note claiming that his presence in Lebanon was jeopardizing normal relations between the two countries.

tine Liberation Army," he said, were receiving instruction in commando fighting and being trained as guerrilla fighters and parachutists. Addressing the first passing-out parade of Iraqi-trained Palestinian commandos on August 11, 1960, Kassem told them: "Very soon you will see with your own eyes that the *jihad* ["holy war"; he twice used the word "holy" which had been the Mufti's stock-in-trade term since 1941] will come into existence. . . . I congratulate you on the birth of the eternal Palestine Republic."[116]

A year later (July 1961) after having inspected the first units of the "Palestine Liberation Army," drilling in Baghdad for the "day of return," Haj Amin finally took the plunge and enthusiastically extolled Iraq's contribution to the "common Arab cause."[117]

A New Alignment

The Mufti's visit and speech in Baghdad spelled out a new alignment of Arab forces, in which he was determined to take sides in order to assert his role and restore his influence. Further tightrope walking became impossible. The lines were drawn firmly and rigidly between Nasser's "Arab socialism," bent on expansion, on the one side, and an odd coalition comprising Kassem's own brand of socialism and the monarchies of Saudi Arabia and Jordan, on the other side. To Nasser, all these three were equally repulsive and hostile. On March 9, 1962, Mohammed Hassan Heikal, chief editorial writer of *Al Ahram*, of Cairo, who was considered Nasser's chief spokesman, wrote that the Cairo regime did not expect any cooperation from King Saud, King Hussein, or Premier Kassem (in addition to Imam Ahmed of Yemen and President Kudzi of Syria) who represented "reaction" in

the Arab world. And two months later, the Cairo magazine *Rose el-Yussuf* wrote: "There can be no solidarity
with Saud, Hussein, Kassem and plotters in Syria. . . .
Arab solidarity begins with the extermination of these."[118]

In this line-up, the Mufti apparently felt that he had no
choice but to throw his lot with the anti-Nasser forces. On
"Palestine Day," Cairo's "Voice of the Arab Nation"
angrily added the name of "the opportunist Haj Amin el
Husseini" to the roster of "many traitors" who were "stab-
bing in the back" the Arab cause.[119]

For several months, Radio Cairo had the field pretty
much to itself, relentlessly attacking Kassem, Saud,
Hussein, the Imam of Yemen, and the Syrian leaders. By
the middle of June 1962 matters changed. Nasser's targets
started hitting back. The counter-offensive came simultaneously from Damascus, Baghdad, Mecca, and Amman.
Nasser had for the first time found himself at the receiving end of the air battle. "It was as if some master-hand
brought order into the anti-Nasser orchestra," commented
the *Jewish Observer and Middle East Review* (June
22, 1962). The identity of this master-hand was easy to
establish. During the years of his service with Nazi Germany, Haj Amin has earned the reputation of a first-class
propaganda broadcaster: aggressive, hard-hitting, dem-
agogic. He applied this experience to launching and coordinating the radio campaign against Nasser.

Coordinated Planning

Kassem, Saud, Hussein, and the Mufti were strange
bedfellows indeed. Nevertheless, some pattern of common
planning seemed to be emerging from their anti-Nasser
stand, with the Mufti as main coordinator.

On May 6, 1962, Baghdad Radio broadcast an official communiqué to the effect that on May 2, Haj Amin el-Husseini arrived in the Iraqi capital, accompanied by his second-in-command, Emil Ghouri, to discuss "the Palestine problem and the joint Jordan-Saudi Arabian plan to solve it." The Mufti conferred twice with Foreign Minister Hashem Jawad, and later discussed "the Palestinian question" with Nagib al Ruba'i, president of the Iraqi Sovereignty Council. On May 5, there took place a "cordial meeting" with Premier Kassem at which were discussed plans for coordination of efforts to "redeem the Palestine homeland for its people" and basic "preliminary steps" for forming the "Palestine Arab Republic," said the communiqué. Kassem urged Palestinian Arabs to follow the example set by the Algerian Moslems in the struggle for their independence and insisted that the Palestinians must bear the greater responsibility for liberating their homeland; brothers in all Arab countries believed in Iraq's idea for establishing an "immortal Palestine Republic." The communiqué quoted the Mufti as fully supporting Kassem's view that the Palestinians should depend on themselves to "liberate the usurped homeland."[120]

It is significant that on the morrow of Haj Amin's arrival in Baghdad this event was displayed on front pages of all Jordan newspapers. It was for the first time in many years that the name of the former mufti of Jerusalem had been allowed to appear so prominently in the Jordanian press. This innovation is obviously to be viewed against the background of the aforementioned "Jordan-Saudi Arabian plan," as opposed to Nasser's scheme of establishing a "Palestine government-in-exile." Arriving in Amman on April 26, Ahmad Shukeiri, former Palestinian lawyer, who became Saudi Arabia's representative at the United Nations, called for "an organization of the Palestine people which should not take the form of a government and does not need to exercise sovereignty over any part of Palestine." During a tour of the Western Bank, Shukeiri was feted as an Arab national hero* and told Arab audiences at meetings held in Nablus, Hebron, and other places:

We have given up any hope for a peaceful solution of the Palestine issue by the Unitd Nations. The new deal policy I am working out with the Jordan Government is one depending upon ourselves only. We shall draw up a well-conceived plan to liberate the plundered fatherland in stages by recruiting the Arabs' entire financial and economic resources to this end.[121]

Special significance was conferred on Shukeiri's mission by the fact that he was accompanied by a delegation of the Mufti's Arab Higher Committee, which included Emil Ghouri, Issa Nakleh (now legal adviser to the Committee's bureau in New York), and Munif el-Husseini (whose first cousin, Dr. Mousa el-Husseini, was hanged in Amman for his part in the assassination of King Abdallah).

Mecca and Baghdad

Haj Amin was functioning as a roving ambassador for the odd assortment of anti-Nasser forces which were backing his "new Palestine policy." After his Baghdad meeting with Kassem, he went to Mecca to attend a "Grand Moslem Congress." The main purpose of the gathering was to rally religious Moslems to resist the heresies of Nasser's "Arab Socialism." King Saud, who pre-

* Only two years prior to that, Amman Radio's official political commentator had described Ahmad Shukeiri as "an old tale-spinner from Acre," while the Jordan press reminded him that "he is the son of a negro mother and should return to the negro female slaves of Saudi Arabia."

sided, urged all the faithful to unite against atheism, raise the standard of the Islamic peoples, and spread Islamic preachings. The Congress denounced "those who disavow Islam and distort its call under the guise of nationalism," as "the bitterest enemies of the Arabs," and called on Moslems to "dispense with all foreign doctrines, such as communism and socialism." As an instrument in the struggle against internal conspiracies, which "aim to tear up the ranks of Islam," it was decided to establish an Islamic League, with English-and French-language newspapers in Africa, to spread Islamic ideals, and a publishing house for Moslem publications. Cairo Radio on May 28 damned the Mecca Congress as a maneuver by the West to line up Moslem states against Nasser and "true Arab nationalism."

Invited to attend the Congress, Haj Amin did not play a prominent, let alone decisive, role in its deliberations and decisions. But he saw to it that "the Palestine issue" would not be forgotten and that the Saud-dominated gathering of Moslem religious leaders would take a hard, uncompromising line on all its aspects. The Congress solemnly proclaimed the partition of Palestine as "void" and cautioned against attempting to settle "the Palestine question" through the United Nations Palestine Conciliation Commission: "This problem can only be solved by the refugees' repatriation." The resolution warned against "liquidating the refugee question through resettlement projects, economic developments, or gradual absorption of refugees abroad." Special attention was paid to the United Nations Emergency Force (UNEF) in the Egyptian-occupied Gaza Strip, which, the Congress said, "freezes the Palestine question and insures stability for Israel"; the UNEF must be withdrawn. Another resolution called for a tighter economic blockade of Israel, insisted that the

Gulf of Aqaba be closed to Israeli shipping, and opposed Israel's use of the Jordan River. A strong appeal was directed to all Moslem states to "prevent Jews living in their countries from emigrating to occupied Palestine."[122]

Without being the central figure of the Mecca congress, Haj Amin had every reason to be satisfied with its proceedings and outcome.

From Mecca, he returned to Baghdad, to preside over the fifth World Islamic Congress which opened on May 29 and was attended by some 200 delegates from Moslem communities in all parts of the world. In his presidential address at the opening of the Congress, the first public speech he had delivered in many years, Haj Amin told the delegates:

> The Palestine tragedy is unequalled in history. The Zionist-imperialist plot against Palestine was most inhuman and base ... world Judaism plans to take over most of the Arab countries to fulfill its so-called historical dream of a homeland between the Nile and the Euphrates. The imperialist-Jewish plot is not aimed against Palestine only but against all Arab and Moslem lands. The Arab and Moslem world is facing a test. . . . If they give in to aggression and conspiracy, they would be proving that they are not worthy of living. . . . But the Moslems will never succumb.

A memorandum distributed by the delegation of the Palestine Arab Higher Committee to the parley urged the participants to "realize the enormous danger of Israeli expansion": Israelis "want to occupy and destroy the Dome of the Rock mosque [in the Old City] and in its place rebuild the Temple of Solomon." The memorandum asked for funds and "volunteers" who could be sent "to the battlefield to defend Palestine." This request was in line with the speech by Kassem who said bluntly that the "people of Palestine" should rely on themselves and expect support only from the Arab nations.

The twenty-seven resolutions on "Palestine," adopted after five days of deliberations, were obviously drafted by Haj Amin. They called on all Islamic countries to reject the present situation in the area and condemned Zionism as "an imperialistic, aggressive movement which has launched war against the free people of the world in general and against Moslems in particular." Other resolutions called for the establishment in each Islamic country of a committee to help Palestinians regain their motherland and for the mobilization of Palestinians to prepare them for "Liberation Day."[123]

Both in Mecca and in Baghdad, though to a different extent, the guiding hand of the Mufti was clearly distinguishable. As a keen American observer put it, "the Mufti rides again." After years of isolation and near-oblivion, he once more forcefully projected himself into the all-Arab picture, betting on the Kassem card and tirelessly laboring at the establishment of an anti-Nasser Iraqi–Jordanian-Saudi-Arabian front, with Kassem as the pivotal force and the "Palestine Entity" as the immediate paramount object.

The issue of the "Palestine Entity" and the "Palestine Army" developed into a triangular conflict between Nasser's Egypt, Kassem's Iraq and Hussein's Jordan. An attempt to assert a major role for "the people of Palestine," the refugees themselves, was made by Dr. Izzat Tannouz, a Mufti man, who was for years the refugees' spokesman at the United Nations. As reported by *Al Jihad* (Jordan) of September 6, 1962, and *Al Hayat* (Beirut) of July 26, 1962, Tannouz submitted to the Arab League and to the Conference of Specialists on Palestine Affairs two memoranda, in which he argued that the Arab governments were not competent to reach decisions on matters concerning Palestine, since "the sons of Palestine are di-

rectly responsible and entitled to determine their fate."
Tannouz insisted that a spokesman for all the Arab states
should announce in the Special Political Committee of the
United Nations that "the Arab States are not entitled to
participate in any negotiations towards the solution of the
Palestine problem. . . . It is the exclusive right of the
Palestinians, just as it was the case in Algeria and other
countries." He also proposed that a large Palestine army
be formed, if necessary by conscription, from Palestine
Arabs residing in the Arab countries, which would be the
spearhead of the Arab forces for the liberation of Palestine: some 100,000 would be recruited in Jordan, 35,000
in the Gaza Strip, 10,000 in Syria, 12,000 in Lebanon, and
500 in Iraq.

A Lost Gamble

For a time, the prospects seemed to be promising. But
Haj Amin's sensitive and seasoned political acumen—
possibly bolstered by well-placed inside intelligence service in the Arab capitals—apparently warned him that he
had badly miscalculated. While for most of 1962 Nasser
was largely isolated in the Arab world, the last quarter of
the year and the first months of 1963 brought a series of
events that catapulted him into a leading role in the
Middle East. On September 26, 1962, the regime of Imam
Ahmed in Yemen was overthrown by a pro-Nasser military junta; a strong Egyptian military force was dispatched to Yemen in support of the new regime, which
was fighting for its life against the Yemeni tribes loyal to
the deposed Imam and helped by Saudi Arabia and Jordan; Nasser thus obtained a firm foothold in South Arabia.
Pro-Nasser stirrings were growing in Saudi Arabia and

the Hashemite Kingdom. The "Casablanca Group" (Egypt, Morocco, Guinea, Ghana, Mali), first established in January 1961, gave Nasser a broad avenue to Africa.

Haj Amin realized that it was foolhardy of him to try to swim against the mighty pro-Nasser trend. With his usual versatility and elasticity, he started toning down his Kassem orientation and looking for approaches to the Nasser camp.

In October 1962 he appeared in Algeria, which had gained independence on August 7 and maintained close ties with Cairo.

The Nasser regime was, however, not prepared to "forgive and forget" the Mufti's defection. He was given the "silent treatment" and was totally ignored. At a protest meeting held in Cairo on the fifteenth anniversary of the United Nations partition decision there appeared speakers from the United Arab Republic, South Arabia, Yemen, Jordan, Iraq, and Palestine. The "Palestinian" speaker was a member of the Husseini's arch-rival Nashashibi clan: Nasser Eldin al Nashashibi, co-editor of the daily *Gomhouria*. When the Cairo weekly *Arab Observer* devoted a long article to Egypt as the "Sanctuary of Free Men," enumerating the names of various Arab leaders who had sought and found political asylum in that country, the name of the Mufti was conspiciously omitted.

Then came the Baghdad coup of February 7, 1963, putting an end to Kassem's rule, and just a month later, the Damascus coup upsetting the anti-Nasser Syrian government. The new Iraqi regime, headed by Abdel Salam Aref, promptly disavowed the Mufti. Asked at a press conference about the attitude toward Haj Amin and his "Arab Higher Committee of Palestine," Hashem Jawad, the Minister of State for Presidential Affairs and recognized spokesman for the Iraqi National Council of the Revolution, replied that the revolutionary government would discontinue its special relationship with the Mufti.

Haj Amin had again lost the gamble.

The Emergence of Ahmad Shukeiri

When the Political Committee of the Arab League met in September 1963, the most far-reaching proposal on the "Palestine Entity" was submitted by Taleb Hussein Shebib, the foreign minister of the new Iraqi government: all Palestinians, wherever they were, were to hold free elections to a Palestine National Assembly, which would then create a Provisional Palestine Government, and to train a Palestine Liberation Army. Jordan challenged the discussion, arguing that no "representative of Palestine" was present (the former representative, Ahmed Hilmi, a Mufti man, had recently died). Overriding Saudi Arabia's negative vote, the Committee then invited the recently discharged Saudi Arabian U.N. delegate, Ahmad Shukeiri, to act as the representative of "Palestine" inside the Arab League; he was authorized to lead a "Palestine Arab Delegation" of his own selection, that would plead the cause of "Palestine" at the United Nations.[124]

Backed by Egypt and Iraq, Shukeiri emerged as "Mister Palestinian," the central figure in the struggle for the "Palestine Entity." Protests by the Mufti and his Palestine Higher Committee were disregarded. This "change of guard" promptly found its expression at the United Nations. Until 1963, Mufti-men—Izzat Tannouz and, later, Emil Ghouri—were permitted to address the Special Political Committee as "refugee spokesmen" representing a "Palestine Arab Delegation." But, at the eighteenth session of the U.N. assembly, all the thirteen Arab League states (Jordan, which had always been opposed both to the "Palestine Entity" concept and to Shukeiri's nomination, did not dare to withhold its signature) submitted a request (Doc. A/SPC/89) for a hearing for "The Palestine Arab Delegation representing the people of Palestine, principal party to the Palestine question." Shukeiri was listed as chairman of this body. He was invited to address the Special Political Committee, and his address —as usual, violent and aggressive—was published as a U.N. document (A/SPC/90).

This was for the Mufti a *capitis diminutio maxima*. He did not take it laying down. The Beirut correspondent of the *New York Times* reported on March 28, 1964: "The opposition to Mr. Shukeiri centers around Haj Amin el-Husseini, the Grand Mufti of Jerusalem, who claims to be the proper and legal representative of the Palestinian people." When Shukeiri arrived at the Lebanese capital, he "got a hostile welcome from several hundred Palestinian refugees," and a police car escorted him to his hotel, while riot squads dispersed the demonstrators. Agents of the Mufti's Arab Higher Committee were distributing large quantities of pamphlets attacking Shukeiri and, according to *Al Difa'a* (March 30, 1964), the Lebanese government felt compelled to warn the Committee against "illegal activities."

It is, however, common knowledge that the Lebanon government, while ostensibly going along with Shukeiri's Egypt-sponsored scheme, was anything but interested in its success and saw in the Mufti a welcome antidote to Shukeiri's campaign. The attitude of Jordan's government was similar. It realized the danger of opposing Shukeiri, behind whom stood Nasser, and whom Soviet Premier Khrushchev had as recently as May 1964 assured of Rus-

sian support for a "just solution of the Palestine problem."[125] Making a virtue out of necessity, King Hussein,
on May 28, in the Old City of Jerusalem, personally
opened a Shukeiri-organized "Palestine National Congress," whose 350 delegates claimed to represent one and-
a-half million refugees from Palestine.[126] Yet the Mufti,
whose Palestine Higher Committee had boycotted the
Congress, was permitted to denounce Shukeiri in a speech
in Jerusalem. "Shukeiri has failed to win the Mufti's followers in Lebanon and Jordan, despite the facilities he
was given for explaining the new scheme," said the "Arab
Affairs reporter" of the *Jewish Observer and Middle East
Review*.[127] The governments of these two countries were
apparently not too unhappy about this state of affairs.
They found the further existence of the Mufti camp—no
matter how dwindling—a most convenient expedient in
the internecine Arab competition. There was no open
identification with Haj Amin, but he was not merely tolerated; he apparently enjoyed as much covert patronage as
it was possible to extend without arousing Nasser's wrath.
The impact of his boycott of the Palestine National Congress in Jerusalem was considerably enhanced by the refusal to attend on the part of Lebanon's president Shebab
and of Prince Feisal, the actual ruler of Saudi Arabia,
which was also inclined to favor Haj Amin rather than
Shukeiri. This indirect backing by Jordan, Lebanon, and
Saudi Arabia, though motivated less by liking for the
Mufti than by antagonism toward Shukeiri and his sponsors, gives Haj Amin, at this writing, some semblance of
a new lease on life. But the longevity of this shadow existence is obviously highly questionable.

7

Close-up

Homo Politicus

THIS BIOGRAPHY OF HAJ AMIN EL-HUSSEINI IS A STRICTLY political one. It is so not merely by choice but also by necessity: next to nothing is actually known about Haj Amin's personal life, his family, his hobbies and friendships—if he had any. We know that he was married (one wife only) and had six children: five daughters and a son. When he fled Palestine in 1937, the family was left behind in Jerusalem and it was still there in June 1946 when he returned to the Middle East.[1] They seemed to have joined him somewhat later in Cairo.

Even for a purely political biography this extreme paucity of data on the subject's personal life—inasmuch as it might have played a part in his impulses, reactions, and spiritual outlook—is of course an essential drawback. Be it by accident or design, this aspect of Haj Amin's image is almost completely omitted in all the extensive material directly or indirectly dealing with the former Mufti of Jerusalem. He appears as a *homo politicus* par excellence, with the noun *homo* almost completely submerged by the adjective *politicus*.

Also regrettably scarce are indications as to the formative forces which have shaped his personality and outlook. We know that, unlike so many present-day Arab leaders, Haj Amin has never studied in Europe or in Western institutions of higher learning in the Middle East; he remained untouched by modern European or American education, ideas, and culture. He abhorred them not because, having absorbed their tenets, he rejected these tenets as contrary to his or his people's ideals and conscience. He did so just because they were strange to him, and therefore hostile and despicable. Until he fled Jerusalem in 1937, his intense and aggressive Palestine Arab nationalism was in its essence locally-minded, devoid of wider perspectives or considerations of international nature.

Local Patriot

The three basic components of Haj Amin's "political philosophy" have always been: pan-Arabian, pan-Islamism, and independence of Palestine. Their respective weights were however far from equal. As mufti of Jerusalem he was the initiator of the 1931 pan-Islamic conference in the Holy City and was elected its President; in 1951 and 1952 he presided over all-Moslem conferences in Karachi. He also was an ardent and articulate advocate of all-Arab solidarity. Yet the core of Haj Amin's thought and action was at all times Arab independence in Palestine. He was a Palestine Arab nationalist first and last, a local patriot above everything. Both pan-Arabism and pan-Islamism served as auxiliary tools, likely to help in achieving the goal of an Arab Palestine rather than as ends in themselves. Palestine was uppermost in Haj Amin's mind, as his very own exclusive domain.

This integral identification of his personality with the collective personality of Arab Palestine, as he saw it, is the key to Haj Amin's stand on several major problems of the country. His ardent advocacy of independence was concentrated on Western Palestine: unification with the left bank of the Jordan was bound to bring into the picture the Hashemite Emir Abdallah, thus affecting the rule of the Mufti's Husseini clan.* It was largely for the same reason that he violently opposed and successfully sabotaged the British proposal of an elective legislative council in Palestine, though it would have considerably bolstered Arab self-government: the mere emergence of an elected legislative body was bound to affect Haj Amin's unique personal status in the Arab community. Throughout his political career he never distinguished between his personal aspirations and Arab national goals in Palestine: both were fully interchangeable in his thought and action. This amalgam of ideal and personality constituted both the strength and weakness of the role Haj Amin played in the Middle East.

The Portrait

Probably the best, most penetrating characterization of Haj Amin is offered by John Marlowe in his two studies, *Rebellion in Palestine* (1946) and *The Seat of Pilate* (1959). In the former work he writes:

He is one of the ablest politicians that the Near East has produced in recent years. There is very little of the Arab in

---

* "As Abdallah grew stronger in Trans-Jordan so the Mufti feared a threat to his own ascendancy in Palestine" (Dearden, *op. cit.*, p. 47).

him either in mind or appearance. He is of midddle height, of a reddish countenance* and with somewhat foxy features. There is in him none of the stridence of the demagogue. He can provoke fanaticism without himself being a fanatic. By oriental standards he is sincere in that he is not motivated by financial self-interest. He is one of those uncomfortable people who love power for its own sake; for whom power is not a means to an end but an end in itself. He is an ascetic in that lust for power leaves no room for other and pleasanter lusts.[2]

Thirteen years later, Marlowe added a few more keen touches to this portrayal. "About Haj Amin was nothing of the graceful melancholy of the Bedu or the half-mocking introspection of the civilized urban Arab. Able, ambitious, ruthless, humorless, and incorruptible, he was of the authentic stuff of which dictators are made. He was the spearhead of the xenophobic, uncompromising Arab nationalism which succeeded the conservative, cynical, easygoing Arab nationalism of Feisal [first King of Iraq], Abdallah [of Transjordan], Nuri [Nuri Said Pasha, prime minister of Iraq], Nahas [Mustafa Nahas Pasha, prime minister of Egypt], Ryad el-Sohl [Premier of Lebanon] and Mardam [Jamil Mardam Bey, Syrian premier]".[3]

British and American writers and newspapermen who, after the Mufti's flight from Palestine, had, at various stages of his career, the opportunity of meeting him or closely observing his way of life and work, contributed several telling descriptions of the man and of the image he conveyed. It seems worthwhile to list these personal testimonies in chronological order.

---

* During the war, British intelligence officers gave him the cover name "Barbarossa." [Author's note.]

Encounter in Baghdad

Freya Stark, the noted British "arabist," met Haj Amin on April 4, 1941, at the Zia Hotel in Baghdad, in the company of George Antonius* and "amid a gowned and turbaned circle." She left a vivid account of the impression he made on her:

The Mufti sat there all in white, spotless and voluminous, a man in his early forties, wearing his turban like a halo. His eyes were light blue, and shining, with a sort of radiance, as of a just-fallen Lucifer. . . . The Mufti was an artist. . . . He had that sort of magnetism by which a man makes a difference to a room when he enters. In his young days he had organized a dramatic society in Jerusalem and taken the comic parts; and he had bewitched George Antonius as securely as ever a siren did her mariner, leading him through his slippery realms with sealed eyes so that George—whom I was fond of—would talk to me without a flicker about the Mufti's "single-hearted goodness." I looked now with deep attention: there was little good and certainly nothing disinterested in that face, but intelligence, and a great bogus charm. . . . We let politics carefully alone and talked pleasantly about modern Arab literature, and when the whole gowned, snakelike company rose to depart, the Mufti alone turned at the door to bow—rather like a cardinal dispensing benediction.[4]

In the four years of Haj Amin's service with the Axis (October 1941—May 1945) no independent journalist had a chance of meeting, or speaking to him. During his sojourn in France (May 1945—June 1946) he was incommunicado for the press. It was only after Haj Amin's return to the Middle East in June 1946 that an opportunity again presented itself to interview the Mufti and to watch him at work.

* George Antonius (1891–1942), an Arab scholar of Lebanese origin and Palestinian citizenship, was considered the brains of the Arab national movement in Palestine. His book *The Arab Awakening* served as standard work for Arab nationalism.

As Viewed in Cairo

Stressing the Mufti's unflagging devotion to his cause, Clifton Daniel reported from Cairo on August 25, 1946,

eighteen hours of his day are given to reading, studying and talking about Arab nationalism and the aims of All-Islam. . . . His political technique is an Oriental version of an interminable series of conversations with everyone with whom he might find a community of interests as a basis for common action. . . . Always solicitous of visitors, he sees them not only to the gate of Villa Aida but into their cars and out of sight. . . . He still exercises the charm and that excessive courtesy which is so highly prized in the Orient. . . . He speaks softly, with a well-modulated voice, in cultured Arabic—another great asset among people who pay great deference to poets and orators. . . . His political theme has the virtues of consistency and simplicity—another advantage among people who are largely illiterate, who require their political ideas to be clear and concise.

Another American correspondent, David W. Nussbaum, who, two years later, succeeded in interviewing Haj Amin in his heavily guarded villa, supplies additional revealing glimpses of the Mufti's appearance, tastes, and personality:

Unlike the Westernized Arab statesmen who have copied European dress, the Mufti wears the costume of a Moslem religious sheik—a floor length, gold decorated black robe, called an *abayeh,* and a tarboosh circled by a white sash. . . . With his Koran-flavored expressions, the Mufti acts the part of a devout and insular religious leader who is instinctively suspicious of outsiders. . . . When he feels himself under attack, he instantly withdraws, tortoise-wise, into a hard shell of silence. His face would be the envy of any pokerplayer. With his large semitic nose and short, gray beard, it is strong and handsome, practically unmarred by the wrinkles that generally furrow the countenance of a man of 54. This granite perfection is the result of a manner habitually cold and inflexible. When he smiles, the movement of his lips is barely noticeable, and his small blue eyes remain somber.

Like most Arab politicians, Haj Amin has a weakness for the more exotic varieties of food, and his chunky, five-foot-five figure has a tendency to bulge. However, he starts each day with Swedish calisthenics, and as a devout Moslem, he neither smokes nor drinks. . . . At eight a.m. he breakfasts on fruit and bitter, black Bedouin coffee, and then takes until eleven to read through his mail, the Arab press, and a pile of clippings selected by his staff from New York, Paris and London newspapers. After this he holds a conference with Arab Higher Committee members and other advisers.

From then until after midnight a stream of visitors from all over the Moslem world flows through his small villa. . . . He seldom rises to greet his callers, but mumbles quickly the traditional Arab salutation and proceeds immediately to the political subject at hand. . . . He hates Western civilization with undisguised passion, and except when he fled to Germany, had always given it a wide berth. Although he speaks fluent French, knows English and German, his reading has been strictly confined to Arabic literature, particularly its highly introspective, intricate poetry. In music the Mufti is devoted to the atonal Arabic chant, and Western harmonies fill him with disgust.[5]

Encounter in Damascus

In the same year (1948), John Roy Carlson, an Armenian-born American writer, who spoke to the Mufti in Damascus, described him as "a short man, with a large white turban wound around his head; a long black cloak covered him completely to the ankles. His eyes were bluish, and his skin fair. His beard was graying softly, and was white at the tip. His ears were conspicuous and protruding. To my surprise, he looked meek and had a rather gentle though extremely alert and sagacious look about him. Perhaps the deliniation of his true character escaped me."[6]

Two More Glimpses

Three years later, a *Newsweek* correspondent reported that "at 58 Haj Amin looks more like an effete intellectual than a rabble-rouser. Except for a prominent Semitic nose, his features are delicate. His blue eyes are pale and soft. His hair and beard, once fox-red, have now turned gray. . . . [He spends] most of his waking hours at the desk in his library office in the Villa Aida. . . . Rarely did he miss a radio news broadcast. . . . Haj Amin rarely leaves his refuge. When he does, he is ringed by his bodyguards, toting .45 and .38 pistols, and cheering him loudly. Haj Amin's retinue of 70 includes his only wife, their five daughters ranging from 25 to 8 years old (his favorite is the youngest, Amina), and their son Salah, a 20-year-old law student. It also includes four male private secretaries and three chauffeurs to drive his two limousines."[7]

The first impression of *Life*'s James Bell, who met Haj Amin in October 1952 in another heavily guarded villa, this time in a small town, an hour's ride from Beirut, was one of mild benevolence: "His face was that of a jolly elf. His blue eyes twinkled above his smiling mouth. . . . He was one of the most kindly gentle-appearing men I have ever seen." The Mufti "handled the small talk in English, sipping sweet Turkish coffee and looking angelic"; but when serious subjects were brought up, he spoke Arabic, which was interpreted by his son-in-law, Haider el-Husseini. When warming up to the discussion, Haj Amin removed his tarboosh wrapped in a gleaming white turban: "The effect was startling. He has only a couple of inches of forehead in front of a bald skull which slopes back steeply. His ear lobes are so close to his head they are virtually indented. Without the headgear he loses the look of angelic amiability."[8]

The Composite Image

In their totality, these lively testimonies by men and
women whose lives are spent seeking out, interviewing,
and observing people of interest, give a composite image
of a man hermetically sealed in a cause, almost frightfully
single-minded: a classical example of a *homo unius rei,* a
man with a compulsive concentration on one, and one
only, cause. It is soley in this context that Haj Amin el-
Husseini has to be viewed. To those who approve of, and
endorse, his cause unreservedly, he is a great patriot and
the torch-bearer of pure Arab nationalism, even though
some among them may have nurtured doubts as to the
moral permissibility and political wisdom of some of the
methods and tactics he used against his opponents in
the Arab camp. To those others who, for whatever reasons, do not accept the Arab total claim on Palestine with
all its implications, Haj Amin is an arch-villian, fighting for
a wrong cause with wrong means, with venom and cruelty
rarely surpassed in recent political history.

Even for those not taking sides in the Arab-Jewish controversy on Palestine, Haj Amin's political record, based
on the principle that the aim—Arab Palestine—justifies
the means, appears damnable. It is unfortunately true that
in the lately prevailing mood of "forgetting and forgiving"
Nazi Germany's crimes against the human race, the memory of the Arab quisling's cooperation with the Hitler regime is gradually fading and is now rarely and reluctantly
mentioned at the international forum in discussions of
Middle East problems. But this chapter of Haj Amin's
biography must not be allowed to be obliterated or con-
veniently explained away. It is an integral and telling
part of his stormy life.

Explaining and Justifying

Ever since his return, in June 1946, to the Middle East, Haj Amin was intent on explaining and justifying the thirty months of his service to the Nazi cause. The main argument was that, having been compelled by "British persecution" to escape in 1937 from Palestine to Lebanon, he went in 1939, again under duress, from there to Iraq. He sought refuge in Teheran after the collapse of Rashid el-Gailani's revolt in 1941, but had to flee again when British and Soviet forces entered Iran. "Through diplomatic arrangements with Great Britian," Turkey refused his demand for refuge. "Therefore," said Haj Amin in August 1946 to the Cairo correspondent of the London *Times,*

finding no Arab or Moslem country in which to take refuge, I had to go to Europe, which at that time was almost entirely under German domination. Since I am not a British subject and there is no treaty between us [i.e., between Great Britain and the Palestine Arabs] and furthermore as there existed no enmity between us [the Palestine Arabs] and Germany, I could see no reason to prevent my taking refuge there at a time when Great Britain was seeking to expel me and to suppress my nation in order to further Zionist aspirations, which were trying to destroy utterly our national integrity.[9]

Irrespective of the accuracy of one or another item in the Mufti's tale of his odyssey of escapes, it may conceivably account merely for his seeking asylum as political refugee in Hitler's Third Reich. But scores of political refugees in recent history have sought and obtained sanctuary in one or another country and stayed there as law-abiding guests, without associating themselves with the political regime prevailing in the country, let alone actively participating in the war this country was waging against other states with different political regimes. This, however, was not the case with Haj Amin.

His association with the Axis powers started (as we have seen in previous chapters) long before he became a hunted exile. He was seeking links with Fascist Italy and Nazi Germany while still in Palestine and was receiving substantial subsidies from them in his Lebanese villa. During his sojourn in Iraq (1939–1941) he sent emissaries to Von Papen in Constantinople and to the Berlin Foreign Office and wrote a servile letter to Hitler, congratulating the Führer on his victories over the Allied forces, assuring him of his devotion, and offering active Arab cooperation. Immediately after his arrival in Berlin, Haj Amin enthusiastically plunged into pro-Axis and anti-Allied activities, from radio propaganda to staging acts of sabotage, to organization of Arab and Moslem units to fight the Allies. All this, of course, was by no means a mandatory ingredient of the status of a refugee seeking merely political asylum. It was the freely chosen status of an "associated belligerent," an Axis satellite—a position which could not be *post factum* explained away by any denials or sophistries. Yet Haj Amin continued to try.

On August 20, 1946, there was issued in Alexandria a statement on behalf of "His Eminence the Mufti" arguing that captured German records establishing that for thirty months he had actively participated in Axis sabotage of the Allied war effort in the Near East, were mere forgeries: "There is a great possibility that Zionists managed to forge these German documents and put them among German official records," the statements claimed.[10] This claim was quietly dropped after the authenticity of the documents had been proven beyond any possible doubt.

In the course of the interview granted to *Life* correspondent James Bell in October 1952, the Mufti brought up on his own initiative the issue of his wartime collaboration with Nazi Germany. After repeating the standard argument that the Third Reich was the only place where he, hunted by the British, was able to find refuge, he assured his American interviewer:

In my radio talks I never spoke against America. I used to mention Britain, but I limited myself to injustices Britain had done to the Arabs in general and Palestinians in particular. Because I did this, he complained, Americans look at me as an enemy.[11]

Even a cursory perusal of Haj Amin's activities listed in Chapter Four of this book is sufficient to establish the fallacy of this "innocent" version, purported to whitewash in American eyes the Mufti's anti-Allied record. An astute and seasoned politician, Haj Amin obviously counted on the admittedly short memory of the Western democracies.

The Pro-German Residue

A residual weak spot for Germany—where he had been treated for two and a half years as an uncrowned Arab potentate and had had ample opportunity to give vent, on an almost world-wide scale, to his anti-Western and anti-Jewish animosities—has remained part and parcel of Haj Amin's credo long after the Third Reich's collapse.

The December 1951 issue of the influential German monthly, *Zeitschrift für Geopolitik*, carried a lengthy interview with the Mufti in which he did not hesitate to reassert his unwavering pro-German feelings:

"The Arab people are bound by ties of friendship to Germany, a country they admire. I send my best wishes to the German people, who in all their history have never done anything to hurt the Arabs and the Moslems. Both peoples have always worked together amicably, in a cooperation which has never ceased. This is true also for the recent period." Underscoring what he called German-Arab "common interests," the Mufti went on: "A common defense front almost always strengthens friendships between peoples. . . . Above all, my wish is that Germany should attain the political prominence she deserves."

There was, however, more than mere good will in the interview: it also contained a practical program for strengthening and developing German-Arab ties. Among the suggestions were: (1) exchange of specialists in various fields, (2) increased commerical relations, (3) education of Arab students at German universities, and (4) tourism by Germans in the Arab lands.

In 1954, Haj Amin started publishing in the Cairo paper, *Al Misri,* his memoirs on the Palestine war. They were so outspokenly and aggressively pro-German that *Der Weg,* the German Nazi journal of Buenos Aires, gratefully acknowledged in its Ausgust 1954 issue, the Mufti's reference, "in general and noble terms," to his relationship with Hitler. "Upright Germans thank the Mufti, that lion of his people, for the true friendship which he always kept with the German nation," *Der Weg* wrote glowingly.

Endorsing the Nazi Claims in 1961

A memorandum submitted, in October 1961, at the United Nations by the "Palestine Arab Delegation" on behalf of "His Eminence the Grand Mufti of Palestine" fully endorsed the entire Nazi concept and justification of their anti-Jewish crusade. With an almost unbelievable frankness the Mufti's statement says:

It is an uncontestable truth that the enmity of Nazis to Jews was one of the most fundamental principles of the Nazi Party, and was based on well documented research and studies made first by the Nazi Party and afterwards by the Nazi Government, and was entrenched in their convictions and plans for the following reasons:

(a) The Nazis believed that the Jews were a strong factor in the defeat of Germany in the First World War because they used their pressure on President Wilson to bring America into the war on the side of the Allies in consideration for the Balfour Declaration.

(b) The Nazis had proof of acts of sabotage committed by Jews in Germany and other parts of Europe against the German war effort after they knew about the Balfour Declaration.

(c) The Nazis were convinced that the domination by Jews of the political, economic and professional life of Germany before the Nazi era was a part of a world Jewish Plan to weaken Germany.

(d) The statements and speeches of Hitler and his book "Mein Kampf", as well as the statements of other Nazi leaders were full of bitter hate and despise for the Jews and their determination to treat them as their bitter enemies.

All these facts prove beyond any doubt that the Nazis needed no persuasion or instigation either by me or anybody else to execute their program against the Jews.

All the above was obviously written to enable the Mufti "to emphatically and categorically state that neither I nor any Arab leader had, either directly or indirectly, any part in, or relation with, what the Nazis committed against the Jews in Europe." Ample excerpts from his wartime broadcasts, with the appeal "Kill the Jews wherever you find them—this pleases God, history and religion," expose this claim as a bland white lie. But in the process of building up his argument, Haj Amin unhesitatingly invokes and sanctions as "uncontestable truth . . . based on well documented research and studies" the entire arsenal of the Nazi anti-Semitic propaganda. In one of the subsequent paragraphs the statement nevertheless virtuously insists that "racial hatred and religious persecution is not in accordance with our principles or convictions as Arabs and Moslems, and we were, and still are, against the persecution of any person whether Jew or Gentile because of his religious belief or racial origin." The only enemy to be combatted is "the Zionist illegal occupation of our country" [Palestine].

What Is in Store for Israel's Jews?

In an attempt to elucidate the full meaning of the Mufti's so often announced determination to "remove" this "Zionist occupation," *Life's* James Bell had mentioned, in the course of an interview (October 1952) in Cairo, "the common assertion that the Arabs planned to drive the Jews into the sea, that in the Arab mind the only solution is a second round which would wipe out all the Jews now in Israel." "Speaking with feeling," reported Bell, Haj Amin answered:

We don't mean at all to eliminate the Jews. Not at all. If Britain and America would stop supporting Israel now, 80% of their extremism and fanaticism would immediately disappear. Then and only then can we come to an understanding with them. When their extremism is gone, we can bring about a right and just solution. No, the elimination of the Jews is not in our program. We have no idea of wiping them out. The Jews lived among us for 13 centuries as a minority and we protected them. This idea you mention is not in our thought and has never been in our history. We Moslems were always known for tolerance with minorities.[12]

The trustworthiness of the assurance that Jews living in Israel would not be molested can be best judged in the light of an interview the Mufti granted, in the Fall of

1951, to Charles Foltz, one of the editors of *U.S. News and World Report*. When Haj Amin insisted that all Arab refugees must return to Israel, Foltz asked: "But if all the Arab refugees went back, wouldn't that mean that some of the Jews now there [in Israel] would have to leave?" The answer was blunt and unequivocal: "Well, how long have they been there? Several months? Several years? What about the Arabs who settled there and lived there for the last 14 centuries? Is it so easy and just and fair to oust people who have lived in a country for 14 centuries and then to worry about people who came into the country and seized it a few months or a couple of years ago?"

This 1951 utterance was not a casual passing remark. Eight years later, in an interview published in the October 1959 issue of the *Middle East Forum*, Haj Amin answered the question "Where do you think the Jews of Israel could go," with the same haughty unconcern:

> They could go anywhere. Already there are 5,000,000 in the United States, which has the resources and space to take more. The Americans like them and they like the Americans, so I don't see why they should not have their own state there.*

---

* In June 1962, Egypt's deputy foreign minister, Hussein Zulficar Sabri, endorsed the Mufti's recipe for Israel's Jews: Mr. Ben-Gurion and all the other Israelis, he told a press conference in Stockholm, should return to their countries of origin. Sabri was, however, prepared to let nine per cent of Israel's population stay on. They were, he claimed, the original Hebrew-speaking inhabitants of Palestine whom he described as "not Jews but Arabs of the Jewish faith." (*Jewish Chronicle*, June 22, 1962.)

Envoi

THROUGHOUT THE FORTY YEARS OF HIS SUSTAINED STRUGGLE for an independent Arab Palestine, Haj Amin rarely left anything to chance. Each stage of the battle was deliberately and painstakingly planned, minutely adapted to the exigencies of the situation as he saw it. In this he favorably differed from most Arab leaders, who so often indulged in hasty and impulsive political improvisations.

Yet, viewed in retrospect, each of his so carefully elaborated schemes were somehow flawed and ended in defeat.

While in Jerusalem, Haj Amin deemed it possible to wage a war for Arab independence on two fronts simultaneously: against the Zionist national aspirations in Palestine *and* against the interests of the British Empire. In this he badly miscalculated, overestimating Arab strength and underestimating the determination and the power of his antagonists. As long as he concentrated on anti-Jewish warfare—both political and physical—and on the elimination of his rivals in the Arab camp, making the British believe that he was just a kind of "British mufti" with some Arab nationalist leanings, he was permitted to operate freely. Yet as soon as he overstepped these limitations and openly challenged the mandatory power, his position became untenable. It is a moot point whether the

British administration would ever have dared to imprison or deport the Mufti of Jerusalem. Haj Amin made this question academic by fleeing the country and becoming a political *émigré* in French-mandated territory.

Once out of British reach, he intensified his earlier ties with Britain's enemies: Mussolini's Italy and Hitler's Germany. Without relenting his anti-Jewish crusade, he increasingly—though still surreptitiously—concentrated on anti-British activities, playing the Axis against Great Britain and getting ever deeper involved in the intricate game of international politics. The breaking point came in Iraq, Haj Amin's next base of operations, where he was instrumental in staging, in May 1941, the anti-British coup of Rashid el-Gailani, and proclaimed a Holy War against the British Empire. He lost again and had to flee for his life.

Since then, Haj Amin's abomination of Britain fully matched, and intermittently surpassed, his loathing of Jews. A great hater by nature, he made these two fierce aversions the guiding stimulus of his entire political strategy. Active association with Nazism was motivated not so much by endorsement of its theory and program— which in the final analysis probably were "too western" and therefore only mildly understandable and attractive for the Mufti's oriental mentality—as by the fervent urge to become a full-fledged partner to the destruction of both world Jewry and Great Britain through the ultimate victory of the Axis, which he considered both unavoidable and imminent.

In this, too, the Mufti miscalculated. The collapse of Nazi Germany seemed to have spelled *finis* to his political career. He became one of the many fugitive Nazi collaborators, liable to stand trial by the victorious Allies. A curious interplay of British double-dealing and bungling and French scheming and fence-sitting, supplemented by an odd American aloofness, saved Haj Amin from such a predicament. He was able (or perhaps permitted) to "escape" from France to Cairo and to be reinstated as the most venerated and feared Arab leader.

He was realistic enough to tone down, in a world dominated by the victorious Allies, his anti-British thrusts, but the anti-Jewish half of his twin-hatred came to the fore again. A great opportunity seemed to present itself after the partition decision of the United Nations. During the initial stages of the 1948 armed showdown between the Arabs and the nascent state of Israel, the Mufti's role was pivotal and spectacular. But—here again—his hopes were frustrated. Israel withstood victoriously the Arab onslaught, and on the Arab side of the barricade it was the Mufti's inveterate arch-rival Abdallah of Transjordan who emerged as the main beneficiary, able to bar Haj Amin's attempt to establish himself as the head of a shadowy "Government of all Palestine," with the seat in Egyptian-held Gaza. It is still uncertain whether, and to what extent, Haj Amin was later (July 1951) involved in the assassination of Abdallah. But the removal of Jordan's ruler in no way improved his political fortunes. Nor was his Pan-Islam card, played in 1951-52, of any lasting avail.

The final blow was delivered by the bloody collapse of the Kassem regime in Iraq—the last big stake in the intricate design of the Mufti's inner-Arab political moves.

This pattern of bold planning and high expectation, followed in each case by setbacks and disappointments, would have broken the spirit of most political leaders. It did not shatter Haj Amin's singleminded dedication to the Arab cause as he saw it. But it all but wrecked his power position in the Arab world. Now, in the year 1964, the former Mufti of Jerusalem is a pathetically lonely, figure.

He is no longer in his prime of age. Yet, at about

302 THE MUFTI AND THE FUEHRER

seventy, he seems to be in full command of his restless,
alert mind. He lost his struggle for the cause he was ob-
sessed by and for which he was so persistently and
vehemently fighting: an Arab Palestine with himself as its
head. The very notion of "Palestine" as he envisaged it
(encompassing the whole of the right bank of the Jordan
River) has actually disappeared from the political map of
the Middle East. The area has been divided between the
State of Israel and the State of Jordan, with Egypt
occupying the narrow Gaza strip. Haj Amin refused
to accept this new reality, vigorously reasserting and
preaching the restoration of what he calls "the Palestine
Entity." But he ceased to be an independent force in any
attempt at restoring this entity. For a time he was able to
play the role of a mastermind, a political idea-man and
promoter. Yet, for whatever action he wanted to take, he
had to appeal to the heads of the Arab states possessing
both military strength and political influence. In one form
or another, they seemed to have, at least in principle, endorsed his program, without however acknowledging his
authorship of it. Since there is no copyright in the world
of political ideas, Haj Amin was compelled to put up with
this plagiarism—a restraint which certainly is not in keeping with his self-assertive ego. The role he was playing
was in essence similar to—though not identical with—
that of a "kibbitzer" in a card game staged by parties
capable of laying out high stakes on the table. The game
itself might have been invented by the bystander, dying
to be recognized as active partner to it; yet, by now he has
become a mere "poor relative," unable to be admitted on
equal footing by heads of established Arab states—a role
which is anything but satisfactory to a man who for so
many years was in the forefront of Arab politics, a power
in his own right.

What is probably torturing Haj Amin most is the proud, and fundamentally correct, conviction that as a political personality he has always been vastly superior to each and every one of the contemporary Arab political leaders. He had no rival in his fanatical and unbending devotion to the Arab cause in Palestine as he saw it and believed in it. His *personal* incorruptibility in money matters is not disputed even by his most ardent opponents, a rare phenomenon in Middle East political mores. If Moslem public funds entrusted to him were used for purposes other than their legitimate destination, these purposes were serving the Arab cause—again, as he saw it—and not his personal enrichment.

In his eventful and checkered political career, Haj Amin showed an almost unbelievable persistence and resilience: he was never discouraged by a setback, never took a defeat as definitive and final. His resourcefulness was truly amazing. After each reverse—and there were many of them—he was instantly looking for a way out, for another avenue, another course of action. There was much of the gambler in his stormy political record. His life was one of high adventure, and he was always ready to take personal risks, and escape a predicament at the very last moment. The roster of his numerous escapes, both genuine and faked, reads as a true cloak-and-dagger story.

The shadowy role he is now compelled to play, with only a dwindling band of his former "Arab Higher Committee" faithfuls still clinging to his flowing robe, must be cruelly frustrating to Haj Amin's proud ego. He is now a leader without an immediate, measurable mass following. Whatever remained of his influence is indirect and at the mercy of the powers-to-be in the Arab world.

Haj Amin el-Husseini is now a lonely, pathetic "has

been." Some call him a "Fallen Lucifer." But, however black are most chapters of his political record, it is difficult not to fall under the spell, the fascination of a life so eventful, dynamic, controversial, intense, adventurous, so rich in ascendances and failures. It left a deep, often bloody, trail in the entire Middle East scene, with ramifications spreading out over other parts of Asia, as well as over the two other continents of the Old World. It is a life begging to be reconstructed. This has been the purpose of the present biography.

Appendix One

Ciano Pledges Abolition of Jewish National Home

Ministry of Foreign Affairs   Rome, April 28, 1942
Eminence:

In response to the letter sent today by you and by His Excellency, the President of the Council, Raschid Ali el Gailani, and in confirmation of the conversations with you, I have the honor to communicate the following:

The Italian Government fully appreciates the confidence placed by the Arab people in the Axis powers and in their objectives, as well as their intention of participating in the fight against the common enemy until final victory is achieved. This is in accord with the national aspirations, as conveyed by you, of the Arab countries of the Near East at present oppressed by the British. I have the honor to assure you, in full agreement with the German government, that the independence and freedom of the Arab countries, now suffering under British oppression, are also the objective of the Italian Government.

Italy is therefore ready to grant to the Arab countries in the Near East, now suffering under British oppression, every possible aid in their fight for liberation; to recognize their sovereignty and independence; to agree to their federation if this is desired by the interested parties; as well as to the abolition of the National Jewish Homeland in Palestine.

It is understood that the text and contents of this letter shall be held absolutely secret until such a time as we together decide otherwise.

Please accept, Eminence, the expression of my highest consideration.

                                                        Ciano

Eminence
Amin el Husseini
Grand Mufti of Palestine
        ROME

Appendix Two

The Mufti's Diary on His Meeting with Hitler

Recording in his own handwriting his meeting with Hitler in his diary, Haj Amin el-Husseini says:

The words of the Fuehrer on the 6th of Zul Qaada 1360 of the Hejira [which falls on the 21st of November 1941] Berlin, Friday, from 4:30 P.M. till a few minutes after 6.

The objectives of my fight are clear. Primarily, I am fighting the Jews without respite, and this fight includes the fight against the so-called Jewish National Home in Palestine because the Jews want to establish there a central government for their own pernicious purposes, and to undertake a devastating and ruinous expansion at the expense of the governments of the world and of other peoples.

It is clear that the Jews have accomplished nothing in Palestine and their claims are lies. All the accomplishments in Palestine are due to the Arabs and not to the Jews. I am resolved to find a solution for the Jewish problem, progressing step by step without cessation. With regard to this I am making the necessary and right appeal, first to all the European countries and then to countries outside of Europe.

It is true that our common enemies are Great Britain and the Soviets whose principles are opposed to ours. But behind them stands hidden Jewry which drives them both. Jewry has but one aim in both these countries. We are now in the midst of a life and death struggle against both these nations. This fight will not only determine the outcome of the struggle between National Socialism and Jewry, but the whole conduct of this successful war will be of great and positive help to the Arabs who are engaged in the same struggle.

This is not only an abstract assurance.* A mere promise would

* This is a reply to the insistent request of the Mufti for an Axis declaration to the Arabs.

be of no value whatsoever. But assurance which rests upon a conquering force is the only one which has real value. In the Iraqi campaign, for instance, the sympathy of the whole German people was for Iraq. It was our aim to help Iraq, but circumstances prevented us from furnishing actual help. The German people saw in them [the Iraqis] comrades in suffering because the German people too have suffered as they have. All the help we gave Iraq was not sufficient to save Iraq from the British forces. For this reason it is necessary to underscore one thing: in this struggle which will decide the fate of the Arabs I can now speak as a man dedicated to an ideal and as a military leader and a soldier. Everyone united in this great struggle who helps to bring about its successful outcome serves the common cause and thus serves the Arab cause. Any other view means weakening the military situation and thus offers no help to the Arab cause. Therefore it is necessary for us to decide the steps which can help us against world Jewry, against Communist Russia and England, and which among them can be most useful. Only if we win the war will the hour of deliverance also be the hour of fulfillment of Arab aspirations.

The situation is as follows: we are conducting the great struggle to open the way to the North of the Caucasus. The difficulties involved are more than transportation because of the demolished railways and roads and because of winter weather. And if I venture in these circumstances to issue a declaration with regard to Syria, then the pro–de Gaulle elements in France will be strengthened and this might cause a revolt in France. These men (the French) will be convinced then that joining Britain is more advantageous and the detachment of Syria is a pattern to be followed in the remainder of the French Empire. This will strengthen de Gaulle's stand in the colonies. If the declaration is issued now, difficulties will arise in Western Europe which will cause the diversion of some [German] forces for defensive purposes, thus preventing us from sending all our forces to the East.

Now I am going to tell you something I would like you to keep secret.

First, I will keep up my fight until the complete destruction of the Judeo-Bolshevik rule has been accomplished.

Second, during the struggle (and we don't know when victory will come, but probably not in the far future) we will reach the Southern Caucasus.

Third, then I would like to issue a declaration; for then the hour of the liberation of the Arabs will have arrived. Germany has no ambitions in this area but cares only to annihilate the power which produces the Jews.

Fourth, I am happy that you have escaped and that you are now with the Axis powers. The hour will strike when you will be the lord of the supreme word and not only the conveyer of our declarations. You will be the man to direct the Arab force and at that moment I cannot imagine what would happen to the Western peoples.

Fifth, I think that with this Arab advance begins the dismemberment of the British world. The road from Rostov to Iran and Iraq is shorter than the distance from Berlin to Rostov. We hope next year to smash this barrier. It is better then and not now that a declaration should be issued as (now) we cannot help in anything.

I understand the Arab desire for this [declaration], but His Excellency the Mufti must understand that only five years after I became President of the German government and Fuehrer of the German people, was I able to get such a declaration [the Austrian Union], and this because military forces prevented me from issuing such a declaration. But when the German Panzer tanks and the German air squadrons reach the Southern Caucasus, then will be the time to issue the declaration.

He said (in reply to a request that a secret declaration or a treaty be made) that a declaration known to a number of persons cannot remain secret but will become public. I (Hitler) have made very few declarations in my life, unlike the British who have made many declarations. If I issue a declaration, I will uphold it. Once I promised the Finnish Marshal that I would help his country if the enemy attacks again. This word of mine made a stronger impression than any written declaration.

Recapitulating, I want to state the following to you: When we shall have arrived in the Southern Caucasus, then the time of the liberation of the Arabs will have arrived. And you can rely on my word.

We were troubled about you. I know your life history. I followed with interest your long and dangerous journey. I was very concerned about you. I am happy that you are with us now and that you are now in a position to add your strength to the common cause.

Appendix Three

The Mufti Proposes an Arab Legion to Himmler

To the   Berlin, October 3, 1944
Reichsfuehrer and Reichsminister
       H. Himmler   *Headquarters of the Fuehrer.*
Reichsfuehrer!

I permit myself to call to your attention the renewal of the
dangerous demands of the Jews, with the support of the Allies, for
the establishment of a Jewish state in Palestine, as well as the
approval given by the British government to the establishment of
a Jewish military unit to fight against Germany with a view to thus
winning title to such a state. According to the last speech of
Churchill in the House of Commons on September 28, 1944, the
British government has declared itself ready to establish such a
military unit and to provide for its training and arming.

This declaration on the part of the British government has
produced the worst possible reaction in all the Arab-Islamic
countries. I therefore propose that as a challenge to this act there
should be announced the establishment of an Arab-Islamic army
in Germany. This army should be established by Arab and
Islamic volunteers and should be merged with the Arab-Islamic
units already in existence. The German government should declare
its readiness to train and arm such an army. Thus it would level a
severe blow against the British plan and increase the number of
fighters for a greater Germany.

I am convinced that the establishment of such an army and
announcement of its purpose would have the most favorable reper-
cussions in the Arab-Islamic countries. I therefore beg you to consider the possibility of making such an announcement on November
2, 1944. It would thus appear on the anniversary of the infamous
Balfour Declaration pledging the establishment of the so-called
Jewish National Home in 1917, and on the anniversary of the
pledge of 1943 by the Foreign Minister of the Reich to destroy
the so-called Jewish National Home.

Accept, Reichsfuehrer, the expression of my highest esteem
                               Yours.

Appendix Four

Mufti Asks Ban on Jewish Emigration as Gesture to Arabs

Berlin, July 27, 1944

To the Reichsfuehrer SS and Minister of the Interior
  H. Himmler
        Berlin
Reichsfuehrer:

In my letter to you of June 5, 1944, I referred back to our conversation in which I reported to you on the inclusion of Jews in the exchange plan of some Egyptians living in Germany.

I asked you, Reichsfuehrer, to take all the measures to prevent the Jews from going. These measures would also be in accordance with German policy in general, especially with the Declaration of the German Government on the occasion of the anniversary of the Balfour Declaration on November 2, 1943, which stated "that the destruction of the so-called Jewish national home in Palestine is an immutable part of the policy of the greater German Reich" and that "the National Socialist movement, since its inception, has inscribed on its banner the battle against world Jewry," as you, Reichsfuehrer, said in your telegram on the same occasion.

In the meantime I have learned that the Jews, nevertheless, did leave on July 2, 1944, and it is to be feared that further Jewish groups may leave Germany and France under the plan for exchanging Palestinian Germans. This exchange of Germans would encourage the Balkan countries to send their Jews to Palestine too. Furthermore, after the Declaration of the German Government, such a step would be incomprehensible to the Arabs and Moslems, and it would create in them a feeling of keen disappointment.

It is for this reason that I ask you, Reichsfuehrer, to do everything necessary to prevent the Jews from emigrating to Palestine, and in this way you would give a new practical example of the policy of the naturally allied and friendly Germany towards the Arab Nation.

Yours, etc.

Appendix Five

Secret Memorandum Addressed by the Mufti to the Governments of All Arab States (November 1959)

(Reprinted from *Jewish Observer and Middle East Review*, London, January 15, 1960.)

The cause of Palestine is at present passing through a delicate stage. The enemies are exerting all their efforts in an attempt to liquidate Palestine and wipe out all trace of its Arab populace, as is evident from the web of plots which they are still hatching against the Arabs.

They are seizing every opportunity of carrying out these plots, whether at the present session of the U.N. General Assembly or at forthcoming international conferences, including the Summit conference. Britain, for instance, is insisting on putting Middle East problems on its agenda.

The statement recently made by the American Secretary of State calling on the Arabs to negotiate with the Jews with a view to liquidating the state of tension arising from the Palestine problem, the statements from time to time that the subsidies to UNRWA are running short and will eventually be exhausted, the brutal maltreatment of the Arabs in occupied Palestine, Ben-Gurion's recent statements during the election campaign that both banks of the Jordan must be merged with the Jewish State, and many other statements, present the Arabs with fresh evidence of the imperialist-Zionist designs for the liquidation of the Palestinian problem.

The memorandum here enters into a dissertation on the history of the Palestine problem, following familiar propaganda lines. It then continues:

On the occasion of the meeting of the United Nations General Assembly, the Arab Higher Committee deems it its duty towards

Palestine and Arabism to express once again the viewpoint of the Palestinian Arabs on this question.

The factors and reasons which led the Arabs and their States to reject and oppose the partition and internationalisation resolutions have not changed. Nothing has occurred to make the Arabs change their attitude.

The partition resolution set aside for the Jews the best, most fertile and largest parts of Palestine, as well as the port of Haifa and most of the coastline. It placed many Islamic and Christian religious sites and sanctuaries under Jewish control. On the other hand, the partition resolution left for the Arabs an area smaller than that of the Jews.

Most of this area is mountainous and barren, and many parts of it are also separated into pieces which are linked with each other by ridiculous corridors. In addition to all this, the partition resolution stipulated the establishment of economic unity between the Palestinian and Jewish States, and the formation of a Supreme Economic Council to supervise customs, currency and other economic affairs.

It was only natural that the Arabs should reject the partition resolution, since no people in the world can possibly concede the partition of their homeland, or allow foreigners to carve out any part of it to set up a State. To this may be added the revoking of the Arabs' natural right to their own country and the infringement represented by this resolution—not to mention the fact that more than one-third of the Arabs of Palestine would be placed under Jewish rule.

As for the establishment of economic unity, this would place the Arab State at the mercy of the Jews, and enable the Jews to attain economic control and to expand economically and financially in the rest of the Arab countries. Economic unity would also necessitate the existence of economic co-operation between the Arabs and Jews, a matter which is tantamount to Arab recognition of the Jewish State and conducive to a peace treaty with it.

This is in addition to the threat to the entire Arab existence by the establishment of a Jewish State in the midst of the Arab homeland. Peace with Israel would make it a member of the Middle East community. Furthermore, acceptance of the partition resolution requires recognition of the borders of Israel—hence recognition of Israel itself. It would also lead to suspension of the boycott imposed on it, as well as any measures against it.

The Arabs rejected the internationalisation resolution because, in addition to the reasons which made them reject the partition resolution, this resolution favours the establishment of bases—or rather, influence—not just for one imperialist power, but for many.

Thus, the internationalised areas would become an imperialist base, a centre for foreigners, a melting pot for espionage against the Arabs, and a springboard for obstruction of the progress and liberation of the Arabs. It would also make the holy Aqsa Mosque and the rest of the Islamic and Christian sanctuaries subject to foreign control. Moreover, it would place the economic and national interests of the Arabs at the mercy of the Jews and foreigners.

Certain Arab States are demanding implementation of the U.N. resolutions on refugees, which give the refugees the choice of repatriation or compensation and resettlement in the Arab countries. Acceptance of these resolutions implies acquiescence in the principle of non-repatriation of Palestinians and their rehabilitation in the Arab countries. This is the object which the Jews and their supporters are seeking to realise.

Also, repatriation of the refugees to a Palestine housing a Jewish State is a matter which is unacceptable to Jews. But, assuming that the Jews would accept it, what guarantees then can be given to protect the Arabs and safeguard their dignity, money and interests? We are witnessing the criminal, terroristic and atrocious treatment accorded the Arabs in the occupied zone by Jews, under the nose of the U.N.

In view of all this, the Arabs are duty bound to confront the enemies with the same readiness and determination which they are employing in pursuit of the achievement of their dangerous aims, aims harmful to the interests of Palestine and the entire Arab nation. Continuation of the policy of leniency and placability will inflict more and graver losses upon the Arabs.

Therefore, the Arabs of Palestine request the Arab States to handle the Palestine question with a view to realising one aspiration—to exert all efforts and employ all methods in conformity with a careful plan for stamping out Jewish aggression against Palestine and purging it of Zionism and imperialism. In this way, the interests of all the Arab countries will be protected and Palestine brought back to the Arab fold.

To realise this supreme aim, Arab interests require that Arab officials should put an end to inter-Arab disputes and work devotedly, firmly and resolutely to mobilise the potentialities of the entire Arab nation to counter the Jewish-imperialist policy of aggression.

Arab officials must stick by the national demands of the Arabs—complete and retracting nothing—and seek to realise the complete unity of the Arabs. This requires the adoption of a firm attitude towards the States which help and assist the Jews, the tightening of the Arab blockade imposed on the Jewish State, the combatting of its efforts to expand economically and commercially in Asia and Africa, the unification of the military commands, the reinforcement of the Arab armies, the training of Arab youth as the Jews train their youth, the postponement of all luxury projects, and the confinement of financial expenditure to military preparation and matters.

In view of the great part which the Palestinians could play in regaining their fatherland, we appeal to the Arab States to take the initiative and bring Palestine back into existence in the manner desired by the Arabs of Palestine, either by a plebiscite or a free popular election.

Such a move must be backed by training, arms, money, etc. All Palestinians from 18 to 50 must be brought under compulsory military training and a Palestinian army must be created, trained and armed to be the vanguard of the Arab forces which will march to regain Palestine.

Chairman of the Arab Higher Committee for Palestine, Beirut.

Notes

Chapter One

1. M. P. Waters, *Mufti Over the Middle East* (London, 1942), pp. 5-8; John M. Bee, "The Ex-Mufti—an Exposure," *Great Britain and the East* (September 5, 1942); Maurice Pearlman, *Mufti of Jerusalem: The Story of Haj Amin el Husseini* (London, 1947), pp. 10-11.

2. I. A. Abbady, "Will Massacre All Zionists, Said Mufti 30 Years Ago," *New York Post*, December 29, 1947.

3. Great Britain, *Parliamentary Papers, 1936-37, Cmd. 5479*, p. 50.

4. Norman Bentwich, *My 77 Years* (London, 1961), p. 73.

5. John Gunther, *Inside Asia* (New York and London, 1942), p. 579.

6. Paul L. Hanna, *British Policy in Palestine* (Washington, D. C., 1942), p. 182.

7. *Palestine Royal Commission Report, Cmd. 5479* (London, 1937), p. 177.

8. Ernest Maine, *Palestine at the Crossroads* (London, 1937), p. 37.

9. *Cmd. 5479*, p. 180.

10. John Marlowe, *Rebellion in Palestine* (London, 1946), p. 74.

11. *Cmd. 5479*, p. 178.

12. J. C. Hurewitz, *The Struggle for Palestine* (New York, 1950), pp. 53-54.

13. H. J. Simson, *British Rule and Rebellion* (Edinburgh and London, 1937), p. 167.

14. Marlowe, *op. cit.* p. 80.

15. *Report of the Commission on the Palestine Disturbances of August 1929* (London, 1930), pp. 71-72.

16. Lt. Col. F. H. Kisch, *Palestine Diary* (London, 1938), p. 191.

17. *Ibid.*, p. 203.

18. Hanna, *op. cit.* pp. 72-73.

19. *Ibid.*, p. 73.

20. Kisch, *op. cit.*, pp. 87, 105, 263, 300.

21. Great Britain, Privy Council, *The Palestine Order in Council, 1922* (London, 1922).

22. *Ibid.*

23. Kisch, *op. cit.*, p. 308.

24. Great Britain, *Parliamentary Papers, 1923, Cmd. 1889*, pp. 3-9.

25. *Parliamentary Debates, House of Lords*, December 8, 1938.

26. Ladislas Farago, *Palestine at the Crossroads* (New York, 1937), p. 60.

27. Humphrey Bowman, *Middle East Window* (London, New York, Toronto, 1942), p. 288.

28. Hanna, *op. cit.*, pp. 83-94.

29. *Cmd. 3530*, 1930, p. 73.

30. *Report of the Executive of the Zionist Organization submitted to the XVII Zionist Congress at Basle* (London, 1931), p. 186; *Cmd. 3530*, p. 70.

31. Horace Samuel, *Revolt by Leave* (London, 1936), p. 46. Sheikh Taleb Morke who called the Arabs of Hebron to kill the Jews declared that an order to this effect had come from the Mufti—Kisch, *op. cit.*, p. 263.

32. Quoted in *Rassvyet* (Paris), December 22, 1929.

33. *Cmd. 3530*, pp. 70-78, 159.

34. *Ibid.*, p. 172.

35. League of Nations, Permanent Mandates Commission, *Minutes of the Seventeenth (Extraordinary) Session, 1930*, p. 41.

36. Walter Z. Laqueur, *Communism and Nationalism in the Middle East* (New York, 1956), pp. 84, 88.

37. Quoted in *Rassvyet*, December 22, 1929.

38. For accounts on the Congress see H. A. R. Gibb, "The Islamic Congress at Jerusalem in December 1931" in Toynbee, *Survey of International Affairs 1934* (London, 1935), pp. 99-109; *The Times* (London), October 19, November 6, 20, 30 and December 7, 9, 12, 18, 1931.

39. Ernest Maine, *Palestine at the Crossroads*, p. 56.

40. *Ibid.*, p. 38.

41. T. R. Feivel, *No Ease in Zion* (New York, 1939), pp. 116-117.

42. Ladislas Farago, *Palestine at the Crossroads*, pp. 62-63.

43. Eliahu Ben Horin, *The Middle East* (New York, 1943), p. 119.

44. Farago, *op. cit.*, p. 62.

45. Ben Horin, *op. cit.*, p. 169.

46. Hanna, *op. cit.*, p. 122.

47. *Ibid.*, p. 123.

48. Laqueur, *op. cit.*, pp. 96-97.

49. *Palestine Royal Commission Report*, July 1937, pp. 104-106.

50. Marlowe, *op. cit.*, pp. 157, 186, 189, 194, 193.

51. Great Britain, C. O., *Palestine Report 1936, Colonial No. 129*, pp. 30-31.

52. Marlowe, *op. cit.*, p. 164.

53. Hanna, *op. cit.*, p. 126.

54. Palestine Royal Commission, *Minutes of Evidence. Heard at Public Sessions* (London, 1939), Col. W. 134, p. 298 and 314.

55. *Palestine Royal Commission Report, July 1937, Cmd. 5479*, pp. 178-179, 181.

56. *The Jewish Chronicle* (London), February 19, 1937.

57. *Ibid.*, February 26, 1937.

58. *Parliamentary Debates, House of Commons*, March 17, 1937.

59. *The Jewish Chronicle*, April 2, 1937.

60. Quoted in S. Levenberg, *The Jews and Palestine—Study in Labour Zionism* (London, 1945), pp. 227-228.

61. Norman Bentwich, *My 77 Years*, pp. 73-74.

62. Great Britain, C.O., *Palestine Report 1937, Colonial No. 146*, pp. 5-8.

63. *The Palestine Gazette*, Extraordinary, No. 675, March 24, 1932.

64. *Ibid.*, Extraordinary, No. 723, September 30, 1937.

65. See an official communiqué issued on October 1, 1937.

66. *New York Times*, October 4, 1937.

67. *Ibid.*

68. Kisch, *op. cit.*, p. 330.

69. *New York Times*, October 24, 1937.

70. *New York Herald Tribune*, October 16, 1937.

71. Gunther, *op. cit.*, p. 585.

72. *New York Post*, October 18, 1937.

Chapter Two

1. *New York Herald Tribune*, October 19, 1937; *New York Times*, October 24, 1937.

2. *Jewish Chronicle* (London), February 2, 1938.

3. Waters, *op. cit.*, pp. 18-19.

4. *Ibid.*, p. 19.

5. *New York Times*, December 19, 1938.

6. Waters, *op. cit.*, p. 20.

7. *Ibid.*, pp. 20-23.

8. J. C. Hurewitz, *Struggle for Palestine*, p. 114.

9. Margaret Boveri, *Minaret and Pipeline: Yesterday and Today in the Near East* (London, New York, Toronto, 1939), pp. 358-395.

10. Quoted in *Jewish Chronicle* (London), March 18, 1938.

11. *Parliamentary Debates, House of Lords*, December 8, 1938.

12. Quoted in *Jewish Chronicle* (London), March 18, May 27, 1938.

13. *Parliamentary Debates, House of Commons*, May 10, 1939.

14. Roger Courtney, *Palestine Policeman: An Account of Eighteen Dramatic Months in the Palestine Police Force During the Great Jew-Arab Troubles* (London, 1939), p. 219.

15. *New Judaea* (London), May-June, 1940.

16. *New York Times*, March 6, December 16 and 19, 1938.

17. *New Judaea*, December 1938–January 1939.

18. Quoted in full in Waters, *op. cit.*, p. 25.

19. *Ibid.*

20. John M. Bee, "The Ex-Mufti—An Exposure," *Great Britain and the East*, September 5, 1942.

21. Duglas W. Duff, *Poor Knight's Saddle* (London, 1938), p. 25.

22. *Documents on German Foreign Policy, 1918-1945*, Series D. (1937-1945), Vol. V; June 1937-March 1939. Washington D. C., 1953.

23. *Jewish Chronicle*, June 14, 1961.

24. *Documents on German Foreign Policy* (Documents 576, 582, 590), pp. 777-780, 789-791, 810-811.

25. *L'Information* (Paris), June 13, 1936.

26. *Palestine Post*, January 28, 1938.

27. *Daily Express* (London), July 19, 1938; and *Daily Telegraph* (London), July 23, 1938.

28. *Parliamentary Debates, House of Commons*, May 22, 1939.

29. John Gunther, *Inside Asia*, p. 552.

30. Raoul Aglion, *The Fighting French* (New York, 1943), p. 217.

31. Carl Raswan, *Escape from Baghdad* (London, 1938), pp. 133-134, 137.

32. *The Times* (London), November 11, 1938.

33. John Marlowe, *Rebellion in Palestine*, pp. 209-210.

34. Paul L. Hanna. *British Policy in Palestine*, pp. 143-144; *Palestine Post*, November 18, 1938.

35. *Parliamentary Debates, House of Commons*, November 23, 1938.

36. *Ibid.*, December 14, 1938.

37. Marlowe, *op. cit.*, p. 211.

38. *The Times* (London), January 24, February 2, 1939.

39. Marlowe. *op. cit.*, pp. 211-212.

40. *Ibid.*, pp. 217-219.

41. Hurewitz, *op. cit.*, pp. 116-117.

42. *Ibid.*, p. 82.

43. *Ibid.*, pp. 148-149.

44. *The Times* (London), October 18, 1939.

45. "Interview with the Grand Mufti," *Arab News Bulletin* (Washington, D. C.), October 10, 1946.

46. Hurewitz, *op. cit.*, p. 148.

47. Lord Birdwood, *Nuri Said: A Study in Arab Leadership* (London, 1959), p. 17.

Chapter Three

1. *Parliamentary Debates, House of Commons*, October 25, 1939.

2. Full text in *The Arab War Effort: A Documented Account* (New York: The American Christian Palestine Committee, 1947), pp. 35-40.

3. Waters, *op. cit.*, p. 29.

4. *Ibid.*, pp. 29-30.

5. *Documents on German Foreign Policy, 1918-1945*, Series D (1937-1945), Vol. XII. The war years, February 1–June 22, 1941 (Washington, D.C., 1962), p. 890.

6. Freya Stark, *The Arab Islands* (New York, 1945), p. 159.

7. Majid Khaddury, *Independent Iraq: A Study in Iraqi Politics from 1932 to 1958* (London, New York, Karachi), 1960.

8. The Nation Associates, *Arab Higher Committee, Its origin, Personnel and Purposes: The Documentary Record Submitted to the United Nations*, New York, 1947.

9. J. C. Hurewitz, *Struggle for Palestine*, p. 150.

10. *Ibid.*, pp. 146-147.

11. In his study, *Independent Iraq*, Majid Khaddury gives a full account, based on first-hand sources, of these negotiations, pp. 178-189.

12. The French text of the letter is reproduced in full in Majid Khaddury's study, pp. 378-380.

13. Majid Khaddury, *op. cit.*, pp. 181-182.

14. C. L. Sulzberger, "German Preparations in the Middle East," *Foreign Affairs*, July 1942, p. 668.

15. *Great Britain and the East*, January 13, 1941.

16. Raoul Aglion, *War in the Desert* (New York, 1941), p. 141.

17. Gerald de Gaury, *Three Kings in Baghdad* (London, 1961), pp. 116-117.

18. Full text of the "fatwa," appeared in *al-Istiqlal* and *al-Liwa*, May 9, 1941; an Italian translation was published in *Oriente Moderno*, 1941, vol. 31, pp. 552-553. It was also broadcast over Iraqi and Axis radios.

19. Philip Guedalla, *Middle East 1940-1942: A Study in Air Power* (London, 1944), p. 140.

20. *The Jewish Herald* (Johannesburg), March 21, September 5, 1961.

21. Bracha Habas, *Achim Krovim Nidachim* (Hebrew; Tel Aviv, 1945), p. 46; Jacob Lestchinsky, *Jews in Moslem Lands* (New York, 1946), pp. 12, 13.

Chapter Four

1. *Documents on German Foreign Policy, 1918-1945*, Vol. XII, p. 959.

2. Khaddury, *op. cit.*, p. 235.

3. Associated Press dispatch, August 18, 1946 (based on captured German records).

4. Arthur C. Millspaugh, *Americans in Persia* (Washington, D.C., 1946), p. 8.

5. Lord Birdwood, *Nuri Said: A Study in Arab Leadership* (London, 1959), p. 192.

6. *New York Times*, October 28, 1941.

7. *Ibid.*

8. Khaddury, *op. cit.*, p. 238.

9. *Ibid.*, p. 232.

10. *Ciano's Diary, 1939-1943* (London, 1948), p. 491.

11. Majid Khaddury, *op. cit.*, p. 232.

12. *Ibid.*, p. 241.

13. Leonard Mosley, *The Cat and the Mice* (London, 1958), pp. 26-29.

14. Khaddury, *op. cit.*, p. 239.

15. *Ibid.*, p. 240.

16. "Jews and Arabs—Enemies? Unpublicized Actions of Unarmed Men," *NER* (Jerusalem) January-February, 1962.

17. *The Arab War Effort: A Documented Account,* published by the American Christian Palestine Committee (New York, 1937), p. 19.

18. *Ibid.*

19. *New York Post,* April 20, 1946.

20. *The Arab War Effort,* p. 20.

21. The Nation Associates, *The Arab Higher Committee: Its Origin, Personnel and Purposes.* The documentary record submitted to the United Nations. May, 1947, p. 7.

22. *The Arab War Effort,* p. 20.

23. The Nation Associates, *The Record of Collaboration of King Farouk of Egypt with the Nazis and their Ally, the Mufti.* The official Nazi records of the King's alliance and of the Mufti's plans for bombing Jerusalem and Tel Aviv. Memorandum submitted to the United Nations. June, 1948.

24. Marc Yarblum, "Open Letter to Mr. Habib Bourguiba, President of the Republic of Tunisia," *The Jewish Frontier,* December 1961.

25. *Palestine* (London), July 1944.

26. Edward D. Kleinlerer, "Mufti and Micado," *Congress Weekly,* February 20, 1942.

27. *Overseas News Agency,* August 28, 1945.

28. Pearlman, *op. cit.,* pp. 59-60.

29. *Palestine,* March 1945.

30. *Osvit* (Sarajevo), April 25, 1943.

31. *Overseas News Agency,* August 21, 1946.

32. *Palestine,* April 1944.

33. *The Arab War Effort,* p. 20.

34. *New York Post,* June 10, 1946.

35. Associated Press dispatch, based on captured German records, *New York Times,* August 18, 1946.

36. *Transocean,* June 10, 1943; *Dagposten,* Stockholm, June 11, 1943.

37. *DNB (Deutsches Nachrichten Büro),* November 8, 1943.

38. *Transocean,* December 18, 1943.

39. *DNB,* November 13, 1943.

40. *Transocean,* January 7, 1944.

41. *DNB,* November 8, 1943.

42. Quoted in John Roy Carlson, *Cairo to Damascus* (New York, 1945), pp. 420-421.

43. Robert M. W. Kempner, *Eichmann und Komplizen* (Zürich, Stuttgart, Wien, 1961), pp. 400-401.

44. *Ibid.,* p. 403.

45. Max Weinreich, *Hitler's Professors* (New York, 1946), pp. 226-227.

46. *New York Times,* November 12, 1943.

47. *Pariser Zeitung,* November 18, 1943.

48. Text in *Palestine* (London), July 1944.

49. The Nation Associates, *The Record of Collaboration of King*

Farouk of Egypt with the Nazis and their Ally, the Mufti. Memorandum Submitted to the United Nations, June 1948.

50. The Nation Associates, *The Arab Higher Committee* (full text of the letter).

51. *Ibid* (full text of the letter).

52. *Ibid.*

53. Kempner, *op. cit.*, pp. 402-403.

54. Quoted in Quentin Reynolds, Ephraim Katz, Zwy Aldouby, *Minister of Death: The Adolf Eichmann Story* (New York, 1960), pp. 174-175.

55. Kempner, *op. cit.*, p. 402.

56. Affidavit of engineer Endre Steiner, dated May 5, 1946, deposed in the minutes of the Nuremberg Trial, read over by Wisliceny himself at Nuremberg and approved for accuracy. Quoted in full in Maurice Pearlman, *Mufti of Jerusalem*, pp. 71-72.

57. Affidavit of Dr. Rudolf Kastner, *Ibid.*, p. 73.

58. *Israel Digest* (Jerusalem), June 9, 1961.

59. *Jerusalem Post*, June 28, 1961.

60. Kempner, *op. cit.*, p. 405.

61. Affidavit of Dr. Rudolf Kastner, quoted in Maurice Pearlman, *Mufti of Jerusalem*, p. 73.

62. Affidavit by Endre Steiner, *Ibid.*, p. 72.

63. *Jerusalem Post*, June 28, 1961.

64. *New York Times,* March 5, 1961; *Jewish Herald* (Johannesburg), March 28, 1961.

65. *Jerusalem Post,* June 13, 1961.

66. S. Wiesenthal, *Grossmufti—Grossagent der Achse* (Salzburg, Wien, 1947), pp. 51, 53-54.

67. Full text of the agreement was published by Drew Pearson in *New York Daily Mirror,* September 15, 1947.

Chapter Five

1. *Parliamentary Debates, House of Commons,* May 30, 1945.

2. *Ibid.,* October 24, 1945.

3. *Ibid.,* November 28, 1945.

4. *Ibid.,* December 12, 1945.

5. *Ibid.,* February 26, 1946.

6. *Ibid.,* March 11, 1946.

7. *Ibid.,* April 5, 1946.

8. *New York Post,* April 9, 1946.

9. *Parliamentary Debates, House of Commons,* April 15, 1946.

10. *New York Times,* May 9, 1946.

11. *New York Post,* July 19, 1945.

12. *Zionist Review* (London), September 7, 1945.

13. *Independent Jewish Press Service,* October 5, 1945.

14. *Zionist Review,* January 27, 1946.

15. *New York Post,* August 31, 1945.

16. *Middle East Opinion* (Cairo), June 10, 1946.

17. *New York Post*, April 9, 1946.

18. *New York Times*, June 12, 1946.

19. In the files of the New York office of the United Zionists Revisionists.

20. *New York Post*, June 18, 1946.

21. Observer, "Dean Acheson's Promise," *Compass* (New York), June 29, 1949.

22. *P.M.* (New York), June 5, 1946.

23. *Independent Jewish Press Service*, June 22, 1945.

24. *New York Times*, October 15, 1945.

25. *New York Post*, November 9, 1945.

26. *Parliamentary Debates, House of Commons*, February 2, 1942.

27. *Ibid.*, December 11, 1943.

28. *Ibid.*, December 1, 1943.

29. Quoted in M. P. Waters, *Mufti Over the Middle East*, p. 9.

Chapter Six

1. Wiesenthal. *op. cit.*, p. 59.

2. *New York Post*, June 10, 11, 13, 1946.

3. *New York Times* and *New York Post*, June 10, 1946.

4. *Parliamentary Debates, House of Commons*, June 19, 1946.

5. *New York Times*, June 20 and 21, 1946.

6. *Parliamentary Debates, House of Commons*, June 21, 1946.

7. *New York Times*, June 22, 1946.

8. *Ibid.*, June 25, 1946.

9. *Palestine Affairs*, August 1946.

10. JTA (*Jewish Telegraphic Agency Daily News Bulletin*), April 2 and 11, 1947.

11. *Parliamentary Debates, House of Commons*, May 6, 1947.

12. Jon Kimche, *Seven Fallen Pillars: The Middle East 1915-1950* (London, 1950), pp. 184-186.

13. J. C. Hurewitz, *The Struggle for Palestine*, p. 252.

14. *The Sunday Star*, Washington, D. C., November 11, 1945.

15. *Jewish Chronicle* (London), February 6, 1946.

16. *Al-Wahda* (Jerusalem), November 10, 1947.

17. King Abdallah of Jordan, *My Memoirs Completed* (*al Takmilah*) (Washington, D. C.), p. 57.

18. Testimony of Jamal el-Husseini in: Anglo-American Committee of Inquiry, *Hearings*, March 12, 1946, pp. 20-27.

19. *New York Times*, April 13, 1946; also Mark M. Krug, "An Unpublished Coup," *New Palestine*, October 4, 1946.

20. John Marlowe, *Rebellion in Palestine*, p. 210.

21. A. Goldstein, "The Nejada: Illegal Army of the Arabs," *Jewish Standard* (London), August 23, 1946.

22. *Jewish Standard*, August 23, 1946.

23. *New York Times*, December 28, 1946.

24. Clifton Daniel, "A New Chapter for the Mysterious Mufti," *New York Times Magazine*, August 25, 1946.

25. *New York Times*, August 13, 1946.

26. *Palestine Affairs*, September 1946.

27. *New York Times*, August 26, 1946.

28. *Ibid.*, August 27, 1946.

29. *Ibid.*

30. *Palestine Affairs*, September 1946.

31. *Middle East Opinion* (Cairo), September 23, 1948.

32. *New Judaea* (London), December 1946–January 1947.

33. *Middle East Opinion*, January 20, 1947.

34. *JTA*, April 5, 1947.

35. Jacob Robinson, *Palestine and the United Nations: Prelude to Solution* (Washington, D.C., 1947), pp. 128, 134.

36. The Nations Associates, *Arab Higher Committee.*

37. *New York Times*, May 12, 1947.

38. *Ibid.*, June 7, 1947.

39. *Ibid.*, October 19, 1947.

40. United Nations General Assembly, *Official Record*, Vol. III. First Committee, pp. 270-272.

41. Robinson, *op. cit.*, p. 137.

42. *New York Herald Tribune*, May 19, 1947.

43. J. C. Hurewitz, *The Struggle for Palestine*, p. 234.

44. George Kirk, "The Middle East 1945-1950," *Survey of International Affairs* (London, New York, Toronto, 1954), p. 24.

45. Hurewitz, *op. cit.*, p. 294.

46. *New York Herald Tribune*, October 9, 1947.

47. David W. Nussbaum, "Hitler of the Holy Land: A First-hand Report on the Mufti, Master of Terrorism," *'48 Magazine*, June 1948.

48. David W. Nussbaum, "The Mufti Plan of Conquest," *Journal-Courier* (New Haven), March 19, 1948.

49. Kirk, *op. cit.*, p. 251.

50. Joseph Alsop, "Crafty Fanatic Organizes Trouble in Palestine," *Evening Globe* (Boston), December 17, 1947.

51. *Parliamentary Debates, House of Commons*, March 3 and 16, 1948.

52. "Jews and Arabs—Enemies? Unpublicized Actions of Unarmed Men," *NER* (Jerusalem) January-February 1962, pp. xi-xiv.

53. Security Council *Official Records*, Nos. 36-51, pp. 137-168.

54. *New York Times*, March 26, 1948.

55. *Ibid.*, March 31, 1948.

56. John Bagot Glubb, *A Soldier With the Arabs* (New York, 1957), p. 49.

57. Sidney Nettleton Fischer, *The Middle East: A History* (New York, 1959), p. 573.

58. *Middle East Bulletin*, April 2, 1948.

59. *New York Times*, April 13, 1948.

60. *Ibid.*, October 10, 1948.

61. *Ibid.*, July 10, 12, 29, 1948.

324 THE MUFTI AND THE FUEHRER

62. *Ibid.*, September 6, 1948.

63. *Ibid.*, September 18, 1948.

64. *Ibid.*, September 21, 1948.

65. *Ibid.*, September 23 and 26, 1948.

66. *Ibid.*, October 2, 1948; *New York Herald Tribune*, September 30, 1948.

67. Netanel Larch, *The Edge of the Sword*, p. 401.

68. *Ibid.*, October 2, 1948.

69. Glubb, *op. cit.*, p. 192.

70. *New York Times*, December 21, 1948.

71. Benjamin Shwadron, *Jordan—A State of Tension* (New York, 1959), p. 284.

72. *New York Times*, December 21, 1948.

73. *Ibid.*, November 11, 1948.

74. *Ibid.*, March 26 and 28, 1950.

75. *Jerusalem Post*, June 13, 1950.

76. *New York Times*, April 14, 1950.

77. *Jerusalem Post*, May 19, 1950.

78. Glubb, *op. cit.*, p. 250.

79. *As Sayeh* (New York), January 16, 1960.

80. Sir Alec Seat Kirkbride, *A Krackle of Thorns* (London, 1956), pp. 164-165.

81. *New York Times*, August 3 and 29, 1948.

82. *Jerusalem Post*, August 7 and 16, 1951.

83. *Times* (London), July 25, 1947; *Jerusalem Post*, July 26, 1947.

84. *Times* (London), July 25, 1951.

85. *Jerusalem Post*, August 3 and 7, 1951.

86. *New York Times*, July 28, 1951.

87. Robert S. Allen, "Mufti Plotting Chaos in Jordan," *New York Post*, August 3, 1951. Also: Ann Dearden, *Jordan* (London, 1958), p. 93.

88. *New York Times*, July 22, 1951.

89. *Jerusalem Post*, April 2, May 19, 1953.

90. Quoted in *India and Israel* (Bombay), October 15, 1950.

91. *Ibid.*, March, 1951.

92. *Ibid.*, July 1951.

93. *Ibid.*, March 1951.

94. *Jewish Chronicle*, February 16, 1951.

95. Quoted in *India and Israel*, April 1951.

96. *Ibid.*, March 1951.

97. *New York Times*, March 1, 1952.

98. *Ibid.*

99. *Ibid.*, March 2, 1952.

100. *Ibid.*, March 1, 1952.

101. *The Jewish Agency's Digest of Press and Events* (Jerusalem), May 23, 1952.

102. James Bell, "Mystery Man of Islam Speaks," *Life*, October 27, 1952.

103. *Times-Herald* (Washington, D.C.), March 3, 1952.

104. Zvi Kaplinsky, "The Muslem Brotherhood," *Middle Eastern Affairs*, December 1954.

105. *Middle Eastern Affairs*, May 1955.

106. *Jewish Frontier*, May 1955.

107. Full text of the memorandum is reproduced in Appendix Five.

108. *Jewish Observer and Middle East Review* (London), January 15, 1960.

109. *Ibid.*

110. *Ibid.*, April 15, 1960.

111. *Ibid.*, January 22, 1960.

112. *Ibid.*

113. *Ibid.*

114. *New York Times*, September 29, 1960.

115. *Jewish Observer and Middle East Review*, September 2 and 9, 1960.

116. *Ibid.*

117. *Congress Bi-Weekly*, July 17, 1961.

118. *Jewish Observer and Middle East Review*, May 25, 1962.

119. *Ibid.*

120. *Jerusalem Post*, May 7, 1962.

121. *Jewish Observer and Middle East Review*, May 4, 1962.

122. *Ibid.*, June 8, 1962; *Near East Report*, June 5, 1962.

123. *Near East Report*, June 5, 1962; *Jerusalem Post*, May 30 and 31, June 5, 1962.

124. *New York Times*, September 21, 1963; *Jewish Chronicle*, September 27, 1963.

125. *Jewish Chronicle*, May 22, 1964.

126. *New York Times*, May 31, 1964.

127. *Jewish Observer and Middle East Review*, April 24, 1964.

Chapter Seven

1. Reuters dispatch in *New York Post*, June 11, 1946.

2. *Rebellion in Palestine*, p. 74.

3. *The Seat of Pilate*, pp. 4-5.

4. Freya Stark, *The Arab Island: The Middle East 1939-1943*, p. 159.

5. Nussbaum, *loc. cit.*

6. John Roy Carlson, *Cairo to Damascus* (New York, 1951), pp. 408-409.

7. *Newsweek*, September 3, 1951.

8. *Life Magazine*, October 27, 1952.

9. Quoted in *Middle East Opinion* (Cairo), August 26, 1946.

10. *Chicago Tribune*, August 21, 1946.

11. *Life Magazine*, October 27, 1952.

12. "Interview with the Grand Mufti Haj Amin el-Husseini. Why Arabs Flirt with Russia," *U.S. News and World Report*, October 5, 1951.

Index